Sun & Moon
An Astrological Lover's
Guide

By the same author:

The Astrological History of the World

Star Quality

MARJORIE ORR

Sun + Moon
An Astrological Lovers' Guide

ASTROInform Publishing

ASTROInform Publishing
Suite 310
176 Finchley Road London NW3 6BT

Published by AstroInform Publishing 2009.

@ Marjorie Orr 1994

This is a revised edition of the Lovers' Guide published by
Aquarian Press 1994.

Printed by Lightning Source Ltd., Chapter House, Pitfield
Kiln Farm, Milton Keynes MK11 3LW.

CONTENTS

Chapter 1:
SUN and MOON
A LOVERS GUIDE TO THE STARS

Is your love life predetermined by the stars? Will they lead you to the one and only perfect partner, custom built for you? Plato, the Greek philosopher, had a belief that we were split in two before birth and that we spend our life searching for our missing half - our soul mate. Is astrology the key to finding this needle in a haystack? The good news is that in astrological terms there are many more than this one solitary ideal mate around who could fit the bill rather nicely for you.

The key lies not just in your sun sign but in the combination of your Sun and Moon signs. That balance holds the real answer to the match that might actually last in your life. When you were born the Sun was sitting against one particular constellation of the zodiac. That is your birthday sign, which is what you read your daily horoscope under - Cancer, Sagittarius, Virgo etc. But the Moon was also against a constellation in the heavens and the combination of your Moon sign to your Sun sign begins to tell you a great deal about how you relate within yourself and what you long for as a lover.

Sun and Moon Signs
You may be an Aries Sun because your birthday is in early April but your Moon could be in Pisces which subtly alters how the Sun energy lives itself out. Aries as a Sun sign tends to be vibrant and outgoing, while a Pisces Moon is sensitive and a dreamer. Another example might be an Aries Sun Scorpio Moon, a mix of fiery, energetic, confident yet with a deeply secretive, moody emotional streak, unusual for an Aries. They need an equally curious mate who can feed their deeply sensual Scorpio Moon without overwhelming all that fiery energy. On the other hand an Aries Sun Sagittarius Moon personality will be a high powered go getting, entrepreneur who opens their mouth, says whatever flits across their brain and has the energy of ten people. They

A Lovers' Guide 8

need an amiable, practical mate who will put up with their high enthusiasm and keep the mundane details of everyday living under control.

Your sun sign (your birthday sign) tells you about the masculine side of your personality, your interests, talents, personality, your identity. Your Moon sign (look on the net for a free birth calculator) tells you about your feminine side, what nourishes you, what comforts you, how you relate to the body, your childhood and your feelings. The connection between the two tells you how your head and your heart are connected - vital if you want a real love affair that breathes. It often tells you about how your parents related or did not relate in your childhood. The patterns you learn in childhood unless you unlearn them will continue to rule your choice of mate, not always with happy results.

First step along the astrological road to relating is a preparatory one - to check up how you get on with yourself and equally how well designed your intended is for a settled match. Look at your personal Sun and Moon connection, just you as an individual (in Chapter Two) ... that is your relate-ability rating. If your Sun and Moon signs are at odds then until you get your head and heart pulling together your relationships will also be disjointed no matter how perfect a specimen of humanity is standing in front of you. Read it also for a straight view of your mate.

Fire, Earth, Air, Water
In astrology simple rules of thumb work remarkably well. The signs are divided into four elements – Fire (Aries, Leo, Sagittarius); Earth (Taurus, Virgo, Capricorn); Air (Gemini, Libra, Aquarius); and Water (Cancer, Scorpio, Pisces). The most common matches are with someone who shares your element – Fire with Fire, Earth with Earth, Water with Water, Air with Air. Some are real mis-matches. Water drowns Fire so not good news unless the Moons help to balance the equation. Earth and Air make for a sensible mix.

A Lovers' Guide

Sun to Sun

Having read Chapter Two on your Sun and Moon sign combination which tells you how to get past the starting gate of relationship as two separate individuals you then proceed to link hands in Chapter Three which tells you how Sun to Sun signs co operate, resonant and spark off each other, or not as the case may be.

Astrology works at all sorts of levels from the simple to the deeply complex. At a party all you are likely to find at a first chat is your fancy's Sun sign. But it can tell you a great deal about their personality and how you are likely to rub together. You are Taurus, they are Aquarius. Is there hope? You are earthy, sensual, possessive. They are independent and quite detached. Could be tricky. You are Taurus, they are Capricorn - getting much warmer. You are Aries, they are Gemini - count down to take off! They are Scorpio, you are Scorpio - almost definitely a hit. You are Leo, they are Leo – tricky since you'll both fight for the spotlight. Some opposites attract like Virgo and Pisces - sweet, kind and refined together. Some don't - like Leo and Aquarius... too stubborn, chalk and cheese. Some adore their own kind like Aquarius (spacey) and Scorpio (sensual passion). Chapter Three will unravel the complications.

Moon to Moon

Sun to Sun tells you how the core of your two identities match up. But your two Moon signs compared and contrasted give you quite a different perspective. The Moon sign tells you what comforts and nourishes you, how you relate to your body, to sexual pleasure, to cleanliness, to your home, your family and your childhood. Your Sun signs can match well but if one has a highly tactile Taurus Moon which is physically indulgent, jealous, rather stubborn and needs cuddled and the other has an Aquarius Moon which really isn't keen on too much intimacy or physical contact then it can raise problems. So Chapter Four tells you how your Moons click. So you start with Sun Moon within yourself, then outside Sun to Sun, then Moon to Moon.

Sun to Moon

The final combination of Sun to the opposite person's Moon sign tells you something quite different... see Chapter Five. Ideally the Sun sign of one lover should be the same as the Moon sign of the other. For example in the long running match between the late Paul Newman and Joanne Woodward - she has a Pisces Sun with Aquarius Moon and he had an Aquarius Sun with a Pisces Moon. Your Moon sign tells you what nourishes and comforts you. His sensitive Pisces Moon needed her gentle caring Pisces Sun personality. While her Aquarius Moon was quite happy to have the space his Aquarius Sun personality gave her.

Astrology does not pre-determine your life. There is no great fate involved. But it is a supremely useful information source. It tells you what you cannot easily find out without two years solid conversation by which time it may be too late. It will certainly tell you if you are still trying to mate a mismatch, a grasshopper with a bull.

This is a before book for those about to embark on the slippery slope of a new relationship to help you understand in what ways your lover is exactly what you need even though different from you. Or so out of step with you that the relationship will just wither or explode out of sight. It is also an ongoing book for those trying to understand why their relationship has hit a snag or just wanting confirmation that it is as good as it feels.

Men are different from women - no matter what the feminists told us. They have different needs, motives, aims and ways of functioning than their sexual counterparts.

In astrology certain Sun signs are different in how they live out depending on which sex is involved. Libra men are often sweet, soft, rather feminine where Libra women, usually their father's daughters, are cool, rational, quite masculine in their approach (a la Maggie Thatcher). Some Cancer men can stay Mom's little boy for ever while Cancerian women grow into matriarchal Queen Bees. Both sexes in Aries are quite competitive and hard driving. Capricorn men on the whole are gentler creatures than their feminine counterparts. Gemini men are wilder, more wayward than Gemini women who tend to be detached. So sex or gender does make a difference.

A Lovers' Guide

Do opposites attract? In astrology some signs do and some do not. Often people early in adult life pick lovers very different from themselves because they fill in for they feel they lack. But really there is not enough similarity for there to be any understanding. So it does not last the course. You need a bit of sameness to feel familiar and comfortable. Too much of the same is bad news though. Too much fire and no one does the tax returns. Too much earth and no one dreams the dreams. Too much water and the relationship overturns in a storm. Too much air and no one feels anything at all.

Learn what your likes, your limitations and your ambitions in the love stakes are. Then travel hopefully. If you know what you want and it is right for you, go for it in your mind, give yourself permission to have it and hey presto it will happen. Good luck.

YOU & YOUR MATE: HOW YOU RATE AT RELATING?

Sun and Moon in the Individual

Relationships may be about two people. But the truth is that if you do not relate well within yourself then you are not going to make it together with even the most perfect specimen of humanity standing in front of you. Also life being what it is you will with the magnetic instincts of a homing pigeon aim straight for the alternative version of your own muddle. The only reason we do not see it is that we do not see ourselves clearly. So step one is self knowledge and therefore a deeper understanding of what you are clinging so firmly onto as your perfect partner. Strip away the illusions before you make that irrevocable commitment. As someone once remarked - no matter who you marry you always wake up on the day after discovering you are in bed with someone totally different. This here is preventative medicine. So read on.

Your Sun sign tells you about your identity, how you relate to the world and about career - basically it is the inheritance from your father. The Moon sign tells you about what nourishes you emotionally, what kind of home life you like, how you relate to your body - it is the inheritance from your mother. The relationship between your sun and moon signs tells you how you relate within yourself, how your parents related to each other and thus what old patterns you carry in your head. Most importantly the Sun Moon contact tells you what you will be looking for and attract in a lover.

Understanding the element of your Sun and Moon also helps. Fire signs are Aries, Leo, Sagittarius - they act first, are confident, flamboyant, imaginative and live in their hopes and aspirations. Earth signs are Taurus, Virgo, Capricorn - they make things tangible, are hard working, practical, often sensual behind a prudish exterior, are tuned into the body and the material world. Air signs are Gemini, Libra, Aquarius - they think first, tend to live in their head, are full of thoughts, ideas, opinions, talk endlessly, can be emotionally detached. Water signs are Cancer, Scorpio, Pisces - they feel first, are highly impressionable, sympathetic, caring, self protective, sometimes self absorbed, moody, creative.

Aries Sun Aries Moon
A bouncing, vital, energetic, noisy New Moon baby you have possibly less need to lean than most. You do not feel a limb is missing if you do not have a permanent partner in life though being a true romantic Aries you always want a dashing romance on the go, the more adventurous the better. It takes you a fair way through life to learn the give and take needed in close relationships. Thinking of the other is not part of your essential nature. Self centred? Well ... not to put too fine a point on it and you always admire honesty even if it causes a fight - yes. Competitive to the point of exhaustion - everyone else's that is - you are a little too combative for the tender souls in life. Though oddly enough you will attract rather submissive geisha-like creatures who seem delighted to make themselves a doormat for your convenience and let you win every time.

Standing still in one place is not a strong point since you are a great starter, not such a hot long distance stayer. Your enthusiasm wanes very fast. Male Sun Moon Aries may remain delightful though maddening Peter Pans far into middle age - growing up is so boring! You need a very special kind of compliant lover who does not object to being abandoned for long periods, will not fuss about odd peccadilloes on the side, yet remain intriguing enough to be a continuing attraction. Female Aries will not be attracted to frills, flounces and the joys of domestic routines. You have strong opinions which you let fly at the slightest provocation. You will need a laid back mate with whom you can compete on an equal basis but who diplomatically lets you win at the same time and most importantly still retains your respect. Another real one-off. The softening down of middle age helps. Sometimes.

Aries Sun Taurus Moon
Your head cries out for ever more adventure, risk, excitement and danger but your heart really wants total security. You are better grounded, more tactile and more earthbound than most Aries but you fight a constant battle within yourself about your need to be free and your need to possess and be possessed. Jealousy crops up more here than you might expect. You are likely to attract yourself

to a lover who is equally ill at ease with their own needs and desires. So at times even with a perfect coupling you are likely to feel that slight jarring of two souls not quite in harmony. What nourishes you is a happy home life, lots of people to cuddle, a great deal of money to buy the ultimate luxuries in life. You adore beautiful clothes in sensuous fabrics, extra comfortable furniture, wonderful food in largish quantities, and drink. Part of you loathes change and too much upset from the quiet routines of pleasuring your senses. You can be fairly selfish about doing what suits you. If your pleasures also happen to suit your mate - great. But you can be very immoveable. So you need a reasonably flexible lover. One who can fulfil your very physical needs for great sex but who is also able to be out of the way when you want to be free to pursue your other interests.

Aries Sun Gemini Moon
Talk? - you had better believe it! You absolutely must have a lover who can stand the sound of your voice since you love to chat. You are bright (beyond belief), noisy, energetic, always on the go (a grasshopper to the nth degree) and exceedingly charming. On a superficial level you have a way with the opposite sex especially at parties but when it comes down to the nitty gritty of committing yourself to anything beyond a ten minute joke that is quite a different matter. The difference to you between a rut and grave as someone once said is only a matter of degree. You simply must have constant variety, change and excitement otherwise you will die of boredom. But the problem is if you attract a mate who has the same needs you will very soon burn yourselves out. You do need some ballast in your life though you are not essentially attracted to earthy people - too tediously practical - and certainly not to watery emotional types - they make you feel as if you were being swamped or drowning. Romances will tend to be short, sharp and fast in younger adult life. What instantly attracts will soon become rather tedious and not substantial enough to hold your interest. There is a two dimensional quality about your emotional responses which is not enough. The knocks of life will bring you deeper into your feelings and make you realise that sacrificing some freedom and excitement is worth the

stronger relationships which develop.

Aries Sun Cancer Moon

At odds with yourself you are constantly on edge, never being able to satisfy your head and your heart at the same time. You did not see your parents as being exactly in tune with each other and because of that you cannot quite get your own relationships together. Certainly you are full of initiative, get up and go and have highly romantic fantasies about what you want but your rather upfront Aries Sun does not let you settle enough to nourish your highly sensitive Cancer Moon. You need a constant, secure happy home life and a great deal of freedom. So what you want is a family oriented lover who can wander independently as much as you, who is not possessive though will not mind your odd flashes of jealousy. An oddly designed animal to be sure but in a way that matches your rather lop sided needs. You can be both highly sympathetic, caring and sweet natured as well as being rather direct about doing your thing no matter what. You will have difficulty committing absolutely to any one person and may, once settled, start to stray which will bother your conscience. Males - you will manage better being able to go out into the world to do your macho act yet able to slither home at high speed when the mood strikes to find comfort. Females - you will find it more difficult to find your lover being ill designed for domesticity in one half of your nature yet craving it with the other. Your Aries machismo is less likely to be fuelled into fantasies about knights on white chargers, more into boardroom battles and beating the competition. You need to be less driven, more receptive, less winning oriented and more tolerant. You also need a fairly soft mate.

Aries Sun Leo Moon

A larger than life, fiery, fast moving, never-say-no, you are a rather dashing personality who will leave weaker souls wilting in the ditch as you fly along at a million miles an hour. Burnout is a real possibility in life since all your energy is in your imagination, your fantasies. Confidence is all. Your instant reaction to any situation is not to feel or to think but to fly instantly into action. You need a lover who grounds you and can cope with the practicalities of life yet you fear between trapped. You need freedom, grandeur, a first class style of living preferably in five star hotels, oodles of excitement, thrills, and no spills. You are, for all your confidence, very easily embarrassed and must, must, must have a mate who will not show you up badly. You think everything reflects back on you. You need a lover who does not mind being a satellite to your sun, or a courtier kneeling at the foot of your throne, though they also have to be a credit to you. Getting your own way is not just a self centred thing it also springs from your genuine inability to change very quickly. You tend to get stuck in ruts emotionally and it takes a real hurricane to push you off course. However this has its merits. More faithful than most Aries you have a long distance quality about you and you are refreshingly honest. Once in a good relationship you tend to stay.

Aries Sun Virgo Moon
An odd mix for sure this since you are brave to the point of idiocy in certain areas of life and timid to the point of paranoia in others. Your Aries Sun could not care less about other people's opinions, needs and lifestyles while your Virgo Moon worries endlessly about absolutely everything and makes you a hypochondriac to boot. However you are more practical, certainly more sensible than most of the over competitive, over fiery Aries breed. But you will take a while through life to get your head and your heart together in love. What you want to mate with is not what you feel you ought to be mating with. Your Virgo Moon does not like infidelity yet you may find that the relationship you want at any one time is not the one you are in. You have to understand that you have two completely different images of yourself and both need a different lover. You want fiery, fairy tale romance and a constantly changing scenario on the one hand and you also want a refined, rather withdrawn existence where you can be protected. What you require is a down to earth, rather sensual lover who can fulfil your needs for physical affection yet is not so gross as to offend your rather more spacey Aries Sun. Who will let you wander but be there to calm down your endless stream of questions, anxieties and invented ghosts who haunt your life.

Aries Sun Libra Moon

A Full Moon baby, you veer between opposites at a great rate of knots. Your life feels constantly tense as if half of you is never satisfied at any given time no matter who you are with. Your conscience and duty are always at odds with your desires. You constantly wish for a composite of the various lovers you have had. "If only I could have Jane's brain and Joanna's body welded together I could be happy. Or "I adore Joe for his chat over dinner but he's so hopeless in bed. Mike is great between the sheets but I wouldn't be seen dead with him out in public." One is never enough. The problems spring from early on where you experienced your parents as very different kinds of people, not really compatible. What they did not get together in their marriage you cannot get together in your head. So you are constantly out of step with yourself - until that is you decide to leave childhood and the old patterns behind. But that means rising above your dilemmas to see that life is not a choice between either this person or that person, neither of whom seems perfect. There is a third way where you can find your composite lover. But the change has to come firstly from you. Your Aries Sun demands total freedom, great excitement and a fiery relationship that does not last for ever. Your Libra Moon on the other hand craves peace, niceness, social respectability and a fairly cerebral mate. You need someone just as contrary as yourself and hope the pieces fit when you come together. But relationships will always be a bit of a struggle.

Aries Sun Scorpio Moon

You are a real puzzle - flying along the cloud tops with a head full of fantasies yet also drawn to the depths where you can indulge your romantic dreams in the most physical and emotional way possible. You never ever admit to being hurt and will hide your feelings away with a determined ferocity. You will probably have handled this conflict early on in adult life by repressing your need for deeply passionate relationships, seemingly a light hearted sprite who does not care about such things. Then one day - you fall! Straight into the bottomless pit and are gripped by such agonies of jealousy and possessiveness that for a while you hardly notice the ecstasies that come along with them. You hate yourself for being so hooked into those love affairs. Yet they give you what your normal dash-in-dash-out flash in the pan flare ups cannot. Your Aries Sun demands that you find someone who will let you win, not mind your me first approach, and not worry when you wander independently off to do your own thing. But your Scorpio Moon wants someone you can wrap your octopus tentacles round and never let go. You need a hybrid like yourself who is transcendently romantic in such contradictory ways and just hope the same facets are on show when you want to be together. You are likely to attract yourself to mates who seem to be as unlike you as anything your friends could ever imagined. But somehow it works. Friends will never see what goes on in the highly secret recesses of your life.

Aies Sun Sagittarius Moon
A fiery, flibberty gibbet you are completely incapable of sitting still for long. Anything that smells remotely like possessiveness or being fenced in will have you running for the open plains. You absolutely must have your freedom but herein lies your dilemma. No restraints at all usually means no relationship either, so life is one long lesson of learning that sacrifices are sometimes worth the hassle. Commitment will never be easy for you since your enthusiasms are notoriously short lived and once you sense that initial ardour waning so you start getting itchy feet again. You need to learn to hack it through the boring patches and understand that obligations need not necessarily be the same as a prison sentence. Not inherently talented at understanding the needs of others you may have problems with more sensitive emotional souls who need you to tune in to their every nuance. Although excitable and exciting, a thoroughgoing adventurer in fact, and a real charmer on the social scene, you can also be overly outspoken in your approach to one to one relationships. You must learn a little diplomacy. Honesty is one of your plus points but too much of it at the wrong moment can be a real downer. You need someone more practical than yourself but who has enough flair not to make you feel stuck in glue, and who is emotional enough to soften you down without becoming

over hurt by your at times careless comments.

Aries Sun Capricorn Moon

Hard working, highly ambitious and rather cool to the touch, you rarely do anything without looking first to see what you can gain. You are probably one of life's winners but happy? ....Probably not early on. You rarely give in to emotional whims and indulgences. Indeed you rarely sit still long enough to find out what those are. Your Aries Sun wants to be first past the post and your Capricorn Moon thinks you will never be loved for just being yourself. You have to achieve to earn love. Which is, of course, a non starter. Because they more you drive yourself to accomplish the further away from your feelings you get and the less likely is it that you will settle down to ongoing romantic bliss. You could settle for rather loveless matches which are good for your social standing. Capricorn Moons do that sadly until one day they fall madly, passionately and very physically in love and all their conventional morality goes straight out of the window. You are a fire earth mix which is more practical and sensible than most Aries. But you lack air's reflective abilities and water's sensitivity to feelings. You can be rather cool and edgy. You need a lover who thinks and communicates, and who is warm enough to heat you up a bit. But that probably comes with age. Capricorn Moons have the happy knack of improving with age. Though you may have to swap partners late in life to find your true depths.

Aries Sun Aquarius Moon

Charming, zany, witty, adventurous and rather racy, you sound like everyone's dream of an exciting lover but the truth of the matter is that you are not at all clear you want a relationship that connects too deeply. You like thinking about love, talking about romance and sex endlessly, fantasising about great passions, even writing novels about the whole affair. But as for actually doing it? Falling in love, making a commitment, trying to find your feelings - not such a hot notion at all. Your Aquarian Moon loves to be bizarre, even slightly shocking just to see the effect it has on others so you definitely need lovers who will not be rattled. It is not that your Aries Sun cannot be fierce, fiery and passionate but sometimes you have a difficulty turning what is in your imagination into real substance. Too many swampy feelings frankly scare you. Once you have got over the adrenalin pumping, love addict phase into discussing mortgages, in-growing toenails and the best brand of laxatives, you really do not want to know anymore. A rather spaced out relationship with plenty of freedom and independence with an intellectual equal is what you need. Any sniff of possessiveness or jealousy will have you taking off like a space rocket.

Aries Sun Pisces Moon

A go ahead type with a heart so desperately sensitive you can hardly bear to let it out to play at all. You fight a constant war in your head between your Aries Sun which despises any kind of cowardice or weakness and thinks you should head straight for what you want and grab it - and your Pisces Moon which operates like an oyster without its shell. It cringes and tries to hide all the time. Most often when your Moon is operating you are too timid to even voice your feelings for a new other person in case of the awful possibility of rejection. More than almost any other Aries type you need a long term relationship to provide you with your shell. Then you can sally out into the world to look macho. Only those close know the real truth. But you need a lover who is exciting enough not to bore you, submissive enough to let you win, yet strong enough to give your feelings the protection they need. You are that ultimate contradiction - a mix of fire and water. What you lack is air for reflection and earth for stability. But an over airy lover will freeze you with too much analysis and not enough action. An over earthy lover will seem too physical and rather blinkered. A practical but emotional type would be your best bet.

Taurus Sun Aries Moon

You are an uneasy combination who wants total stability and security as well as constant change and excitement. Your Taurus Sun wants a solid, unchanging, settled family life where you can root yourself preferably for ever. But your Aries Moon wants nothing of the sort. When it is in charge you never know quite what you want - except that the routine and constancy which your other half yearns for is certainly not it. In early adult life you probably attract yourself to zany, whacky, wild adventurers who love you and leave your heart bleeding. You are much more possessive and jealous than you ever want to admit. The lover you need is home-oriented yet freedom loving, physically warm yet able to leave you free to fantasise as you want. Taurus is a highly physical energy, very sensual at a body level, which does not suit your Aries Moon. So you need a very special combination in your mate who will probably be as complex and contradictory as you are yourself. A solid home base is a must but from there you must be able to flee when you please, to roam the wide open spaces and do what suits you. You would do better with reasonably undemanding lover or at least one who will take your whims and desires as being theirs.

Taurus Sun Taurus Moon
A very earthy New Moon baby, you have less need to relate outside yourself than most. Which does not mean you will not have good relationships. Just that you are less desperate than most to find your other half. A strong sense of mission usually goes with you through life which sometimes gets in the way of love. You undoubtedly adore the good things of life, especially the ones which pleasure the body - food, drink, clothes, a luxurious home. You are extremely tactile even in non sexual situations so you must have people around you who are not too spacey or reserved about body contact. Love to you must be expressed in highly physical ways. It is not an imaginative experience as it is for fire signs, or one to be thought and talked about as it is to the air signs or even felt deeply in a watery emotional way. You must see tangible expressions of love and affection before you will be satisfied that it exists. The problem is being both Sun and Moon in Taurus you would naturally be attracted to other Taureans but it is a rather dull pairing. You need flair, sparkle and variety from the lighter signs. You can be immoveably stubborn so you need a flexible, sometimes

submissive mate. You can be ever so slightly self centred when it comes to getting your own way so there is no sense in marrying or trying to mate with a Prima Donna. Jealousy and possessiveness can be problems. You can sulk for ever at slights and hurts. You are a real one-off.

Taurus Sun Gemini Moon

You are solid, stolid, very earthy yet a real grasshopper at the same time. Part of you is so securely anchored it hardly moves at all and would be happy rooting itself to one spot for ever. Your Gemini Moon, however, which is your other part regards with horror all this unchanging-ness. To a Gemini Moon the difference between a rut and a grave is only a matter of degree. So your life is one long dilemma of how to keep your head and your heart happy at once. Your prime requirements for a lover are an intelligent mind and a witty flow of conversation with enough physical passion to keep you satisfied but not so much you feel pulled down by it. You absolutely must have someone who shares your rather indulgent approach to life - adoring good food, drink, clothes and luxurious furnishings. One tricky area is sex about which you are highly ambivalent. Your Taurus Sun is very physical and needs tangible displays of affection. Your Gemini Moon is very spacey and would rather think, talk, analyse it all, than do it. So you need someone who understands only too well your fleeting mood changes. What you wanted last night or last week or even ten minutes ago is not what you want now. Being an earth and air mix you may veer over into being a tiny touch cool at times so you probably need a partner who is slightly fiery to give you a bit of sparkle, or just passionate enough to stir your deeper feelings without scaring your Gemini Moon into flight.

Taurus Sun Cancer Moon

This Sun Moon combination looks to others very well balanced. You feel as if you were at ease with yourself. Socially you operate very smoothly, flirting and having fun especially with the opposite sex. But you do not always have the smooth life on the inside that you crave. You are fairly stubborn and a past master at the art of passive resistance. Nothing can shift you when your mind is made up. Your earth water mix means that you recharge your own batteries very successfully indeed though you can at times be a little heavy. You need some fire to sparkle you up and detachment to allow you to think clearly. That would stop you hanging on quite so tightly. Physical passion is always hugely important to Taureans but to Cancer cuddles are more gestures of family affection rather than anything deeply sexual. So you will never be quite sure what it is you exactly want. What you will undoubtedly end up with is a solid home life. You adore the idea of staying rooted in the one place surrounded by a large brood. When you do settle you are faithful, definitely designed for the long haul relationship rather than anything that is likely to chop and change. Disloyalty is not either in your best interests or really in your nature. Jealousy can be a problem since you are possessive as only Taurus can be and with all the Cancerian insecurities about being abandoned or hurt. You need a lover who is tactile and generous hearted enough to put your indulgences at the top of their priority list. A home loving raver in short.

Taurus Sun Leo Moon
Wow! A really strong combination but not an easy one. Always at odds with yourself, you never feel totally satisfied with anything or anyone. Your head wants a practical, earthy, sensible, sensual mate while your heart really wants a flashy, flamboyant, rather regal personage. You always feel you get one or the other, but never both at the same time. What you want to have is never what you ought to have. This rather gritty, restless, at-cross-purposes streak in you should ease as you mature and separate yourself from childhood. You certainly saw your parents as being highly different people not totally in tune. You need in time to rise above their differences to find your own way of relating. You are obstinate to the nth degree, determined to

fulfil your own indulgences and be centre of attention. An earth fire mix you are known in the astrological business as a "steamroller" type - always charging ahead when everyone else is sagging by the wayside. So you obviously need a lover with stamina. Your insistence on living life at a first class not to say five star level could cause problems - you also need a rich mate. But you are at heart a sign who needs love, passion, romance and real connections before you feel alive.

Taurus Sun Virgo Moon
Socially very much at ease, given to the good life and never happy if you body is not being indulged, you are lucky that your earthy mix makes you work hard. You could otherwise end up as a slightly decadent character. In early adult life you were probably rather restricted by a lack of imagination and too practical an outlook. If anything you were probably a little heavy as a personality, needing mates who would sparkle you up a bit. Your Virgo Moon worries endlessly about everything under the sun and invents quite a few things to agonise over that do not even exist. You need a mate who is calm enough to handle your jitters, tolerant enough to stand your hypochondria, yet flexible enough to let your Taurean side have its way most of the time. What is also necessary is a good life style that will give you the good food, drink, clothes and luxurious house that allows you to feel comfortable. You are not flashy but you are acquisitive and need to indulge your sensations. Jealousy can be a problem though you will hide it well since your refined Virgo Moon does not like to admit to such primitive feelings. You need to learn to be more objective about yourself. Standing back far enough to see yourself clearly is not easy and self analysis always seems a waste of time to you. But relationships will not work until you learn to see yourself as others see you.

Taurus Sun Libra Moon
Although you are never quite at ease with yourself this can be a rather lovely combination since both Taurus and Libra are ruled by Venus so you can be charm itself, rather creative, always superbly in good taste and very calm. You

are at the refined end of Taurus. What you need around you are the luxuries, indulgences and extravagances of life and the beautiful people. And you certainly loathe the great unwashed, the lazy, the idle and the unemployed. Being earth and air you are practical, sensible, communicative and fairly detached. What you lack at times is warmth, dash and craziness. You need a lover who will push you towards the edge. That Taurus grit of yours and need for total stability sometimes makes you just a touch dull, safe and rather boring. That Libra Moon too can make you just a touch superficial. If you always want life to be nice, sociable and clean, you miss out on a great deal that can be alive, human and invigorating. A rather restless spirit within you never quite lets you settle. You are never totally satisfied with life or your mates. Your Taurus Sun really does want a cuddly armful but the Libra Moon makes you standoffish. Finding an accommodation between the two conflicting sides of you is your life's challenge.

Taurus Sun Scorpio Moon
Strong, often silent especially on the subject of your feelings, you are definitely a force to be reckoned with. A potent combination of sultry desire, simmering jealousy and unresolved tension ensures that your love life will never be boring. It may not always make you happy but you do live your life in depth. You are stubborn - which is the understatement of the year. Having a Fixed Sun and Moon, your normal reaction to change is to dig your heels in and steadfastly refuse to budge an inch. Since acquisitiveness and possessiveness lie at the core of your being you never let old love affairs go easily. What you want is what you want and that is all there is to it. If anyone hurts you, though, there will not be a flicker of emotion shown. You hide away from public gaze what wounds you. There is nothing milk sop or middle of the road about your feelings. You take them extremely seriously. You either love people to distraction or you loathe them. Once you have finished an affair you can never be friends. You ought to have a lover who is flexible to fit round what you want but you need someone who can stand your depths so a weakling won't do. What you will probably find is someone as stalwart as yourself

and end up in a continual power struggle. Life will not be easy emotionally but you never give up trying.

Taurus Sun Sagittarius Moon

You want almost everything you do not want and vice versa so life is not easy on the relationship front. Your Taurus Sun wants to hang on to an unchanging, long term relationship that provides earthy stability and lots of cuddles. Your Sagittarian Moon on the other hand wants freedom first and foremost. You do not expect to have to ask permission to roam the world as it suits you at the drop of a pin. Possessiveness makes your hackles rise and you reach for your running shoes. What you require is the impossible lover who is sensual but not too physical, loves being cuddled but will stand being abandoned frequently, can offer you security but does not make you feel fenced in. In return they will be given a wonderfully fiery, flamboyant relationship with indulgences, extravagances, and luxuries thrown in since you adore the good life. Restlessness will always be part of your nature so you need to have a lifestyle where you can keep on the move. Entertaining is one of your skills since you are both practical and given to colourful displays of largesse. Your parties are the talk of the town because you feed people so well in a highly original way. So lovers and future mates must be reasonably sociable creatures and communicative. That Sagittarian Moon loves to philosophise about life. Being an earth and fire mix you have tons more energy than everyone else.

Taurus Sun Capricorn Sun

Earthy, practical, very attached to the body and very hard working, you will be more at ease socially and at work than you will be in close relationships. Somehow you have the idea that to be loved you have to achieve. No one loves you for just being you. Which is a great mistake but you will take most of your life to unlearn it. Your Taurus Sun wants to be hugely indulgent but your Capricorn Moon is a hard taskmaster keeping your nose to the grindstone or sending you after lovers who are socially useful though hardly a bundle of laughs. You need to unhook your upwardly mobile tendencies from your love life and go for sensual pleasures. Being an earth earth mix you have a tremendous potential for real physical passion though you need also to learn of the realms that lie beyond the body in the spirit, the heart and the mind. You will be inclined to pick rather serious, sometimes older lovers, but what you need in your life is more sparkle, fire, craziness and general chuztpah. Your sense of humour will probably develop late in life. You will, also, find the last third of your love life makes up for all the coolness of the first third. You will with a little encouragement turn into a merry, mischievous geriatric who oozes sex appeal.

Taurus Sun Aquarius Moon
This is rather a square edged combination which makes you resolutely earthy, solid, stubborn and quite sensual on the one hand. But you fight a conflict within yourself with the other half of you which is airy, talkative, detached and rather anti anything too physical. How do you come by and resolve these dilemmas? Well take a good hard look at your parents - they were hardly in tune. What they could not get together between themselves you cannot get together in your head. So you constantly want what you do not have, or have what you do not want. Lift yourself out of your childhood battles and see life from a new perspective. It is possible to have your cake and eat it. To get what you want and still be doing what you ought to do and at the same time! But you will always be slightly restless in relationships and you certainly need an oddly constructed mate - someone who can let you have your way since your Taurus Sun is both super indulgent and slightly self centred. (Both your Sun and Moon are fixed signs so you expect the world to adapt around you.) But your lover will also have to be detached enough to let you fly free when you want, and not mind being shocked along the way. You love being eccentric, slightly wild just to see the effect on people around so mates need to be of an unshakeable temperament. Your earth air mix could probably do with some sparkle in your mate and a little emotional warmth.

Taurus Sun Pisces Moon
Steadfast, stalwart and unflappable on the outside, you are

a real shrinking violet where your feelings are concerned on the inside. You hardly dare voice your inclinations for fear of the dreadful hurt of rejection. So sometimes in life you miss out on relationships because you are scared to reach out. Emotional courage needs to be fostered though you will never be upfront about your feelings. Your earth water mix makes you sympathetic in a highly practical way which is wonderful for those whom you trust. So you have a great deal to give if you can get over your feelings of self pity. You belong to the refined end of Taurus and though you share the general characteristics of indulgence and love of the good life you conduct yourself in a highly tasteful manner always. The fixed side to Taurus is largely lacking or at least mellowed because you know the heart is just as important as the body and its pleasures. What you need is a lover who will be flexible enough to let you have your way, yet strong enough to protect your sensitivities which are legion. You need an intimate confidante to whom you can unburden your heart and soul without being scared that the instant you open up they will savage you or abandon you. That takes time to find and ultimately trust. Once you settle you will do so for a lifetime or what is left of it. You want security, roots, unchanging-ness and a feather bedded home.

Gemini Sun Aries Moon
Fun loving, chatty, butterfly brained and grass hopper footed you are not exactly the stay at home type. On the social scene you appear at ease with yourself and happy to flirt with everyone in sight. Nothing about you stays the same for long since you crave variety in yourself and in your companions. What you want now is not what you wanted ten minutes ago, never mind ten days ago. You can appear like a will o' the wisp. One moment here, the next moment there, so you absolutely do not want a deeply possessive mate. Being an air fire mix you easily burn yourself out since you do not have a natural way of recharging your batteries. You are neither earthy and grounded nor are you watery and emotional. So you probably want a lover who can provide you with some ballast, a bit of practical know how and an anchor. Other fire air types are marvellous fun for you to be around since both of you brim over with

liveliness but it is a fire that flares up and dies down quickly because it consumes itself. Stocking to one of anything is not always your strongest suit since Geminis always like to hedge their bets and absolutely must have a range of choices. Your Aries Moon also wants freedom and constant excitement. What nourishes you is getting all the attention and coming first which is easier in a constant series of new relationships than in one that has had to learn about compromise. So you need a mate who will give you a very long rein indeed.

Gemini Sun Taurus Moon
Air headed and earthy footed might be the uncomplimentary description of you but it is true that you are made up of very different elements. Your Gemini Sun is quick witted, rather cool, freedom loving, restless and given to sudden whims. Whereas your Taurus Moon is of a heavier cast. Solid, stalwart and affectionate, it loathes change, especially the kind of sudden change which your Gemini Sun often precipitates. What nourishes your heart is a secure, rather physically passionate, certainly sensual match but the other half of you is frankly not too tuned into the body. So you will need to find relationships which give you just enough cuddles, kisses and tangible gestures of love without smothering you or making you feel tied down by the earthy realm. You have a jealous streak and a wandering eye which is a quirky combination. You crave faithfulness and loyalty in others but are not always good at finding it in yourself. What you really need is an anchor at home who will provide all the indulgences of life for you - good food, drink, beautiful clothes and luxury furnishings but leave you free to roam at will. Your darker side sometimes draws you into frankly undesirable relationships because you need to experience the profound depths. But luckily you quickly flit on somewhere else.

Gemini Sun Gemini Moon
Airy in the extreme you think everything through before you even dare to feel it. You prefer to talk, analyse, debate and argue over life rather than actually get in and live it. Cool and a touch unemotional at times you learn

eventually that detachment has its drawbacks. If you do not give emotionally to others, you will not get support and affection back. But being born at the time of the New Moon you are more self sufficient and have less need for close relationships than most. You do not feel half a person without a partner. You do have a strong sense of mission that drives you on and can push relationships to one side so you need a long suffering mate whose ego will survive being rejected or abandoned every so often in favour of the grand plan. If this makes you sound like the Iceman or the Snow Queen you are far from it. As far as short lived affairs are concerned you can heat up along with the best of them. You adore the excitement, the risk and the thrills of a new romance blossoming. But long distance staying was never going to be your strong point. Variety really is the spice of your life. Though part of that is an artificial way of avoiding facing the desert in the middle of your emotional life which you do want to fill with a meaningful relationship at some point. You just do not have enough faith to believe that will ever be possible. Lovers absolutely must have a sharp mind and be good conversationalists. A meeting of minds is the sine qua non of any match for you.

Gemini Sun Cancer Moon
A stay at home Gemini is a contradiction in terms yet it is precisely what you try to be. Family relationships and a secure, unchanging base in life are your sheet anchor, yet your Gemini Sun yearns to fly free and be unfettered. A compromise is what you feel your love life always is, never quite everything you want. Whatever the emotional atmosphere of your childhood it stays around you for most of your adult life and colours what you think relationships can and should provide. You find it difficult to stray far from what is known or you stop feeling nourished. So you fight this continual battle in your head about wanting too entirely different ways of life. It is tiring but in a curious way it also keeps you alert. Being an air water mix you are more emotional than many Geminis, not so cool and detached. But you lack earth and fire so partners who can provide you with a little chutzpah and some practical grounding would help. Though not too much. Your Cancer Moon can

make you jealous since at heart you are so desperately insecure and terrified of losing what is nearest and dearest to you. Attachments to mother and your childhood family continue too long and can cause problems in relationships. But letting go is causes such pain. You need security and a long rein.

Gemini Sun Leo Moon
Communicative, attention seeking, restless, fiery and determined to live life the five star way you are certainly no shrinking violet. Highly persuasive, blissfully charming when it suits you and rather entertaining on the social scene, you can oddly take offence very easily. Your vanity is a real weak spot. Standing on your self importance can unsettle mates who do not have your sense of ego. Not always too tuned into the needs of others in early adult life you may take a while to settle. Faithfulness is not easy for your Gemini Sun but your Leo Moon is essentially loyal and honest. Which does not mean to say you will not stray but at least half of you will disapprove or at least feel that the lying and petty deceptions are beneath your dignity. Your air fire mix is a heady one keeping you constantly on the go, always looking for excitement, variety and thrills. What you need from a mate is stimulation and adoration, but also some common sense to keep you anchored down otherwise you are likely to take off like a hot air balloon or just plain burnout. Recharging your batteries is always necessary for you. Another fire air type would drive you wild but exhaust you rapidly. You need a touch of earth in your lover to get you tuned into your body and maybe a touch of water to let you find your heart. But too much of either and you will feel you are being weighed down or swamped by soggy feelings.

Gemini Sun Virgo Moon
Fidgety, restless, highly adaptable and quite incapable of sitting still, you need a rock of Gibraltar onto which to anchor yourself. You are communicative with an extremely bright mind. Your witty rather precise way with words makes you entertaining on the social scene but you never seem satisfied with yourself or anyone else. You want what you do not have and have what you do not want. In

childhood you were aware of tensions in the atmosphere at home and have internalised these in your adult life with the result that you feel relationships will always pull you in two. They will not, but you do need to try lateral thinking. Life is not about either or. There is a third solution, if you leave childhood behind and rise above those conflicts. You worry incessantly about everything on earth and quite a few things that exist no where. Trying to continually impose order on the chaos of your life tends to make you over rigid. Sometimes you can even appear prudish which is almost impossible for a Gemini but you manage it. Hypochondria can send you rushing off anxiously for advice, remedies and reassurance so you need a calm, stable mate who will listen sympathetically but not get irritated by your constant harping on. Your nervous system is over wound up causing your digestive system to act up at times. So you need a physically supportive lover as well. Being an air earth mix you can be a little dry at times but you are warmer than some Geminis because of your earthy Virgo Moon.

Gemini Sun Libra Moon
Cool, communicative, and at times rather cut off from feelings is how you come across to others. You can be extremely sociable, very friendly and charming, yet you reach out to people with your head and your tongue not your heart or your body. Flirting comes easily, almost as second nature to you as long as it is conducted with decorum since you have a horror of social embarrassment. You are extremely sensitive about how other people see you. Your status in society is a crucial factor in all your deliberation whether about work or relationships. Being a slight snob does not bother you at all since you know your tastes are impeccable. Gemini does have a dark, sometimes sensual side, but your Libra Moon is not happy about plunging into the depths of passion, nor about anything too physical or claustrophobic. You abhor people who do not wash or are socially unacceptable. So you need a mate who is happy to meet at a more surface level and allow you the freedom you need to continually be exploring new vistas, new interests and new acquaintances. You adore meeting successful, fairly wealthy and rather well bred people so your friendship

circle will be wide, varied and rather elegant. Traditionally having the Sun and Moon in the same element - here in air - was supposed to make you at ease with yourself and the opposite sex. But it often indicates a social ease rather than a real yearning to connect. So you have to watch that you do not become too 'up in your head', too detached. A fiery lover would make you sparkle though you might cringe at their brashness. A watery one would make you feel swamped. But you do need anchoring and grounding. A rather earthy type might help to give you warmth and a connection to life.

Gemini Sun Scorpio Moon
Drawn to the dark side you are undoubtedly amongst the most heavyweight of the Geminis, certainly the most secretive. You never ever let on when you are hurt, keeping your wounded pride to yourself, but allowing yourself the minor pleasure of getting your revenge at some point. Air and water are an odd mix since your Gemini Sun basically prefers talking and thinking to touching and feeling. Whereas your Scorpio Moon adores passionate clinches, intensely lived emotions and even deeply messy love affairs. Finding a balance which will suit both sides of your conflicting nature will not be that easy. Early adult life will contain wild and way out relationships and passing flings which you would not like to see in print or have brought up in front of your mother-in-law. But your need, quite compulsive at times, to find another half, a perfect mate for your desires will push you into a determined search to find that special someone. Although Gemini can be a wayward sign when it comes to fidelity, your Scorpio Moon will provide you with stability. It gives you a streak of jealousy and possessiveness which will eventually teach you that your insecurity demands a reliable lover. Loyalty is a real Scorpio quality which is a blessing though you will always be slightly uneasy about being trapped.

Gemini Sun Sagittarius Moon
Restless, flighty, fiery and liable to burnout from non stop go, there is no danger of you ever being bored or boring because you never sit still long enough. You talk endlessly, entertainingly with a real gift for lifting other people's

interest yet you are wary of being trapped in a committed relationship. Being fenced in is close to your idea of suffocation and at the first whiff of jealousy you are off at the run. Freedom is what you thrive on but you tend to be naive. You learn about the harder side of life through knocks and bad experiences. Disillusionment comes hard though your sense of humour will always bounce you back. There is an inner conflict between what your head wants and your heart yearns for which come from a childhood sense of tension between your parents. When you get the lover you think you wanted you start wanting someone totally different. You need a mate who can bring you down to the ground a little without restricting you too much. You need to learn to recharge your batteries, rather than trying to stay high all the time. You are warmer than many Geminis because of your fiery Moon and more flamboyant so you will have little trouble in attracting a stream of lovers. Finding the right one will take more time.

Gemini Sun Capricorn Moon
Talkative, ambitious, hugely determined yet inclined to be just a tiny bit dull unless you can find a lover who will drag you away from work and your need to be socially acceptable. Gemini can be zany enough but you grew up thinking that achieving was the be all and end all. Success would make you loved and deep down you never think you do enough to earn your happiness. Which is, of course, all the wrong way round. You need a lover who is warm and centred enough to make you realise how magnificent a human being you are in yourself. Although you will always want a solid life style with the better things liberally sprinkled around. You are not one for slumming or mixing with life's failures. Being an air earth mix you thrive on situations and people who are not too fiery, impulsive or erratic. Your sharp mind demands mates who are intellectually stimulating rather than a bundle of passion. But you do need someone who makes you take yourself less seriously. You mellow with the years, gaining a livelier sense of humour, becoming quite a snazzy geriatric but it does take time. Relationships are important to you but you need to gain more confidence. You may look cool, controlled and together but inside you

often feel lonely, vulnerable and insecure so you take slights to heart more than others realise.

Gemini Sun Aquarius Moon

Zippy, zany, wildly communicative and quite impossible to tie down, you are quite a character and very up in your head. In the strict sense that emotions are thought about, talked about but not always felt too deeply. An Air Sun and Air Moon together make you dabble endlessly in a wide variety of interests but you often need prodded to help you turn your ideas into reality. A lover with fire in their belly or an earthy attachment to reality will help you get into life more. A watery emotional mate would make you run a mile because anything that smells like possessiveness has you very much on edge, ready to flee. You are more nervous than you appear, at times even hyper sensitive, which belies your cool, chatty exterior. But you positively must get away from routine at times, especially out of domestic ruts, to clear your mind from its eternal worrying, planning and fidgeting. Friends are hugely important to you and often you irritate more romantic lovers by always inviting the gang along just when a moment of cosy intimacy offers itself. This is your real challenge. Because your Gemini Sun deep inside really wants another half in life, the mythical twin you feel you have lost way back before the beginning of time, and very much wants to water the desert that seems to exist where your heart should be.

Gemini Sun Pisces Moon

Highly adaptable, rather gentle, always fidgeting, and a more emotional Gemini than the norm you really do want to find a tender love in life. But it is not easy to settle your wayward tendencies and fear of being trapped, never mind your fear of being rejected. Often you cannot find the courage to voice your feelings so prospective lovers pass by never knowing they were the object of your desire. In childhood you were aware of a difference in outlook between your parents and it may take you well into adult life to settle the inner conflict that rages inside you as a result. Your heart points you in one direction and your head in another. You marry one person and promptly fall in love with someone else. What is over the fence always looks more attractive - until you hop across and get what you thought you wanted. Then the whole process starts over. You need to find a way in your emotional life of doing what you want and what you ought at the same time. An air water mix between your sun and moon helps you be creative, makes you good at counselling other and is a highly sensitive combination. You just need to watch that you do not dream too much. Your escapist tendencies can get out of hand. A fiery lover would help you act out your fantasies and an earthy one would pull you into reality more. Though they need to be tactful on the one hand and not too physical on the other. You dislike brash ill mannered mates and dull clods. You need variety alongside stability in your mate. But someone who can centre you and anchor you without making you feel fenced in really is the ideal.

Cancer Sun Aries Moon
Emotionally super sensitive and home loving, you also have a real determination to get out into the world and make it happen. A watery sun and a fiery moon make it difficult for you to settle to what you need. One part of you yearns for family togetherness and suburban bliss, the other part of you is a hard driving, over excitable, go getting raver. It may take you half a lifetime to find the balance but you will once you learn to rise above the either-or conflicts in your life. Your head and your heart can be made to agree. What usually happens early on is that you commit to one person and immediately find you want someone else. Nothing satisfies you totally. Your Aries Moon wants nourished by a lover who is fierce, courageous, romantic and a great adventurer. But your Cancerian sun is looking for a more stable, suburban mate altogether. Someone to cling onto who will be dependent on you. You can be completely contradictory in your moods even more so than the usually fickle Cancerian so you need a steady mate who will protect your more sensitive feelings yet can also give you the excitement you absolutely must have. Getting out to make your career happen is almost more important to you than anything. You will tend to over react to criticism,

even where none is intended, so a tactless lover is a no no. Great physical passion is not really your scene. You like cuddles and you dream of wonderfully ecstatic clinches but you get bothered by mates who want total exclusivity.

Cancer Sun Taurus Moon

Home loving, security conscious, possessive, indulgent, caring and considerate you are one of the world's family people. The better things of life are a must for your happiness and fulfilment - comfortable home, classy and sensuous clothes, good food and drink, plush friends and an abundance of cuddles. Being a water earth mix you are creative in a highly practical way. Starting new projects is never a problem but once on track you have more staying power than most Cancerians. You like to wrap yourself round lovers, anchor them to the spot and never let them go. Jealousy runs deep in your nature and you react with great speed to any threat to your emotional well being. Part of you is amazingly physical and passionate but part of you wants the emotional contact as much as anything. Cancer is not given to deeply erotic relationships though Taurus is, so you need to find a balance in your mate. You can be stubbornly determined to get your own way in relationships and at home which can cause problems. You need a pliable, flexible partner who does not mind giving in. Throwing tantrums is not really your style except at the Full Moon but you are a past master at the art of passive resistance. Cancer the crab digs itself into the sand at the first whiff of danger or disagreement and Taurus, the bull, stands firm at all times. You are slow to anger but quite a sight when you do erupt. You absolutely must have a faithful mate.

Cancer Sn Gemini Moon

A fairly untypical Cancerian you can blanch sometimes at too much emotion, hate being swamped in sentiment and really long for the wide open spaces. You are supposed to be a home lover, yet at the first opportunity you fly the coop. Restlessness is inbred. Gemini Moon people regard ruts and routines with something akin to horror. You feel as if you might implode if you have to keep at the same repetitive, drudgery for ever. So you have a conflict on your hands going on inside you between your Cancerian half which wants home, family and the suburban life and your Gemini half which wants excitement, travel and mental stimulation. You can be jealous though you loathe to admit it. You need an oddly assorted lover who will not cling on too firmly, and can give you enough security without making you feel trapped. You are not terribly good at intensely intimate physical relationships where it is all heavy breathing and hot passion. You need space and a lighter touch. The ability to communicate in your partner is a must. If they cannot talk, think and sparkle, they will not last long. You are a water air mix so maybe you need a touch of chutzpah and common sense in your mate. Being highly sensitive can make you a dreamer and rather fantasy prone but you are still able to get your act together very effectively. You can laugh at yourself better than most Cancerians.

Cancer Sun Cancer Moon
Deeply emotional, hyper sensitive and curiously rather self sufficient, you feel as if you were almost too swept around by your feelings at times to be able to open up easily. Like a raft cast adrift on the sea you are blown hither and thither by the winds and the currents. Consideration and care of others in a general way is central to your nature but sometimes you find it easier to relate to the sufferings of the world and give to everyone rather than give to someone very close. You need to pick mates who will not hurt you in any way. It is said that Cancer is the sign most deeply afraid of being hurt. Fear of separation is the worst and you have it in double quantities. Jealousy runs strongly in your nature and you can sulk endlessly if things do not go your way. Leaving the past behind is difficult, at times feels almost impossible and you can be wildly, wonderfully sentimental. Curiously enough being a New Moon baby you do not have a driving need to have a partner around all the time. You can prop yourself up quite happily and your self absorption may upset mates cause you do not rely enough on them. But you do have all of the Cancerians love of family though you may make mates feel more like children or siblings after a time than intimate lovers. You are full of initiative, get up

and go and will doubtless have an active career. When life gets tricky, you pull your socks up and start a new project to keep you occupied.

Cancer Sun Leo Moon

Water and Fire do not mix they say but you have to find a way, since you are emotional and dynamic at the same time. Living life to the full in the most flamboyant way is your aim. Extremely creative, very colourful, full of initiative you keep your life moving along at a fair pace. The grand style is important to you. Life as you see it should be travelled first class staying only in five star places. You adore surrounding yourself with wealthy, elegant friends. Charm comes as second nature and entertaining is one of your great joys. Your reputation is perhaps a touch too important to you so a partner who can boost your status is a must. Home and family are deeply important to your wellbeing and you cling firmly onto those you love. Jealousy can be a problem but in addition to loathing separations of any sort you also loathe criticism, even the merest whisper of it. Hyper sensitive was never the word for it. So you need a mate who is the soul of tact and diplomacy, endlessly patient and willing to put up with your foibles, dislikes and mood swings. At best you can be simple, direct and very straightforward. At worst you can be given to loud outbursts. You can be amazingly stubborn at home so lovers have to be bendable.

Cancer Sun Virgo Moon

Kind, considerate, highly practical, socially charming, a mover and a shaker in a very quiet, refined way, you are one of the world's special people. Worrying is your great downfall. You are a past master at nit picking over every tiny anxiety and when they are used up you invent a few more! You crave order a little too much and need to watch a tendency to be prudish. Luckily your Cancer Sun keeps you on the move, starting new projects, creating a little beauty or comfort for yourself and others. Being of service is extremely important to you though you are remarkably good at standing up for yourself when the moment comes. You are no pushover and indeed have more inner determination than most. A family is important to your wellbeing, both when unmarried and married. So you need lovers you can introduce round your relatives as well as one who wants to settle with children eventually. You also need one who understands your deeper fears and phobias. In your off days you can be amazingly scratchy even sometimes slightly paranoid and need to be made to feel secure. You can be both possessive and quite adaptable. What could be a problem as you age is a tendency to turn lovers into just another one of the brood at home or to become slightly shrivelled up with worry. You have to stay open to life and live that Virgo Moon out to its fullest physical expression.

Cancer Sun Libra Moon
Successful, creative, sensitive, considerate, charming and rather elegant, you are definitely one of the world's beautiful people. You love surrounding yourself with tasteful objects and even more tasteful people. The great unwashed hold no fascination whatsoever for you. Dare it be said - you can be just a touch snobbish and at times too much on the surface. Home loving but definitely not the stay at home type, you are constantly on the move, working for success. But you are also perseveringly trying to find the answers to your inner dilemmas because you always have a sense that you never get quite what you want. Your life is always half wonderful. But you feel discouraged about ever getting total satisfaction. What you want is never what you ought to do. Your Cancer Sun pushes you towards emotionally sensitive, home loving people who can be part of your larger family but that Libra Moon wants a one to one partner who is also fairly spacey and detached. Finding the right balance is tricky and much of it comes from the incompatibility which you sensed as a child between your parents. They did not feel that together so you cannot feel that together within yourself until you leave childhood behind and begin to find your own identity. You are an escapist so you need someone rather practical and grounded, within limits.

Cancer Sun Scorpio Moon
Creative, caring, strong, intense and very determined, you always know inside yourself exactly where you are aiming though often you do not let on. You are awash with emotion

and sometimes feel cast adrift like a small boat on the ocean, blown hither and thither by the winds and currents. Your feelings run deeper than almost everyone else but you never ever admit when you are hurt. Taking great pride in concealing your vulnerabilities you sometimes come across as uncaring or rather tough but quite the reverse is the case. Standing far enough back from yourself is not easy so you can rarely be objective. Over reacting to slights or hearing criticism where none was intended makes life not only difficult for you but also for mates. Some people need to balance up by finding lovers the opposite of themselves but you could not stand an airy, unemotional sort. Or one who was too fiery and up in the clouds. Earth types can ground you a little and make you feel more stable and secure. But at the end of the day you really want a mate who can join you in those oceanic feelings which are times threaten to swamp you. You never take your love life lightly. It's all love or war! Once you are off people that is IT. At times you may not want any mate at all because you do get so pulled into your depths. Often you find yourself giving and getting emotional nourishment from larger groups of people. But you cannot live without love for long. Families are hugely important to you.

Cancer Sun Sagittarius Moon
No one could ever accuse you of being boring or stodgy. A wonderfully colourful mix of fire and water you thrive on fun, constant activity and impulse decisions. A contradictory mix is what you are - fiercely emotional, home loving and caring on the one hand but also freedom loving, independent, devil-may care and tactlessly honest on the other. You fight a constant battle with yourself over your inner conflict. One part of you wants family, security, stability and roots - the other wants the wide open spaces, stimulating friendships and the odd thrill to keep life exciting. You need an equally odd mix in a lover who will give you space and support at the same time. Hot strong physical passion is not your scene. What you really prefer is emotional warmth and perhaps the romantic illusion of an adventurous relationship. You certainly will never settle for anyone dull. But you do not like to be too crowded. As you grow older lovers may feel as

if they had been added in as just another member of the family which could cause problems. On your best days you are wonderfully, refreshingly direct and on your worst given to firework displays of bad temper. You love to entertain both socially and professionally. You will never feel totally satisfied about your emotional life because you need such totally different things in a mate.

Cancer Sun Capricorn Moon
Emotional and earthy, caring and practical, creative, successful, you are always on the go. You have oodles of initiative and never sit still. New ideas new projects, new people constantly float through your life. Whatever is not working well is abandoned as you sail off to start afresh. Beginnings are relatively easy. It's keeping going which is difficult for you. Routine and long distance jobs are a bore. But somehow you never feel quite satisfied with life or love. A Full Moon baby you are constantly living on a see saw. You veer from extreme to extreme, wanting what you have not got. Once you have it then wanting something else. In childhood you felt your parents as being quite opposite types. You have absorbed the split between them inside yourself so that what you ought to do is never what you want to do and vice versa. You commit to one person and promptly want another. At times in life you will not have stopped working long enough to find a satisfactory love life. You never feel acceptable for just being you. You feel you have to earn love by achieving all the time. Your Cancer Sun years for roots, protection, reassurance of a family while your Capricorn Moon pushes you out into the cold, hard world to keep working. You need a mate who will drown you in love and boost your self esteem to the extent of making success less necessary.

Cancer Sun Aquarius Moon
Bright, sharp witted, caring, creative, very restless and rather sensitive, you are never quite sure what it is you want in life. Emotionally quixotic you want quite contradictory, incompatible qualities in a lover. They need to be into their feelings enough to give you security and protection yet spacey enough to let you roam free. You are desperate

to continue your childhood family life into adulthood yet you shy clear of one-to-one involvement and commitment because you fear being trapped. You are a compulsive joiner of groups, teams, crowds of friends. Safety in numbers is one of your mottos. You are constantly pulled between your head and your heart. At times the only solution seems to be to disappear into your daydreams. Escapism is a failing but it brings discontent and dissatisfaction. You do have a fertile imagination which can be put to better use than creating fantasies. What you lack is real trust in life and practical common sense. But if you try to find these qualities in a lover you get unsettled by their fiery over confidence or their boringly mundane approach to life. Great physical passion is not at all to your taste. Indeed your Aquarian Moon really wants to be separate from the body at times. What you need is a highly sensitive thinking type.

Cancer Sun Pisces Moon
Deeply sensitive and caring to a degree which hurts, you feel pain for almost everyone to the extent that you sometimes need to shut yourself away from the world and people just to settle down your surging emotions. At times you are so impressionable you feel cast adrift on a wide sea, helpless to anchor yourself or be at rest. Your extraordinarily creative and considerate temperament can be put to good use either in artistic careers or in helping others. But you sometimes shy away from revealing your feelings in intimate relationships because you fear rejection, abandonment or worse. Though you are very seducible and often find yourself dragged into relationships out of pity. Finding the courage to voice your feelings is a challenge for you. So you absolutely need a lover who is not a rough clod around matters of the heart. Someone who can sooth away your worries, protect you against the troubles of the world, and give you a secure harbour. Mates also need to be strong enough not be blown around by your emotional extremes which can be very extreme. At times you can appear and probably are very self-absorbed just because your feelings do swallow you up. Maturity usually brings you some ideal in life to dedicate yourself to which helps to pull you out of yourself. Resentment can be a tiny failing since you so

often feel a martyr to other people's needs. Escaping off on a daydream trip is your way out but not always helpful. You need love and a family.

Leo Sun Aries Moon

Bright, brash, colourful and highly active, you live life at a pace which exhausts most people. At times you even threaten to burnout yourself. An energetic go getter, you are great at creating, at starting up new projects, thinking of new ideas and you have all the courage and daring in the world. Common sense is not always your long suit and neither it has to be said is emotional sensitivity. You just never sit still long enough to consider other people's needs which obviously can bring relationship problems in its wake. As a red hot Leo you need an audience of adoring, admiring fans and courtiers. With an Aries Moon you even more need to stand out as an individual. Co operating, sharing, caring and being half of a duo is a difficult concept for you especially in early adult life. So you tend to aim for rather submissive lovers who will agree and anticipate your every whim. Though they have to be classy enough to fit in with your idea of your station in life. You always think of yourself being highly romantic and often wish you had been born in a more glamorous era. You will have some sizzling escapades but they may not survive for ever. Since love is essentially about Being and not Doing you are somewhat at a loss. Your reactions change constantly, you loathe restraint in any form and the idea of compromise makes your hackles rise. Your pride often gets in the way of love. The knocks and disappointments of life will hopefully eventually soften you down a touch, giving you a connection to your own suffering and thus to the suffering of others. Then partnerships really begin to work. You are basically faithful, want a solid home and family life and once settled can be loyal. But you also will need space to do your own thing.

Leo Sun Taurus Moon

Fun loving, power and attention seeking, determined to follow your own pleasures in life, there is no doubt that you carve your own path. A determined steam roller of a personality you will do whatever is necessary to fulfil your ambitions. Your fiery Sun can make you just a touch vain or pompous but luckily your earthy Moon adds a touch of grounding, common sense and humility. Self indulgence, however, is a large part of your make up and you rarely listen to advice which tells you to cut back, give up or be hard on yourself. Pleasuring your senses is high on your list of priorities. So you eat and drink well, insist on living in style and comfort and really cannot survive without an abundance of cuddles. Your great strength can be a blessing or a curse. Hugely stubborn, you obviously need a mate who will adapt to your needs rather than the other way round. If you hit difficulties you stand rooted like an oak tree until other people and circumstances adapt to you. But once on track you have a great deal of staying power. Indeed there is little that will shift you. Your head and heart rarely agree so you often settle in one relationship then your wandering eye starts to look over the fence. But you can be loyal and faithful once settled though you will always be jealous and fairly possessive. You do need to acquire an appreciation of the finer subtleties of life and love, perhaps at some point dedicating yourself to serving others rather than the other way round.

Leo Sun Gemini Moon
A never-sit-still individual you are everyone's idea of heaven at a party. You talk entertainingly and non stop, feeding titbits of fascinating information to anyone who will listen, quite often about yourself. You revel in attention and admiration, the more the merrier. Routine and drudgery are but one step away from the grave to you. Your life must be filled with variety, spice, excitement and glamour otherwise you get very bad tempered. Committed relationships are a mixed blessing in your view. Your Leo side really wants a burning passion which will fill your life from now to infinity and in that mode you can be extremely faithful. But your Gemini Moon is a real social butterfly. What you want one moment is not what you want three second later. You need a partner who is just a erratic, unpredictable and quirky as you. You also need a mate who will put up with your need to be centre spot of the limelight. They have to be

grand enough to share your regal lifestyle (Leo being king/ queen of the beasts) but not so uppity that they threaten to upstage you. It often takes you a while through life to learn compassion or sensitivity to the needs of others which can prove a stumbling block to early relationships. What you lack, being a fire air type, is water and earth. So you must get more in touch with your feelings in tiny ways in all aspects of life. Lack of earth makes you impractical and rather unrealistic so it would help to find a mate with some common sense to balance you up. You give them fiery enthusiasm and trust in life. They keep your feet on the floor.

Leo Sun Cancer Moon
Two words spring to mind - one is family, the other is grand. You certainly love the better things of life, you need socially elevated friends, the more the merrier, and you want a solid, settled family base. No one is going to upstage you at home, that is for sure. Leo always wants to be top dog in the family and your Cancer Moon makes very certain that the older you get the more you will pull the strings of power in the family. Being a fire water mix you are a person of extremes, excitable, impulsive, intense and highly sensitive to criticism. You are over reactive even where no slights were intended which can make you a prickly minefield for lovers. They have to tread very delicately around you. Jealousy can be quite a problem. Certainly you hate being separated from those you love both in the emotional sense and because you absolutely loathe being humiliated. Your mood swings can be quite severe though you are usually able to express yourself with a refreshing directness. You can be highly unpredictable or thoroughly warm hearted. Showbusiness personalities often are of your type and you certainly would adore the glamour, razzamatazz and romance of the public life. What you possibly need more than anything else is an earthy type who would offer you warmth but tempered with common sense. You do lack air and the objectivity it brings but airy types - Gemini, Libra and Aquarius - would seem too cool and detached.

Leo Sun Leo Moon A fiery combination this both for

yourself and for mates. You are so centred in yourself and your needs, so determined to be grand, be admired and be loved that you genuinely find it difficult to step beyond the boundaries of your own world to see the needs of others. It will get better as you grow older and learn a few tough lessons about love, suffering and life. Few people recognise quite how insecure, unconfident and empty you really feel you are. They only see the regal gestures, the flash, the show, the public performance. Inside you are often very frightened, not knowing whether you really exist at all so you absolutely must have a mate who can boost your fragile ego and does not mind being a slave to its demands. Your moods can be extreme opposites - one moment demanding, proud and arrogant, the next humiliated, feeling worthless and powerless. You can be stubborn to nth degree but are not always sensible, to put it mildly. You lack earth to give you a sense of your body and to put your feet on the floor. You lack water so you are not always well in touch with your feelings which could nourish you. Burnout is a real problem since you have no sense of when to slow down. Being a New Moon baby you are more self sufficient than most, have less need to have a constant other half. But you do need a passion. Not for nothing is Leo known as the sign of the burning heart.

Leo Sun Virgo Moon
You work very hard to stay in a prominent position in life. Two quite contradictory traits vie with each other inside you. One wants the glamorous life full of attention, admiration and money. The other is rather self effacing, workaholic, almost timid and a great worrier about the tiny trivia of life. But you are a great deal more realistic than most Leos which is a help since you pay attention to your body and do not delegate the boring tasks of life loftily to others which is the norm with most other of your sun sign compatriots. Being fire earth, you are what is known in astrology as a steam roller type who keeps going long after everyone else has dropped by the wayside out of sheer exhaustion. You have the energy and determined of ten. So you obviously need a partner with stamina to keep up with you though not, of course, to knock you off centre stage, which is the

cardinal sin in your book. You do lack contact with your feelings and are often not good at standing back far enough to see yourself clearly. But a highly emotional mate would make you feel too swamped and an airy mate would feel too cool and detached. You need a flexible partner who will give way when you dig your heels in.

Leo Sun Libra Moon

You could never be poor, unwashed or a down and out. You need to be grand, to move in the best circles, to live a luxurious lifestyle with a group of highly elevated friends. Upwardly socially mobile is the name of your game. Your Leo Sun wants attention, excitement and colour. Your Libra Moon wants peace, harmony and elegance. You certainly have great taste - in clothes and interior decor. Being fire and air you move at speed, rarely slowing down to ask your body or your feelings what they want. So you need a mate who can anchor you a little without making you feel suffocated or swamped. You find it difficult to connect with the darker side of life. If anything you can come across as being slightly superficial because you like to stay sociable, stay on the surface and not face depressions, pain or misery. Hard experience in life will teach you to connect to the depths which can give you more stability and solidity. Your sense of humour is usually a strong point and you can always look on the bright side of life. But over optimism sometimes trips you up. You often accuse others of being critical or gloomy where in fact they are just being realistic.

Leo Sun Scorpio Moon

Sunny on the outside and deep, dark and determined on the inside. You rarely show that you are hurt, indeed you rarely show your feelings at all. Your Leo Sun is all show and you certainly adore being centre stage when admiration and attention is going. But emotionally you play your cards very close to your chest and are a much more complex being than the normally straightforward Leo. Your Scorpio Moon makes you hang onto grudges and you can even be vindictive when people have hurt you. Forgiveness does not come easily. You are stubborn to an extraordinary degree so need a mate who can bend and flex to your will without feeling aggrieved. Change is not easy for you and in general you will withstand most pressures, digging your heels in to maintain the status quo. You assume circumstances and other people will give way before you do. You are the most controlled of the fire water types but even your moods swing from extreme to extreme. Unpredictable, excitable and rather impulsive you often have little discipline about life. What you want is what you want and that is all there is to the matter. You can express yourself very directly at times and can be warm and supportive though you will always hold part of yourself back. You will jealously guard what is yours.

Leo Sun Sagittarius Moon
Wild, restless, charming, self centred and absolutely determined to do what you want at all costs, you are in danger of burnout because you will not settle down ever. You ignore the signals from your body that it has had enough, ignore advice from everyone around and generally ignore life's warnings until you are forced to face up to reality with a bump. Sometimes you come across as warm, charming, outgoing and generous but you do have a genuine difficulty about seeing other's point of view or understanding partner's needs so you can also seem less than sensitive. You are an entrepreneur at heart, a real go getter and promoter so you need a mate around who can support you in your aims and does not mind being abandoned for long stretches while you go chasing after your visions. What can let you down in relationships is your inability to stay with your heart. Very watery, emotional mates make you feel swamped but you do need to learn to take in nourishment from your feelings and not fly along the cloud tops all the time. Lovers and partners will often be accused by you of being critical or gloomy whereas they are probably only being sensible in refusing to be totally caught up in your wild enthusiasms.

Leo Sun Capricorn Moon
You want to look grand but are willing to put your back into making it happen, rather than indulging in vague dreams. The attention and admiration of others are your life's blood but you are much more insecure, under confident and

deprived than you let on. You have always felt that you need to achieve to be loved rather than being accepted for just being yourself. You certainly make more of a success of your life than most but along the way you do not always feel as happy as you should. You can come across as vain, even arrogant, but in reality you are terrified no one will notice you. Criticism hurts you deeply. Being a fire earth type you are what is known in astrological parlance as a steam roller, able to keep going long after weaker souls have dropped by the wayside. You have formidable energy and the vision to sustain your interest. Love may be pushed to one side for the sake of work and ambition for longish periods in your life but you are basically a warm hearted person underneath all that rigid self discipline. Your Capricorn Moon can be sensual, cuddly and pleasure seeking when you let yourself relax which does happen more easily as you get older. You need a mate who will adapt to your needs since you are fairly stubborn and perhaps also can survive times when your interest is either on yourself on your ambitions.

Leo Sun Aquarius Moon
A Full Moon baby you never know what you want. Your head says one thing, your heart quite another. When you have a lover, you promptly want someone else. But that never quite works either. Your Leo Sun wants attention, admiration, is rather traditional and is quite self centred. But your Aquarian Moon is friendly, is happy to be one of the crowd and could not care less about the limelight. It is also zany, whacky, eccentric and unconcerned about the social niceties of life. So you are constantly at war with yourself. This conflict stems from a childhood in which you saw your parents as being incompatible. What they could not get together in their marriage, you cannot get together in your head. So you need to rise above their differences of long ago and find new solution to your problems. It does not have to be a question of either this or that. There is a third way. Very close relationships make you claustrophobic and fight shy of anything that smells remotely like jealousy or possessiveness. You want to be free to follow your own unconventional life style. Often you set out to startle or shock companions just to make an effect so you need a

mate who is spacey, tolerant and fairly unflappable. Being a fire air type you could probably do with a lover who is slightly earthy to give you warmth and grounding. Watery, emotional people make you run a mile.

Leo Sun Pisces Moon
Fun loving and attention seeking on the outside, in reality you are a deeply sensitive, rather timid soul inside. Those who know you well, and few probably do, realise that you often pass up chances for relationships because you are so scared of rejection. Often you indulge more in day dreams than in actual romances. You need to make more of an effort to get into reality. Being a fire water type, you are excitable, impulsive, restless and prone to fairly extreme mood swings. Over reacting to others' comments can make you seem prickly and unreasonable but you do genuinely hear slights in anything that is not unabashed admiration. Feeling a martyr often makes you seem self pitying and you need to make an effort to pull yourself away from the past. Restraining yourself is not always easy through life and you are possibly more addiction prone than some. At best you can be refreshingly straightforward and direct though you can also be way off beam at times. You are highly creative, probably musical, and would fare well in show business or entertainment careers. You need a mate who is adaptable and willing to put their needs aside to allow you centre stage. But you are more giving than many Leos, able to understand the distress and needs of close partners. Emotional types would suit you well though some earth in your mate would also help to bring you down to the ground occasionally. You are not remotely practical.

Virgo Sun Aries Moon
A restless personality, you are in truth a slightly odd mix. Your Virgo Sun makes you hard working, modest, rather refined and a great worrier. Whereas your Aries Moon makes you excitable, slightly brash, go getting and fairly pushy. Being an earth fire mix you are a real steam roller of energy, crashing on when other weaker souls have dropped by the wayside. You have determination, persistence, an eye for detail and an appetite for grand schemes. In love

you want excitement and a slight element of danger. Sitting still at home tending to the domestic chores is not your idea of heaven. You somehow manage to be highly critical, a bit of a perfectionist, and wildly impractical all at once. You never feel you have everything you want in life at the same time. Something is always missing. You certainly need a similarly unsettled personality as a mate. Ideally an Aries with a Virgo Moon would be your choice. You adore to work and you channel your energies with great dedication. But your reactions change constantly and you tend to leap into activity often without thinking matters through carefully enough. You need a mate who is more fixed than you, able to stand still while you dash around like someone possessed.

Virgo Sun Taurus Moon
Earthy, warm, charming, hard working and very rooted, you are certainly concerned with giving yourself what feels good in life. Luckily your Virgo Sun gives you a strong sense of service otherwise you would be totally given over to your own comfort. Although reasonably adaptable you essentially loathe change of any sort especially in your home life. You are affectionate and more demonstrative than some Virgos. The Taurus Moon makes you extremely tactile and always in need of a good cuddle. Life to you is about the pleasures of the senses and as long as you find a mate whose pleasures coincide with yours then you should have relatively little trouble. You do lack slightly in imagination being all earth. You can have a rather narrow vision of life and do need to channel your formidable energies into some challenging task. A perfectionist where others are concerned you can be a touch critical or analytical and that sometimes freezes emotions before they have had a chance to develop. Luckily your Taurus Moon warms up that rather detached side of Virgo. You need an emotional mate who can breathe some real life into your heart. Fire types will drive you wild with their impracticality.

Virgo Sun Gemini Moon
Restless, adaptable, a great worker and worrier, you find concentrating over a long span difficult. More likely to

be a jack of all trades than a specialist you always have several strings to your bow. The difference to you between a rut and being half dead is only a matter of degree. You need to learn to settle in life just a little and would be the better of a fixed partner - Taurus, Leo, Scorpio or Aquarius either Sun or Moon to give you some anchorage. Though sometimes security makes you feel suffocated and trapped. Nervousness can be a problem because you are highly strung, possibly more so than others realise. So you also need an unflappable mate who can cope with your panics and phobias without getting exasperated. You can be both intellectual and practical but what you are not is impulsive or emotional. You come across as cool, reasonable even a little chilly. You need to attract more fiery excitement into your life and a little more feeling. Though there is no sense in you mating with an over watery type since too many emotions threaten to swamp your finely balanced system. You need to get fully into life at some point. You are in danger of drying up if you do not. Virgo has a tendency to be too much the observer, not enough the participant.

Virgo Sun Cancer Moon
A charming, helpful, hard working, home loving person you are not one of the world's ravers but all the better for it. Being practical and adaptable you can fit into most situations rather happily and go well out of your way to make sure companions are well looked after. You do tend to be over serious at times, and self protective but you have the capacity to hang on in there through almost any crisis. Your inner strength is considerable but you can be too attached to the past or need to maintain your security to an obsessive degree. This can cause problems in relationships as can your tendency to manipulate. But you have an adaptability and a sense of initiative that are highly useful. What you lack sometimes is staying power and the insight to understand your unconscious fears. Your Cancer Moon makes you sentimental rather than realistic about your past and present family life which is not always helpful. Breaking away from your childhood family is difficult for you. You absolutely need to settle down with a family as an adult so keep your Virgo perfectionist streak well under

control. It sometimes destroys feelings before they have had a chance to blossom.

Virgo Sun Leo Moon
You want to live life the five star way and are willing to work extremely hard to make it happen so it is not all a pipe dream. You are a curious mix being both modest, self effacing, rather shy and also being charming, entertaining, at times vain. Your ego never quite knows where it is - being pushed into the background or being allowed centre stage. More outgoing than the normal Virgo, you love putting on a show and being flamboyant. Your vanity is easily dented and you loathe criticism in any form though being a Virgo you can be quite a perfectionist about others. You appear more flexible than you really are. That Leo Moon does not give way easily to anyone else's needs or wants. Your personal magnetism gets you your own way most of the time. Being an earth fire mix you charge through life, leaving other weaker souls exhausted by the wayside. Your workaholic tendencies combined with flair and vision make you a formidable achiever. But you need sometimes to look at the subtler sides of life and not be so determined to keep on the move all the time. A mate with a touch, not too much, water in them would help to nourish you, slow you down a little. Staying in touch with your feelings is important.

Virgo Sun Virgo Moon
A workaholic and a worrier, practical, self contained and rather critical, you do not always need a partner in life. Being a New Moon baby you can survive better on your own than most. Being a Virgo in addition you are fairly good at staying within your own boundaries. Which does not mean you do not want to relate, just that you are not desperate for a soul mate in the way some are. A double earthy aspect can give you too narrow a vision in life and an obsessive concern with what works. If you career lets you down you panic so it always has absolute priority. You do not always let your imagination free to push you in the direction of your dreams and visions. You need to find more trust in life, more chutzpah and daring, and to stop worrying. They

always say that the Virgo Moon raises worrying to an art form. You have it in double doses. Emotions can sometimes be analysed to freezing point before they have had a chance to blossom. You need to allow your feelings more space though they worry you a great deal so you control them. A spontaneous outgoing lover would probably do you the world of good. Though you will object to having your neatly ordered life upset. Getting into life is important since you can turn out to be rather spinsterish (no matter which sex you are) if you stay on the sidelines and only ever observe which is a tendency.

Virgo Sun Libra Moon
Refined, elegant, rather retiring, and very hard working, you would never knowingly put a foot out of line socially. You are one of the world's goodies though you need to watch that you do not become too precious or indeed too much of a superficial observer on life's scene rather than an active participant. You are fastidious, slightly snobbish and loathe the great unwashed and the idle. Your Virgo Sun makes you a great perfectionist about other people and your Libra Moon makes you want everything to be "nice" - blissfully harmonious and peaceful. This can make relationships tricky since it leaves no room for flaws, faults and the odd off day. You are adaptable and full of initiative so you usually pick yourself up and keep things ticking over. What you are exceptionally good at is creating a beautiful home full of beautiful things and you entertain like a dream though you are not an indulgent party person yourself. You like working at everything including your social life. Being an earth air mix you can sometimes come across as too practical and cool. You lack impulsiveness and emotional sensitivity. So perhaps you need a lover who is just a touch more daring and has more connection to their feelings. Getting down into the depths of yourself is not easy for you.

Virgo Sun Scorpio Moon
An intriguing combination, you can appear rather prudish on the surface but passions burn deeply within. Your workaholic tendencies obscure your deeply emotional nature at least to the outside view. What is sure is that you

will not be one of life's dried up spinsterish Virgos who view it all from the sidelines. You throw yourself intensely into whatever you are doing emotional or professional. Your Scorpio Moon is deeply secretive and few ever know the turmoil of feelings which churn inside you. You will never let on when you have been hurt. Forgiving and forgetting does not come easily to you. At times you have been known to be vindictive though you dislike yourself afterwards. As an earth water type you have tremendous stamina and endurance. You can survive through any calamity but have a tendency to cling too firmly onto what is past rather than try to move ahead through changes. What you need is a lover who wants to live life at the same emotional depth as you, preferably a water sign, ideally a Sun Scorpio, who can put up with your slightly manipulative tendencies. Fire does not sit happily with your nature but maybe a mate with a touch more daring than yourself could give you the courage to be less fearful.

Virgo Sun Sagittarius Moon
Restless, fidgety, talkative to a startling degree and rather wise, you are certainly not a stick in the mud personality. But you never feel quite settled with yourself. Your head and your heart always want different people and different things. As soon as you settle with a lover, you promptly lose interest and look elsewhere. You need to find a way of combining your duty with your desires. Jealousy and possessiveness make you run a mile so an insecure mate who tries to fence you in absolutely will not do. You need to have intellectual and emotional freedom to wander as you please. Friends are hugely important to you but they need to be relatively thick skinned since you are honest to a staggering degree. Being an earth fire person you keep going constantly. In astrology you are known as a steam roller, able to forge ahead when everyone else is dropping by the wayside. You have a way of combining flair with practicality so you can turn your visions into reality though at times you do get bogged down in details. Work is your main interest and a life of unvarying sameness is one of your ideas of hell. You need a lover who can introduce you to the subtler aspects of life and maybe even get you more

in touch with your feelings.

Virgo Sun Capricorn Moon

Earthy, over worked, a worrier, a touch too practical, you can be surprisingly sensual if you let yourself go. But you tend to assume you will only be loved if you achieve so you can go through ambitious, workaholic phases and even be celibate for longish periods. You are undoubtedly charming though you never relax much on social occasions. You have a sneaking feeling that indulgences are a sin which other people can manage but you cannot. You come across as someone who is relatively at ease with themselves though it is partly an illusion. Being a double earth type you are a touch narrow in your vision of life and obsessed with what works, what is practical, rather than what could be a dream or an ideal. Money could become too much of a god for you or social status. You need to let your imagination roam free and have more faith in life. Take the odd risk. A mate with water Sun or Moon (Cancer, Scorpio or Pisces) would get you in touch with your feelings more. But you really love a partner who makes you feel needed, secure and someone who is worth while. Your self esteem is not great. If your career fails at any point you panic like mad.

Virgo Sun Aquarius Moon

You constantly surprise yourself by being what you are not. An odd mix of the highly traditional and the frankly way-out you manage to be at the same time rather prudish, fairly retiring and wild, whacky, eccentric. You almost deliberately set out to shock mates at times just to see the effect. Friends are the mainstay of your life and you are never happy with the idea of claustrophobic, possessive relationships. At the first whiff of jealousy you are off. Being an earth air mix you can come across as too cool and practical. Although impulsive in some respects you are not given to emotional flights of fancy. In fact you often stand so far back from feelings that others wonder whether you have them at all. You run the risk of never getting into life but becoming the expert observer and analyser who stands on the sidelines all the time to watch. Dissecting every lurch of your heart before it has taken time to root will freeze a relationship. You need to learn to trust feelings more and to go with the flow. Highly watery, emotional mates would be too difficult and threaten to swamp you. But a touch of sensitivity to that side of life would help.

Virgo Sun Pisces Moon
A Full Moon baby you are constantly out of step with yourself about what you want. Your head wants one person and your heart quite another. You settle and suddenly the grass looks greener elsewhere. You need to rise above the conflicts of your childhood to see that you can get your duty and your desires together though it will not be easy. Adult life can be a long search for emotional happiness and stability. You are restless, adaptable and rather kind in nature so you should be able to find what you want ultimately. You have a self sacrificing streak and genuinely want to be of service. But because you are so sensitive to rejection you sometimes shrink back from exposing your feelings. Romantic opportunities are often missed because of your timidity. Daydreams can often fill in for what your relationships fail to provide. Often you feel self pitying, almost slightly martyred because of your predicament. You need to find courage to get out into life. You have warmth and sensitivity. A lover who is fixed would give you an anchor. Maybe one with a touch (not too much) of fire would give you a sense of daring and trust in life. But you need a lover who is as refined as yourself. No one brash, crude or too direct would suit you.

Libra Sun Aries Moon
A Full Moon baby, you never know quite what you want. It usually is not what you have got. Settle with one lover and the grass immediately looks greener on the other side of the fence. You rarely get your head and your heart together which is a great shame since you desperately need a mate in life. Librans are never good at being solo flyers. You just do not feel whole without another half. But you are insecure, rather excitable, move around far too much and tend to be rather outspoken at points which ruffles feathers around. Libran ladies more so than men in this respect since they are anyway rather direct in their approach to life and an

Aries Moon adds to their dynamic, assertive energy. Libran men tend to be sweeter and softer. Being an air fire mix you are rather combustible and can flare up very rapidly. You also tend to burnout because you never slow down enough to recharge your batteries or listen to your body. A mate with a touch of earth about them to ground you and give you common sense, or one with a hint of water to teach you to nourish yourself emotionally would help. You can at times come across as rather superficial because you are highly sociable and shy away from the deeper, darker side of life and love. It is only through painful experiences and being disappointed that you learn to plunge into those very feelings which can give you strength and stability. Your sense of humour and wonderful way with words are real blessings for you.

Libra Sun Taurus Moon
Both your Sun and Moon are ruled by Venus, otherwise known as Aphrodite, goddess of love, parties, indulgences and the high life. You certainly know how to enjoy yourself and no mistake. You have superb taste in clothes, decor, entertaining and you eat and drink rather to excess. You were never designed to be poor and absolutely must have a mate who either provides you with the luxuries of life or will allow you to spend as you please to pleasure yourself. You need another half in life, so a partner is a must. You are more earthy, sensual and body oriented than some Librans so must have a good sex life. You can be stubborn about getting your own way at home and you dislike change in your emotional life. Being an air earth mix you can come across as rather cool. Certainly you are not given to wild impulses or flights of fancy except where your comfort is concerned. A hard worker you are never happy with lazy lovers, certainly not those who are idle about personal hygiene. You dislike the great unwashed. Your Taurus Moon can make you possessive though Libra on the whole is not a jealous sign. A refined Sun Taurus would suit you down to the ground.

Libra Sun Gemini Moon
An airy, detached, talkative, nervy, restless personality you

certainly know how to put yourself across to people in a highly persuasive manner. You rarely sit still and loathe settled routines of any sort so you need a mate who can fly along at your pace or at least let you have your head. Being a double air person you tend to live up in your head, in your idea, opinions and thoughts. You will tend to attract yourself to similar kinds of people because you absolutely must have stimulating conversations but two air types together become very cool and so detached eventually you will hardly touch at all. Emotions, do however, make you feel swamped and you basically distrust watery people (Cancer, Scorpio, Pisces). Earthy types also make you feel weighed down and suffocated. Fiery types are much more exciting but together you are too reckless and burnout could be a problem. So you need to compromise and find a way of connecting to what can nourish you in life without being overwhelmed by it. Happily your Gemini Moon though exceedingly restless does have an inclination to the darker side of life and this could be your saving grace because you will be pulled at some point towards the depths which will give you some stability. But staying too high will always be a problem.

Libra Sun Cancer Moon
You are basically at odds with yourself so will not find it easy in early adult life to get your head and heart together. What you lust after is not always what duty tells you is right. But both Libra and Cancer have relatively similar interests in life so you will fare not badly as long as you can set up a comfortable, beautiful home; a coterie of elegant, sophisticated friends; and a career that allows you to be constantly on the move. Being an air water mix you swing between detachment and deep sympathy, being thinking and feeling. You are highly sensitive and can be a real dreamer and escape merchant. What is vital is an outlet for your helping skills. Your Cancer Moon does make you security conscious and at times jealous. You loathe the idea of separation, indeed any kind of emotional pain makes you wince so you need a highly sensitive mate. But you also need one who will put up with your cool, airy rather detached side which frankly does not want to swim around

in too many swampy feelings. This is your inner conflict and the challenge which you must face up to in your relationships...how to combine air and water. You must just find a way of living out both.

Libra Sun Leo Moon
Vibrant, sociable, colourful, charmingly persuasive, not a shrinking violet, you are certainly one of life's more noticeable people. You want to live the five star way with the best of everything. Certainly you were never designed to be poor and you loathe the idle, the unemployed and the great unwashed. You have great taste in clothes, decor, friends and entertaining. A gourmet not to say a gourmand you may have trouble with your waistline at times because you party so much and so wholeheartedly. Vanity can be a tiny problem and you certainly react very badly to any kind of personal criticism. People who put obstacles in your way also get to be highly unpopular. You need another half in life who will pander to your whims as well as being a great support. Being an air fire mix you are likely not to listen to your body's needs and exhaust yourself at times. So a mate with an earthy touch who can ground you would help. Emotional people make you confused so you'll avoid them. Libran ladies are always more masculine where Libran men are more feminine so the female of this species with a regal Moon thrown in will be a considerable challenge. You need a lover who can cope.

Libra Sun Virgo Moon
A sweetly diplomatic, rather refined, possibly fairly quiet individual who will put themselves out for other people's needs is how you come across. Libra always thinks of the other and Virgo is deeply into service and being self sacrificing. You can be at times rather cool, sometimes highly critical and always a great worrier. But you are warmer than most Librans though possibly less sociable. You never find you can relax totally at parties though you adore them. You always feel the need to be doing rather than just being. Being an air earth mix you can think in a highly practical way though you do worry too much about the details of problems and are an obsessive tidier. Getting

down into the murky depths of life, into the blood and guts of it all, is not really your scene yet you need to find your roots otherwise you will shrivel up eventually. Mates need to be slightly more fixed than you to give you an anchor, perhaps with a tiny hint of fire to give you daring and chutzpah. If anything you will be too conservative, traditional and slightly snobbish. Mates certainly should not be brash and social embarrassments but you do need a little jolt once in a while to liven you up.

Libra Sun Libra Moon

A New Moon baby, you should have less need to relate than most outside yourself and yet the idea of a Libra without a mate is like a cart without a horse. So you need a relationship in which you can maintain your boundaries where you can feel half of a whole and yet still be self sufficient at times within yourself. Being a double air person you live up in your head, in your ideas and your thoughts. So you are not well tuned into your body or your feelings and perhaps do not trust life quite enough. Libran ladies are usually quite direct in their approach to life - crisp and cool, not frilly and feminine - and this is a double emphasis of that rather cool, argumentative temperament. Libran men on the other hand tend to be sweet and rather feminine, more tactful and less assertive than their counterparts. So double the difference here. You are more highly strung than your appearance would suggest. At times you need to step away from your worries to wind down. You will tend to attract yourself to similarly cool, airy types but it would be a mistake because you will eventually hardly relate at all. Your suspicions are aroused by emotional lovers and earthy ones make you feel trapped. Fiery types will excite you more though together you can take off like hot air balloons and as a combination lack common sense. A hint of water or a hint of earth would help. You will spend your life trying to find the right balance.

Libra Sun Scorpio Moon

Interesting combination this since you seem cool, detached and rather laid back but only those in your intimate circle know quite how deep, dark and passionate you really are. Nothing in the world will make you admit when you are hurt. Indeed your feelings are rarely on public display at all. But you are a little at war with yourself. What your Scorpio Moon wants is intensity, depth and an emotional tussle... the agonies are worth it for the ecstasies that come along for the ride. But your Libra Sun hates all that angst and really wants permanent peace, bliss and harmony with nothing to ruffle your calm. There is no way you will satisfy both sides of yourself totally. A compromise is needed somewhere along the way. Perhaps a mate with a touch of elegant, sensitive Pisces which is at the lighter end of the water spectrum would keep your Moon nourished while not swamping your Libra Sun. Being an air water mix you swing between thinking and feeling, but you have a way of putting your ideas into practice with sympathy. You have a very jealous streak which you dislike intensely but can never quite stamp out so why try? You can be vindictive which comes out of this rather unforgiving side of your nature as well. Sex interests you more than most Libras. At times you can be positively preoccupied with it.

Libra Sun Sagittarius Moon
High flying, highly sociable and rather scatterbrained, you rarely sit still. Life to you is about staying on the move, having fun, chatting up a million different people. As you mature your ideals become more important to you and you aspire to greater ambitions. Usually fair and honest, you can be trusted with making sensible decisions though the process may take some time. But you do stay too much on the surface of life. For air fire people like yourself burnout can be a problem since you are not tuned into your body enough to listen to its demands. You need to stop once in a while to recharge your batteries. Only through the years with disappointments and suffering do you begin to plumb your depths to connect with those feelings which will give you stability and solidity. Finding a mate like yourself would be a mistake as you would take off like a hot air balloon together. You need a lover who can ground you, a little, and teach you to become more sensitive to your emotions. Partners who are too emotional will terrify you and if too earthy would bore and suffocate you. But just a hint would help. You loathe being fenced in or made to face

up to petty details but a mate with more staying power than you could help to anchor you enough to make you commit.

Libra Sun Capricorn Moon

Definitely upwardly mobile you are a restless personality, full of ambition and initiative, and determined to get to the top professionally and socially. You grew up believing that only by succeeding would you be loved so you really do not accept that you are worthwhile in yourself. You need to patch your self esteem together before you will get the relationships you need and deserve. The Capricorn Moon though earthy and quite sensual can also be so work oriented it switches off altogether from emotional and sexual relationships for longish periods. But being a Libra you basically need another half in life. You need to watch a tendency to pick partners who will help you up the social or professional ladder. You cannot compromise your feelings for ever. Essentially you are in a minor war with yourself about what you want. Your head and your heart never seem to agree. Find a mate and the one over the fence promptly looks more attractive. But you are highly motivated to find the answers to your problems and eventually will rise above your desire/duty dilemma to find what you need. But you probably want a mate with a touch of emotional sensitivity who can put you in touch with your feelings and one with a little fire in their belly to give you the courage to risk more.

Libra Sun Aquarius Moon

Traditional, slightly snobbish in your outlook at one level you can also be outrageously eccentric at another. You want a mate and yet you fear close intimacy. You want life to be balanced, blissful and peaceful yet you also adore startling and shocking people around you just for the effect. So you find it difficult to understand yourself - how can others cope? Being a double air person you live up in your head, in your ideas and thoughts. You are not tuned into your body or your feelings. You run on extraordinarily high levels of nervous energy. But finding your opposite will not do. Because earthy, practical mates who might ground you will also stifle you and make you feel weighed down. Watery, emotional lovers will make you nervous since you fear being swamped by emotions which you basically distrust. Finding another of your own sort will not do since you would disappear eventually into a pair of book ends. Fire is probably your best bet so a lover with Aries or Sagittarius for their Sun or Moon is what to seek out. Though watch for exhaustion since neither of you will know how to slow down. You will always need to keep a wide circle of your own friends since you hate being fenced in. Lovers need to be pals as well.

Libra Sun Pisces Moon
A sweet, sensitive, creative and highly diplomatic soul you can be really timid when it comes to love since you are terrified of rejection and often pass up romantic opportunities because you are scared of failing. But you need a mate in life. Librans cannot function alone. Being an air water mix you are slightly at odds with yourself. Half of you thinks and the other half feels. Your Pisces Moon is deeply romantic and wants a real daydream of a love affair. But Libra is cool, detached and rather laid back about anything too smoochy. So your Moon may become evasive and disappear into your fantasies rather than try to go out into the world to make it together in reality. At times you feel self pitying, almost martyred because of your fears and phobias, and you need to find courage. This is easier for a Libran lady who will be reasonably direct in approach than for a Libran man who tends to be sweet, soft and more timid. Certainly you need a mate who has superb taste in clothes, decor, art and entertaining. You are supremely elegant yourself and loathe being embarrassed socially. A sensitively emotional lover who is not too clinging would suit you.

Scorpio Sun Aries Moon
To say you are a person of extremes is putting it mildly. You are deep, dark, passionately intense and high flying, fiery, very upfront. Your mood swings are a sight to behold as you flip from one end of the spectrum to the other. Hugely stubborn at times and rather immoveable you can also be constantly on the move seeking new challenges at every turn. Emotional, excitable and impulsive you rarely put

restraints on yourself. On good days you are refreshingly direct and can express yourself freely. On bad days you explode with frustration and anxiety. You almost always act out of a sense of insecurity or impatience. You dislike your need to get back at those who have hurt you but it always seems to pop up. You are never wishy washy in your approach to love - it is all or nothing. Once an affair is over you let it drop. Being friends with old lovers is not really your style. You can be warm, supportive and highly entertaining. What you need is a lover who will cope with your agonies and ecstasies, the highs and the lows, the erratic whims, and the need to win. A Scorpio Moon is probably a must in your mate though you have to realise you will never find your ideal fantasy lover. You need too many contradictory things. A compromise has to be reached.

Scorpio Sun Taurus Moon

A Full Moon baby, you can never quite get your head and heart together. What you desire is not what your sense of duty tells you is right. When you settle with a mate, you promptly want another more attractive lover on the other side of the fence. You are deeply passionate, very jealous and stubborn to a staggering degree. So you absolutely need a mate who is flexible and adaptable. But finding one who is intense enough to satisfy your highly sexual and sensual needs but is not so jealous that they object to only having half of you is going to be tricky. The problems lie in your childhood where you felt your parents to be inherently incompatible. What they could not get together in their marriage you cannot get together in your head. You will need to separate from the past and rise above those conflicts before you find that there is a third way of relating. Your head and your heart can be satisfied at once. Your Taurus Moon needs a tactile, cuddly lover who can really look after you. Your physical comforts are hugely important to you. But you also want a lover who can transport you to positively transcendental realms. At times you wallow around in the depths of your darker feelings. You must have a lover who is able to meet you there.

Scorpio Sun Gemini Moon

Intensely emotional, hugely determined and very restless you are an enigma even to yourself. The darker side of life definitely appeals to you though you are more of a butterfly brains than most Scorpios. Your restless streak fights a war with the part of you which wants to stand rooted to the spot. You can be immensely secretive and very swayed by your deeper impulses but your airy Gemini Moon pulls you back from the edge more often than not. Being a water air mix you swing between feeling and thinking. This can give depth to your ideas and at times will detach you from your over strong feelings to lend perspective to your actions. But you do feel pulled and pushed by your conflicting needs to stay high and to dive deep. The Gemini Moon does not want to be fenced in, nor to be closeted in a claustrophobic relationship while your Scorpio Sun wants love that is hot, passionate, jealous, possessive and angst ridden. A compromise is inevitable and you may never feel wholly satisfied with your love life so some needs have to be met elsewhere. But luckily Gemini, though airy, does have a leaning towards the darker side of life albeit in a rather laid back way. It likes to know rather than to directly experience. But it is an easier combination than an Aquarian or Libra Moon would be. You need a lover who can offer you the impossible. The ecstasy without strings.

Scorpio Sun Cancer Moon

Wonderfully emotional, deeply sensitive, certainly intensely jealous, you are a water person through and through. Though you give out the appearance of being strong, dark and silent you feel half the time as if you are on a raft on the high seas being driven hither and thither by the winds. For you the hidden undercurrents are deeper than almost anyone else on earth. You act on compulsion, at times quite blindly and certainly never forget a hurt. Your vindictive streak gets you into trouble and does not always make friends but you cannot help yourself. Often you hear slights when none were intended so you create more emotional tension than is necessary. Being deeply impressionable you soak in the atmosphere from those around so always have to be choosy about who you keep in your close circle.

You need both an intimate soul mate and a family which sometimes creates dilemmas. Scorpios adore one-to-one exclusive relationships which are so intertwined there is no room for anyone else. But you absolutely must have a tribe of your own around as well from childhood and in your adult life. Jealousy is a great stumbling block for you and there is no middle way in romance. You love them or you loathe them. Lovers never become friends later. They are erased. An earth water person might suit you since they would provide you with an anchor or even a water air type to give you a sense of perspective on your actions. You are often so swamped by your feelings that you cannot see yourself clearly.

Scorpio Sun Leo Moon
A powerhouse of determination, energy and (dare it be whispered) vanity, you are a mystery even to yourself. Your Scorpio Sun is intensely emotional and secretive. Yet your fiery Leo Moon wants to let it all show. You are a real contradiction and find it difficult to marry the desires of your heart to the dictates of your conscience. What you want is never what you ought to do. If you settle with one partner, you promptly fancy someone else like mad. And so it goes on. Your head and your heart are split because you grew up in an atmosphere of mutual incompatibility or at least great difference between your parents. What they could not get together in their marriage you cannot get together in your head. You can - with effort - separate from the past and rise above those conflicts to find a third solution. But it will take time and you find change enormously difficult. You are stubborn so need a flexible, gentle partner, but one who can cope with your ego and your slightly manipulative tendencies. They also need to be reasonably unflappable to cope with your mood swings and lack of restraint. Living life the five star way is always your wish so a wealthy mate would help or at least one who will not cost you. You can get explosively frustrated about life's setbacks so you need a warm, comforting lover who will reassure you. But you need to find peace with yourself before you will find it with another.

Scorpio Sun Virgo Moon
Intense, highly determined but more practical than most Scorpios, you have a way of making life work for you that others envy. Certainly you worry incessantly but that often pushes you into building up more security for yourself. You are extremely self protective, with the ability to survive through difficult times and catastrophes. Endurance is your middle name. Where romance is concerned you can be passionate and rather prudish by turns, so lovers never quite know whether you will be blowing hot or cold. Your obsessive tidying streak can also exasperate more chaotic companions but you do like everything in its place. If you can unhitch the prim side of your Virgo Moon you can be warmly physical as well as emotionally sensual. Being a water earth personality you lack a clear vision of yourself. You also could do with more chutzpah, more daring and recklessness. A touch of sparkle from a fiery mate would help though not too much since you are essentially opposites. Jealousy can be a problem since you loathe losing control over close partners and you basically hate the idea of being humiliated by rejection. You are less vindictive than some Scorpios but the kickback is still always there. A warm Capricorn could do you the power of good.

Scorpio Sun Libra Moon
An odd mix this since you live in the depths of your emotions and can be superficially sociable. You never quite know what to do with your feelings. Part of you wants to be passionately, emotionally intertwined with another. Part of you wants a spacey, chatty, harmonious relationship which includes friends and not too much hassle. Unfortunately while your Scorpio Sun is prepared to put up with the agonies for the sake of the ecstasies, your Libra Moon is not. It wants everlasting peace and niceness. Scorpio knows you have to go down into the gutter sometimes to find the gold nuggets. Libra is too fastidious to conceive of anything being bearable which is not elegant, expensive and socially acceptable. You will find trouble marrying the two parts of yourself together never mind finding a mate who fits. But it will happen because your Libra Moon needs another half and your Scorpio Sun certainly wants a strong connection.

Being a water air person you veer between feeling and thinking. Because you are a highly sensitive being you sometimes disappear into your day dreams and fantasies as a way of escaping the difficulties of real life. You are peculiarly sensitive to the opinions of others.

Scorpio Sun Scorpio Moon

A New Moon baby, you are intensely self protective, self sufficient and self contained. Not only do you have less need to relate outside yourself than most people, being a double water personality, you have a fear of being swamped or overwhelmed by others. So you retreat into your own private emotional world and it needs fair persuasion before you will venture forth into relationships. You are secretive, stubborn, jealous but never ever admit when you have been hurt. You take your emotional life incredibly seriously and anyone who ever hurts you will never be forgiven. With you there is no half way house - it is all or nothing, love or hate. Once lovers have blotted their copybook or been abandoned, it is very final. There is no turning back. Your problem is in finding a mate who will cope with your intensity and deep undercurrents. Ideally in one way another Scorpio would suit but the pair of you would wrap yourself in your own secret world and never emerge. A touch of earth to ground you would help so a Scorpio with an earthy Moon might be the best compromise. You need to watch your manipulative tendencies.

Scorpio Sun Sagittarius Moon

A wondrous combination this, full of fiery intensity, and conflicting urges. You want passionate closeness yet you loathe being fenced in. You want to plunge to the murky depths to find your soul and yet you are equally convinced that only by sailing high on the cloud tops will you satisfy your spirit. A water fire mix you are emotional, excitable and impulsive and remarkably sensitive about how others see you. Your mood swings are frightening to behold. On good days you are refreshingly, even scorchingly, direct and encouraging. On bad days you are ready to explode with frustration. You can be warmly supportive but you need to learn moderation in all things. Lovers will need to be sensual enough to fulfil your deepest longings for transcendental sex yet with the sense to give you a long rein. You are jealous yet you hate being possessed. You are a born entertainer at heart but not easy to live with. You need a strong sense of purpose about your life.

Scorpio Sun Capricorn Moon

A real heavyweight personality, you rarely let the grass grow under your feet. A supreme strategist you always have your eye on the main chance or your secret ambition and you will shift heaven and earth to get to where you want to be. Scorpios are known as the miracle makers of the zodiac because they never take no for an answer and Capricorn is the sign of high achievement so which ever way you look you are hardly a rabbit. But you are always torn about your love life. Your Scorpio Sun wants a love so intense and so passionate you will never be parted. But your Capricorn Moon believes sadly that you will never be loved unless you achieve so you disappear off into your career ambitions for longish periods which leaves you and your mate dissatisfied. Being a water earth personality you have fairly traditional values and need security. You have the ability to survive through calamities and catastrophes and have great inner strength. But you can be manipulative and too attached to the past. You need a mate with more of a sense of detachment and perhaps a bit of sparkle. Your strong sense of destiny sometimes pulls you away from love but you always bounce back.

Scorpio Sun Aquarius Moon

The oddest combination of them all you hardly know what to make of yourself. Your Scorpio Sun wants emotional intensity, deep and dark passionate affairs yet your Aquarian Moon shies away from any kind of commitment in close one-to-one relationships. It wants to be friends not lovers and prefers a platonic group to a sexy clinch any day. You have to sort out the conflict within yourself before you will settle into a happy duo. Part of the problem stems from childhood where you felt your parents were not in tune. They were opposites. What they could not get together in their marriage you cannot get together in your head. What you want is never what you feel you ought to be doing. You find a lover, then immediately fancy someone over the fence, preferably who is committed elsewhere. You must find a way of resolving that desire/duty dilemma within yourself. Being a water air personality you veer between feeling and thinking. One moment you act blindly from your guts, the next up in your head you are so detached you freeze every feeling before it has had a chance to blossom. You are sensitive to the degree that you will escape into your daydreams and fantasies to get away from hard reality. You need a mate who will love you to the end but give you space and a long rope to wander. In short you need someone as oddly assorted as yourself.

Scorpio Sun Pisces Moon
Deeply emotional, passionately intense yet very sensitive, you swim around in a universe full of feelings. You are so impressionable that at times you feel like a raft adrift on the ocean blown this way and that by the winds and the currents. Because of your instability you sometimes withdraw into your own little universe or you find it easier to be a healer and counsellor to those around than to make very close relationships which might conceivably overtax your highly charged emotional system. Because your Pisces Moon makes it difficult for you to approach others out of a fear of rejection you sometimes miss out on romantic opportunities. But at the end of the day your Scorpio Sun really needs a close, committed relationship and it certainly does not lack courage. Being a double water personality you have to watch a tendency to become too self absorbed. Finding an ideal mate is tricky because although other water types would share your sensitivities you would sink each other in the swamp of your feelings. You need a water air type who can give you a little distance and perspective on your life. Or a water earth type who will anchor you to the ground. You are certainly charming on the social circuit so should have few problems ultimately in finding a soul mate.

Sagittarius Sun Aries Moon
Lively, energetic, boisterous and exuberant you are one of

the world's movers and shakers. Never one to hold back when you could be leaping into action, you can get yourself at times into hot water. You frequently do not engage your brain before letting your tongue loose and find it difficult to empathise with other people's feelings. So you do have a reputation for being just a touch upfront in the way you relate. Life's harsher lessons of pain and disappointment may well mellow your sharper edges and teach you compassion along the route. You act often out of insecurity and your reactions change so fast and frequently that mates become confused. Certainly they feel they cannot trust you to be in the place they want you to be. You adore challenge and excitement - too much. As a lover you obviously need someone of unflappable and reasonably secure. You are allergic to anything which even hints at possessiveness. Being fenced in is close to your idea of suffocation. A very grounded earthy lover would make you feel weighed down and possibly offend you. Too much of a concentration on earthly physical pleasures is not your thing. You like fantasy in romance not sweat and dandruff. Emotional types you distrust. They make you feel swamped. Airy, up in the head chatterboxes do suit you but as a combination you are likely to take off like hot air balloons. You need ballast.

Sagittarius Sun Taurus Moon
Fiery, restless, outspoken, demonstrative and affectionate you are a bit of an enigma. You may feel odd because of your contradictory and conflicting attitudes to life, love and sex but there is merit in having the grounded energy of Taurus added to your flyaway Sagittarian Sun. The only trouble is that you need to be both free and rooted at the same time. You live half the time in your ideas, dreams and fantasies. The other half of the time you are greedy for your physical comforts. Sometimes you are desperate for variety, excitement and challenge. Then you flip into moods where you yearn for sameness, security and the status quo. Being a fire earth mix you are what is known in astrological parlance as a "steam roller" personality able to keep going long after weaker souls have dropped in to the ditch with exhaustion. You are a powerhouse of determination and

can translate all those wonderfully fiery visions into tangible realities. What you are not enormously good at is starting new projects. You are stubborn and flexible but initiative is a touch lacking. Getting in touch with the subtler aspects of life possibly through a lover with just a hint of water would help you enormously. A whiff of the airy signs also might just do good. Though in neither case do you want too much.

Sagittarius Sun Gemini Moon
A restless, talkative Full Moon baby, you never know quite where you are at or what you want. You are butterfly brained and grass hopper footed, loathe settled routines, obligations and heavy commitments. Whenever you find one lover who sparks your interest and you start thinking about mating long term you promptly find your fancy wandering off across the fence to another. And so life goes on. You grew up seeing your parents are basically opposites and what they could not get together in their marriage you cannot get together in your head. The only solution long term is to separate from the past and rise above those old childhood conflicts. Then you will find that life is not about either suiting your head or your heart. Duty and desire can be made to coalesce in the same mate. But it takes time, effort and energy. It will not happen if you look the other way and just hope. Being a fire air mix you are volatile in the extreme. Think of the mixture of helium gas and flame in a hot air balloon. You can take off effortlessly enough. But you find it difficult to stay attached to the ground, reality or your body. Love is fantasised about or thought about but it does not really blossom in your feelings or your physical senses. You could do with a lover who has a hint of water or earth just to help you recharge your batteries once in a while otherwise you will burnout from constantly being on the move.

Sagittarius Sun Cancer Moon
Fire and Water are a mix that handled properly can produce a boiling kettle but allow it to go wrong and you find the water boils over and the flame goes out. You are impulsive, excitable and emotional with wild mood swings and a marked inability to restrain your whims. Your lack of self control lands you quite literally at times in hot water. You

veer between fantasising and feeling. You want freedom, then you want security. You are an enigma even to yourself. You cannot ever make up your mind what you really want. Your Sagittarian Sun needs to be able to roam to the ends of the earth without being fenced in. It is basically not a domesticated animal at all. But your Cancer Moon desperately wants a happy home base, a tribe of children and close relationships to wrap yourself round. Somehow you need to satisfy both parts of yourself. It makes more sense to find a good family set up and then give yourself the elbow room to fly free when you want. The other way round really will not work. So give your Cancer Moon what it wants and needs but reserve the right at all times to be without strings. So you probably need a lover or a mate who is willing to provide that anchor at home and will not fuss too much when you disappear off across the perimeter fence for days at a time. Too much physical sex is not your style but you do need closeness at times.

Sagittarius Sun Leo Moon
Over active, restless and probably over concerned with making things happen in the world you are a real go getting entrepreneur... one of life's movers and shakers. Relationships are not that simple partly because you hate being fenced in and partly because being all fire you genuinely have difficulty empathising with the emotional needs of others. Fire is basically a self centred energy and you can approach lovers in a way that seems insensitive. In the process of maturing through life's darker passages and disillusionments you do learn more compassion which helps. Humility is not a strong feature of your nature and you do think you deserve to live the five star way. Your reputation is hugely important to you and vanity can be a weak spot. Criticism wounds you deeply and you certainly do not tolerate people who get in your way. But you can when you try be charmingly persuasive, highly entertaining and very generous. Lovers have to be flexible enough to move around your needs which are quite demanding and, of course, to give you constant admiration which goes without saying. The problem is to assess what kind of personality you need. A little earth to ground you but not so much

that you feel suffocated. You are not a deeply physical lover. Perhaps a little water to give you more subtle sympathy though a highly emotional lover would cringe at your scorching directness and you would feel swamped by their hidden undercurrents. A lover with an air Moon would offer you intellectual stimulus without too many problems added.

Sagittarius Sun Virgo Moon
Certainly restless, you are very talkative, slightly at odds with yourself but on the whole a pleasant combination. Your Virgo Sun helps to anchor that flyaway Sagittarian nature which never happily settles to anything for long. You can be over verbose and at times sharply critical but there is a warmth about a fire earth mix which mellows your rougher edges. You do have the strength of ten and are usually still going strong when weaker souls are dropping by the wayside. But you do worry - endlessly and inventively. Once all your anxieties are settled - you think up a few more. Sometimes chaotically fragmented, you can also have moods of obsessive tidiness. Partners have to put up with your contradictions since you are fickle and wayward at times. Because you had from childhood a sense of parents who were not exactly in tune you cannot get your head and your heart together in adult life. Where duty lies is not what you desire and vice versa. So settling with one exclusive partner always feels like an unsatisfying compromise. A Sun Virgo could suit you. An emotional watery type would be a disaster. A hint of Gemini around your mate could appeal.

Sagittarius Sun Libra Moon
Wonderfully communicative, lively, energetic and sociable, you never let the grass grow under your feet when it comes to making new friends or seeing new places. You like to keep on the move. At times scorchingly honest and at other times highly diplomatic, you can be mellower than some Sagittarians because you genuinely care about other people's approval. You have high ideals and in general dislike dishonesty and sleazy behaviour. You like a life that is clean, above board and straightforward. Mates need

to be hard working, well scrubbed and solid members of society. The unemployed and the unwashed are not your cup of tea. Being a fire air mix you are not good at coming down to ground level. Learning about the darker side of life is important for your development but it will not be easy. Through disappointments and emotional suffering you will learn compassion and sensitivity. If you do not then you will continue to fly high and run the danger of exhausting yourself. Recharging your batteries is a must. You generally have a wonderful sense of humour and a wicked way with words but you do need more depth. Lovers need to give you a long rein since you hate being fenced in. The first whiff of jealousy and possessiveness and you are off like a shot. But with a Libra Moon another half in life is a must for you. You need a sweet, harmonious, easy going mate who will not hassle you or rock the boat too much. They must also have a keen intelligence.

Sagittarius Sun Scorpio Moon
Sunny, outgoing, communicative on the surface you are also secretive, stubborn and fairly controlling at an emotional level inside. A curious combination of contradictions make up your personality. Your Sagittarian Sun makes you freedom loving, tolerant, very direct and highly sociable. But your Scorpio Moon can be jealous, possessive and will never let on what is going on inside your turbulent feelings. If you are hurt you will stand coolly and never let on. But you never forget or forgive. Being a fire water mix you are impulsive, excitable and given to mood swings. You can be surprisingly sensitive to what others think of you. On good days you are straightforward and highly encouraging. On bad days you are explosively frustrated and unpredictable. It is a good combination for show business and business affairs in general. Your lover will need to give you the intensity required by your Scorpio Moon which adores deep, dark passions but they will also have to give you space to roam free. They will have to be a complex personality to please all of your different needs. A hint of earth in your mate would help to anchor your extremes of mood, perhaps even a hint of air since you often lack the detachment which might give you perspective on your actions.

Sagittarius Sun Sagittarius Moon

Impulsive, overly active, hugely restless, you are one of the world's non stop movers. Being double fire you tend to hare into situations without stopping to think before you leap. At times your way of relating to others can seem less than sensitive just because you get so fuelled up with your own enthusiasms that you do not see their needs. It is genuinely difficult for you to empathise with others or indeed to stay in contact with your own feelings. You probably do not see this as a problem but it becomes one through life if you do not slow down enough to nourish yourself. Burnout from exhaustion or addictions is sometimes a problem. Being a New Moon baby you have less need to find the support of another half in life so finding relationships does not have the edge of desperation is does for certain people. You certainly dislike being fenced in and since your enthusiasms are notoriously short lived you like the kind of affairs where you can move on very rapidly. Long term commitments are not easy. Most of your energy is kept for work projects with you attack with formidable courage and determination. You are a self motivated go getter, a real entrepreneur at heart. But for all that you are immensely popular. You have a way of keeping other people stimulated intellectually. Your ideas are wide ranging and you do have strong beliefs. You hate being involved with petty details so a mate with a tiny amount of earth about them would be of use, since they would handle the practical side of life.

Sagittarius Sun Capricorn Moon

More serious than some Sagittarians, you work very hard in life to achieve because that is the only way you think you will be loved. You constantly strive to justify yourself and gain approval. It all comes from a rather restricted childhood where you did not feel valued. You need to learn self acceptance before you will be happy in your relationships otherwise work will always come first. But for all that you do have a helpful mix of fire and earth which allows you to be practical as well as enthusiastic. You are what is known as a steam roller personality able to keep going long after weaker souls have dropped in the ditch from exhaustion. You have a way of turning your ideas and ideals into reality.

But you do need to develop a sense of the subtler side of life. Sometimes a Capricorn Moon can settle for security or social advancement rather than love but your passions will catch up with you one day because underneath all that driving ambition is a streak of purely self indulgent sensuality. You are a slightly odd mix since one half of you is whacky, upfront, very honest and uncaring about approval, while the other side of you is genuinely traditional and easily embarrassed at a social level. Your lover needs to be able to give you a long rein and a stable base in life. You need physical contact and cuddles, but not too much. You do tend to blow hot and cold which can be confusing.

Sagittarius Sun Aquarius Moon
Zippy, zany, friendly and highly talkative you have a million ideas, endless enthusiasms and a restless lifestyle. You are rather scared of highly committed one-to-one relationships which feel claustrophobic to you. You would much rather be one of the crowd with friends than stuck in a passionate clinch. At times you can be startling or shocking just to see the effect it has on others. A born anarchist at heart you love to rebel and upset the status quo. Being a fire air mix you are inclined to fly too high above life and need to come down to see the dark side at some point. Burning yourself out through exhaustion is a real danger since you rarely give yourself a chance to be grounded or to stay in touch with your feelings, either of which would give you stability and inner strength. You are optimistic in outlook, hugely idealistic though not very realistic. You need a mate who can give you extra long rein because you absolutely must be free to do what suits you. You loathe jealousy or possessiveness in any form and will run at the first sniff of a restriction or a tie that might bind you. Settling long term is difficult since you worry about commitment. But because of your social charm you should have little problem in keeping a constant supply of partners running.

Sagittarian Sun Pisces Moon
Restless, excitable, impulsive you tend to go to extremes and do have mood swings. But you are highly adaptable and good at fitting round most situations. Most often you

are at odds with yourself over what you want. Your head and heart rarely coincide. What duty tells you to stick to is not what you desire. You find one lover and promptly one much more fanciable pops up elsewhere and so it goes on. This stems from a childhood where you saw your parents as very different personalities. Because they were not in tune in their relationship you cannot quite get in tune in your head. But these inner conflicts can be left behind if you rise above them and leave childhood behind. However it will take a fair way through life before you are able to commit yourself wholeheartedly to a settled relationship. Your Pisces Moon is not brave indeed you will miss romantic opportunities because you are too scared of rejection to even voice your feelings. Being a fire water mix you are surprisingly sensitive to others opinion of you and will hear slights where none were intended. You can sometimes wallow in self pity, because you resent your situation. Daydreaming or escaping into fantasies is one of your ways out. You need a compassionate, intuitive mate who will understand your anxieties. They need to be stable enough to ground you a little but not so possessive that they make you feel fenced in.

Capricorn Sun Aries Moon
Ambitious, restless, always starting new projects and very, very determined to reach your goals in life, you can sometimes come across as rather hard edged. You have a very sensual, earthy side which you keep well hidden behind your workaholic tendencies. You can go without companionship for longish periods while you concentrate on your more materialistic aims but then you fall deeply, violently and passionately in love. But standing still for long term commitments is not easy for you. You need constant challenge and change. Often you act out of a feeling of insecurity and because your reactions change all the time you often confuse companions who feel they cannot rely on you. Being an earth fire mix you have the energy of ten and keep going long after everyone else has dropped by the wayside from sheer exhaustion. You need to learn about the subtler aspects of life which you tend to miss by flying along at such high speed. Lovers obviously

have to be reasonably self sufficient to stand the times you are away working and ignore them totally. They also have to be unflappable to put up with your flare ups. Because your Sun and Moon are rather at odds with one another you often feel you are never totally satisfied. What you have is never quite what you want. You have to overcome these inner conflicts before you can settle happily.

Capricorn Sun Taurus Moon
Charming socially though too much of a workaholic to settle easily into emotional relationships, you are very definitely in touch with the material world. You love to have a challenge to sink your teeth into and to channel your formidable energy towards. But you can be too narrow in your outlook since you see the world in highly practical terms. You dislike abstractions and daydreams but really you need to have an uplifting vision in life to give you a sense of purpose. If your career sags at any point you panic because it gives you a sense of self worth. A tendency to be too cynical or sceptical can upset close relationships. But underneath it all you are very earthy and have a strongly sensual streak. A Taurus Moon certainly gives you a liking for the physical comforts in life, including cuddles. You can be warm and affectionate when in the mood and highly possessive. You loathe change in your home or emotional life and will dig your heels in hard if forced to shift for any reason. You need a lover who can broaden your view of the world perhaps one with a hint of water about them. Emotional sensitivity is lacking and they could introduce you to a softer approach to relationships. You are highly conventional and must never have a mate who will embarrass you socially.

Capricorn Sun Gemini Moon
Although enormously restless and a real social butterfly you also have a dedicated, determined streak when it comes to work, ambition and achievement. You will do almost anything to fulfil your aims and have been known to cut corners. But your overly active mind sometimes makes it difficult for you to concentrate over the long term. You really prefer to be knowledgeable across a wide range of interests than specialise too heavily. You are a wonderful

propagandist but your interests rarely stay still for long. Being an earth air mix you can be rather cool, unemotional almost and need a lover who can give you more sparkle, more chutzpah and a feeling for taking risks. Underneath your driving ambition you have a sensual streak which needs to find an outlet. For periods in your life you can be almost celibate then all of a sudden you fall into times of physical indulgence and sensuality. But you do find emotional commitment tricky because your wants are so changeable. Your moods flit around and what you want two days ago is not what you want now. Sometimes you have been known to settle for partners who are helpful at work or in boosting your social reputation but it never works long term. An Air Sun with an Earth Moon would suit.

Capricorn Sun Cancer Moon
Being a Full Moon baby you are constantly pulled in two opposite directions in life. What your head wants is not what your heart needs. Wherever you are is not where you want to be. Find one lover and another across the fence promptly looks more fanciable. Your Capricorn Sun makes you work oriented, highly ambitious and determined, at times rather detached. Your Cancer Moon on the other hand wants nothing more than a happy home and family life, is highly emotional, rather jealousy and desperate to hang onto anything that belongs to the past. You are at odds with yourself because you had a sense in childhood that your parents were not compatible. Since you inherit traits from both of them you cannot get together in your head what they could not get together in their marriage. You need to leave the past and childhood behind, rise above those conflicts and find a new way of relating that is entirely yours. But it is not easy. Being an earth water mix you tend to be self protective, rather over serious. Indeed you often do not feel happy unless you are carrying a heavy burden through life. You have a great deal of inner strength so surviving through difficulties is never a problem. You are highly traditional in your outlook and want to maintain the high standards of the past. Lovers who are whacky, eccentric or likely to embarrass you socially will not do.

Capricorn Sun Leo Moon
Highly ambitious, rather grand, you are determined to work as hard as it takes to give yourself a five star life style. You loathe doing anything cheaply and will do almost anything to boost your reputation. You can be charmingly persuasive and generous to others but you do like to have admiration in return. Your vanity is a weak spot and you absolutely cannot stand being criticised. Being an earth fire mix you are a real steam roller of a personality able to keep going long after weaker souls have dropped by the wayside. But you do need a lover who can teach you about the subtler side of life which you often miss because of your driven lifestyle. At times you have a tendency to settle for partners who can offer you advancement through work or a leg up the social ladder but it is always a mistake in the long term to compromise with your feelings. You are extremely traditional in your outlook and fairly stubbornly attached to the status quo emotionally. So sudden changes unsettle you. You need a lover who can adapt to your determined, sometimes slightly self centred wishes and who will endlessly devote themselves to your needs but not worry too much when you fly off on work ventures which leave them abandoned for long periods. You do have fairly strong physical needs which you deny at times but you always come back to fulfilling. Your Capricorn Sun is earthy, sensual, at times almost wickedly indulgent.

Capricorn Sun Virgo Moon
Seemingly at ease with yourself, you can cope well socially though your primary drive in life is towards work. You are highly ambitious, very determined to fulfil your aims and willing to put in any amount of energy in that direction. A great worrier, you do sometimes invent anxieties where none exist. They always say that Virgo Moon types raise worrying to an art form and when you have cleared the decks of everything that has been plaguing you, then you seek out new problems to burden yourself with. Being a double earth personality you can be too narrow in your outlook in life. You want everything to be practical and your aims tend to be materialistic. You can lack imagination and a sense of vision in life. So you need a lover who can

broaden your approach give you a little sparkle, chutzpah and maybe even an inclination to risk. A water type might threaten to swamp you emotionally but a lover who is a hint more in touch with their feelings than you would help to connect you to the subtler side of life. You also need a lover who will not be manipulated by your excessive need to keep order in life. You have a prudish streak which in early adult life can make you seem rather defensive. Launching yourself wholeheartedly into the middle of life with all its murk, muddle and problems will curiously make you a happier person and better able to enjoy your emotional life.

Capricorn Sun Libra Moon
Full of initiative, restless, energetic, work driven, ambitious professionally and socially you certainly never let the grass grow under your feet. You will seek to better yourself at every turn. You were not designed to be poor. The idle, the unemployed and the great unwashed are not your cup of tea at all. You abhor drifters, derelicts and under achieving members of society. Being an earth air mix you can appear rather cool, logical and not given to impulsive gestures but in fact you have a fairly earthy, sensual streak underneath. You just repress it far too much. You are surprisingly sensitive to others' opinion of you. Social approval is exceedingly important, perhaps too much so. You need to relate more to the essential values of other people and indeed your own feelings. Allowing yourself to be pushed around by everyone else's value judgements eventually makes you seem superficial and lacking in integrity. Your Sun and Moon are at rather gritty angles to each other so you do not find it easy to get your head and heart together. What you want and what you ought to do are usually two entirely different things. Overcoming this desire/duty conflict is not easy since it is rooted in a childhood where you felt your parents were incompatible but as you leave your past behind you should find there is a warm solution.

Capricorn Sun Scorpio Moon
An intense personality who is both deeply emotional and very work oriented, you are highly self protective. Your tremendous inner strength and stamina mean you can

survive through any calamity. Your ambitions usually come first and you are able to look as if your feelings do not matter to you. In fact you are just highly controlled and rarely let the seething turmoil of emotions inside you be seen even by those closest. Your privacy is almost more important than anything else. You are jealous, possessive and sensual but you never ever let anyone see when you are hurt. It is a matter of pride for you to look calm but you rarely forget or forgive a slight. Plotting revenge can be a weak spot in your temperament. Your Capricorn Sun is highly ambitious and will usually go to any lengths to achieve its aims but underneath it is very earthy and indulgent. Your physical comforts are given a high priority. Your Scorpio Moon can make you preoccupied with sex, though usually in secret. You act often from secret compulsions which others do not understand. Your undercurrents are deeper than most peoples. You need lovers who can cope with your intensity, your need for passion and your need to be free at times to follow your ambitions.

Capricorn Sun Sagittarius Moon
More happy go lucky than some Capricorns, who can be very serious, you never quite know how to settle your restless spirit down. You are very work driven but you also need to be able to roam free. Your Capricorn Sun makes you practical, earthy and determined to fulfil your ambitions in life whether professional or social. You love being regarded as someone of status and high reputation. But your Sagittarius Moon makes you a bit of a gambler, a great talker and someone who is un-inclined to pay attention to too much detail. The two opposing sides of your nature do not always sit happily together. Though being an earth fire mix you do have tremendous stamina and once you find beliefs in life which matter to you, nothing is allowed to stand in your way. You have the energy of ten and can keep going long after everyone else has sagged with exhaustion. What you are not good at is empathising with the needs and sensitivities of others. So you need a lover who can connect you to the subtler aspects of life and love. But who will not be dismayed when you disappear off after your own projects. You adore friends in large numbers and can chat

endlessly. Once you have learned to devote yourself to some cause you will find yourself much steadier in love.

Capricorn Sun Capricorn Moon
Deeply serious, very practical, too much of a workaholic, you will be half way through life before you begin to mellow, find a sense of humour and give yourself time to relax. You were a very old child but the good news is that you will be a young geriatric. Life may have seemed a struggle early on either through emotional or financial deprivation. But your old age will be a paradise in comparison. What may stop you finding an ideal lover early on in adult life, apart from being too tied up with your material ambitions, is that you are quite self sufficient. Being a New Moon baby you have less of a desperate need to find another half in life than some people. You can be celibate for long stretches or settle for a mate who can bring you social or professional advancement. Your view of the world is too narrowly practical. You need to find a broader sense of vision, to make your imagination work more. There is more to life than work, money and social position. Unfortunately early in life you got the message that love only came if you earned it. So you struggle to achieve to get attention but along the way you may lose partners because you give them so little time. A lover with a hint of water would get you in touch with your feelings though you do not want a highly emotional mate since you basically distrust feelings and they would never settle for coming second to work.

Capricorn Sun Aquarius Moon
An odd mix, you are both highly conventional and rather eccentric. Your social reputation is important to you and yet you can leap off into rather startling comments or activities because you adore shocking companions. Close one-to-one committed relationships are not easy for you and you tend to surround yourself with crowds of friends as a way of avoiding them. Possibly you distrust relationships which put value just on you as a person. You feel you have to achieve to earn acceptance. Being an earth air mix you tend to be cool, rational and unemotional. You examine feelings rather than letting them blossom which can sometimes

turn you into an observer rather than a participator in life. Stubbornness is a fault in your emotional life and you can be immensely hard to shift. So you need a lover who is adaptable and can put up with your highly variable whims. They also need to be of unflappable temperament when you set out to be rebellious. Often you put on a show of being outrageous or slightly eccentric just to make others sit up. Though often it means very little. You do mellow through life and become warmer as middle age approaches. A lover with a hint of water to give you more connection to your feelings would help. And perhaps one with a hint of fire to give you more sparkle.

Capricorn Sun Pisces Moon Serious, self protective and a very hard worker, you can give the impression of not being emotional. Yet behind your rather ambitious front you are deeply sensitive. Often you miss romantic opportunities because you are so scared of rejection that you fear to state your feelings. You can easily become a martyr to work and complain of your lot in life. But you just need more courage in your love life to say what you need. You are good on the social scene, able to charm and flirt with an ease which often surprises you but when it comes to closer relationships you can become a little manipulative. You are basically highly insecure and attach yourself firmly to the traditional values of your past. You have a great deal of stamina and can cope with crisis well. What you find more difficult is to cope with the pleasanter, more settled aspects of an ongoing emotional relationship. Luckily you mellow through life, gaining a stronger sense of humour through middle age and approaching your older years with a warmth that was missing early on. Escapism can curiously be a problem for you either through daydreaming, or the addictions. Capricorn is usually known as a practical sign but it does have a highly indulgent physical side and the Pisces Moon very definitely wants to lose itself in some orgiastic or boundary loosening activities. You need a lover who can keep you gently in touch with reality and give you more courage.

Aquarius Sun Aries Moon

Zany, funny, wildly energetic, highly talkative, desperately keen always to keep on the move, you are one of the world's live wires. Rebellious, quite disruptive at times, you do not sit still and accept what comes your way. You act often out of insecurity and your reactions change constantly. Others sometimes think you cannot be counted on because you are never in the same place twice. Constant challenge and excitement keep you alert but settling down to committed relationships or a stable existence is not easy for you. On the social scene you always appear at ease with yourself and the opposite sex but coming deeper into your feelings through intimate relationships is something you shy away from. You are idealistic and rather high flying but you need to face up to the darker side of life. Usually through the years with disappointments and suffering that goes with love you do begin to connect to those deeper feelings and needs which can give you inner strength and stability. You need more grounding and more emotional contact in your life otherwise you burnout because you have no way of recharging your batteries. Being an air fire personality you take off like a hot air balloon and really need a lover who can give you ballast, anchor you to the ground.

Aquarius Sun Taurus Moon

Stubborn, solid but curiously in constant disagreement with yourself, you can never decide whether to stay spacey and friendly or to aim straight for cuddles and physical comforts. Being born at the time of the waxing quarter moon you never quite get your head and your heart together. What you want is never what you have got. If you find a lover you promptly want someone else. Part of this duty/ desire dilemma is rooted in a childhood where you saw your parents as being quite different people. Because you inherit their traits you cannot get together in your head what they could not get together in their marriage. You will need to leave the conflicts of the past behind before you are able to find the wholehearted emotional satisfaction you seek. Being an air earth mix you come across as cool, logical and unemotional. Though your Taurus Moon is, underneath that front, very warm, affectionate and demonstrative.

This can create a difficulty for your Aquarian Sun which is basically friendly rather than passionate. You need a lover who feeds your needs for physical closeness but is happy to give you a long rein which you need. Although you can be jealous and possessive, you hate being fenced in yourself.

Aquarius Sun Gemini Moon
Communicative to an extraordinary degree, you are a real jack in the box personality, who never sits still if there is a chance of excitement, variety or fun to be had. You feed off challenges and constant upheavals. Being both stubborn and very changeable you are an enigma to most people around you. A born rebel at heart you do not often take other people's approval into account when deciding on a course of action. Indeed frequently you will aim to disrupt the status quo as a way of making yourself feel better and trying to establish a better future. You are tolerant about other people's foibles which makes you popular though you are not easy tie down in close, committed relationships. You basically hate sitting still so you need affairs that give you elbow room to race around at high speed. You are more nervy than you appear because you are a double air personality. Running down your nervous energy is very easy since you are so highly strung. You do not always have a way of replenishing your batteries because you are so out of touch with your body and with your feelings. You need a lover who is more sensitive than yourself emotionally though not too much so. You basically distrust feelings and a highly emotional type would not take kindly to your up-in-the-head approach which rather freezes emotions before they have had a chance to develop.

Aquarius Sun Cancer Moon
A contradiction in your own lifetime you both want space and a happy home life. You fight for your freedom yet you are jealously possessive of those close. You need a long rein but it always has to come back to a protective niche that is filled with your own tribe of people. Your Aquarian Sun basically is happier being friends with an enormous number of people and not getting into claustrophobic clinches. But your Cancer Moon definitely wants the wrap

round factor. Neither your Sun nor your Moon is physically very passionate but your Moon needs cuddles, affection and a feeling of belonging. Letting go the past or childhood is exceptionally difficult for you which can make you sentimental in the extreme. Being an air water personality you have a highly sensitive, rather escapist streak. You often want to get away from harsh reality by disappearing into daydreams and fantasies or even addictions. You need a mate as contrary as yourself who will give you the warmth and security you seek but not tie you down or object to you having your own circle of friends. A mate who is highly emotional will appeal to half of you but frighten the other half witless. So you must compromise and find a family oriented but laid back individual.

Aquarius Sun Leo Moon
Fiery, restless, talkative, rather flamboyant, you definitely like living the five star way. Nothing but the best for you. You are much grander than the usual run of the mill Aquarian and more sensitive to the approval of others. You are curiously pulled in two directions since half of you is eccentric, wayward, a real rebel at heart and the other half desperately wants to be accepted as the creme de la creme. A powerfully stubborn Full Moon baby you are never clear what you want in life. Whenever you find a mate you promptly think the grass on the other side of the fence looks greener. So you wander restlessly from one partner to another. This conflict between what your head tells you and what your heart wants stems from a childhood where you saw your parents as being quite different types. Because you inherit traits from both of them you find that you cannot get together in your head what they could not get together in their marriage. So you need to leave childhood behind and rise above their conflicts to find your own solution to a totally satisfying emotional life. But it is not easy especially since you are resistant to change. You need a lover who is flexible and can adapt to you rather than the other way round. Also one who can make you see the darker side of life. Being an air fire personality you tend to fly too high and be wrapped up in your ideals and visions. Being brought down into the depths of your feelings and having more

connection to your body will give you more inner stamina. You will also not exhaust yourself so much by constantly giving out all the time.

Aquarius Sun Virgo Moon

Wildly rebellious, rather eccentric and quite modest, you worry yourself sometimes by your outrageous gestures. You do have a strong need to be of service to people and to make a better society for others to live in so you can channel your revolutionary tendencies in acceptable ways when you try. Being an air earth mix you can appear rather cool, logical and unemotional. But behind your rather spacey image you have a warm heart. You do worry too much and are a perfectionist which can come across as critical. But you want the best for those you love. It is said about the Virgo Moon that is raises worrying to an art form. Whenever you have cleared your desk of problems you promptly invent a few more anxieties to gnaw over. You can be a touch prudish or over obsessed with neatness and order but there is a streak of pure anarchy in you which can reduce life at times to chaos. So you fight a private war with yourself. You need a lover who will give you a long rein because you hate being crowded or possessed. But maybe also one who can give you a touch more sparkle and fire. You are fairly out of touch with your feelings and need a connection to the more sensitive realms of love.

Aquarius Sun Libra Moon

Airy, communicative, restless and rather more socially adapted than some Aquarians you very much want the better things of life for yourself. Aquarius at heart is a rebel, an anarchist and a revolutionary but your Libra Moon shudders in horror at anything which would upset the status quo. You desperately want to be accepted by all the proper people in your circle and you have fairly traditional values. Home to you should not be a hang out for hippies or the wild eccentrics of life but for nice people, with elegant tastes, cultural values and upwardly mobile tendencies. You loathe the idle, the unemployed and the great unwashed. Although you are socially at ease and appear happy within yourself, you are in fact a contradiction in many ways.

Certainly you are more highly strung than you appear and have to watch out for nervous exhaustion. You very much need periods of calm, meditation or retreat in your life to take you away from your constant worries, anxieties and endless thinking. You live too much up in your head and need a lover who can bring you a little more in contact with your body, your feelings and perhaps more give you more trust in life. It is all very well being brilliant but you are more than just a brain. Too much emotion makes you suspicious and uneasy. Too much physical contact makes you feel weighed down and suffocated but you must allow a little more feeling and cuddles into your life in small doses.

Aquarius Sun Scorpio Moon
An intense personality you think widely, feel deeply and find change rather difficult. You are stubborn and fixed in your ways so must find partners in life who can adapt to your way rather than the other way round. You are at odds with yourself since your Aquarian Sun makes you spacey, friendly and fearful of close one-to-one commitment. Whereas all your Scorpio Moon really wants are passionate clinches, intertwined relationships and a fairly transcendental sex life. What your head wants is never what your heart yearns for. What duty tells you is not what you desire. This inner conflict is rooted in a childhood where you felt your parents to be very different people. Because you inherit traits from both of them you cannot get together in your head what they could not get together in life. So you need to leave your childhood behind and rise above those conflicts to find your own way of relating. But it will not be easy since you do hate change. You loathe being possessed and yet are fairly jealous yourself. You never show when you are hurt and take pride in concealing the turbulence of your emotions from outside view. But you never forget hurts and rarely forgive. You plot revenge years later though you hate yourself for it. You are sensitive and can be an escapist daydreamer. You need a lover who can ground you and give you more courage.

Aquarius Sun Sagittarius Moon
Whacky, wild, energetic, highly talkative and always honest,

you rarely sit still or fit into accepted moulds. You want to be a one off who is not fenced in especially to the domestic scene. You have wonderfully expansive ideas and are a stimulating conversationalist. Your enthusiasm allows you to be a good teacher and you must always have a strong sense of purpose about your life though at times you do come across as being quite irresponsible. Being friendly and open with a large crowd comes more easily to you than close one-to-one commitment or passionate, sexy clinches. You are not well connected to your body or your feelings and avoid at all costs facing up to the harsher realities of life. You prefer to fly high with your head in the clouds. So you need a lover who can gently bring you down into the depths of your feelings and in contact more with the ground. That way you will gain in inner strength and be able to recharge your batteries. Otherwise if you stay high you will burn yourself out from exhaustion. You can be fairly stubborn out in the world though at home you are more adaptable. Your sense of humour and wicked way with words makes you popular at a social level and probably eases you over domestic hiccups. But you need a partner who will give you a long rein and allow you to keep up your own circle of friends.

Aquarius Sun Capricorn Moon
A wonderful mix of wildly way out and rather conventional, you often have a fight with your conflicting traits. Part of you could not care less about social acceptability and is really a rebel at heart. Part of you desperately wants to be respectable, indeed to be upwardly mobile on the social ladder. Sadly in childhood you got the message that you had to earn being loved by achieving so you work too hard. Your self esteem is not high and you do not understand about just being valued for being yourself. This early feeling of being under loved has resulted in you seeking emotional security at every turn but you sometimes pull yourself away from the very nest you seek by struggling out in the world to do everything you feel you must. Being an air earth mix you appear cool, logical, and practical rather than emotional. You need a mate who can gently pull you more into contact with your feelings and give you sparkle. You lack trust in

life and need to develop faith that everything will be alright. You can be very ambitious and use any means to achieve your ends which does not always bring you happiness. You will mellow through middle age, gain a stronger sense of humour and a sense that you do not have to try quite so hard.

Aquarius Sun Aquarius Moon

A zany, highly individualistic personality who cannot bear restraints of any sort. You buck convention and the status quo at every opportunity. Being a New Moon baby you have less need to find a partner in life than some. You feel whole within yourself. Being a double Aquarian you prefer space and a friendly approach to crowds of people than being stuck in passionate, sexy relationships over a long period. You are rather cut off from your body and your feelings and live more in your head and ideas. You may give the impression of being highly sexed but much of that is an illusion. You know it all in your head but are not always so keen on the practice.   Examining emotions intellectually comes easier to you than feeling them intensely. You certainly need a mate who is flexible since you are immensely stubborn and cannot easily adapt to other people. Your nervous system is more highly strung than others ever see and you are prone to butterflies in the stomach or emotional digestive disorders. You need times of retreat, rest or meditation to pull you away from your constantly active mind which runs over and over plans, anxieties and worries all the time. You need a lover who will give you a long rein but will also bring you slowly more in touch with your feelings and the more sensitive side of life. You also need to connect to your body in a more grounded way.

Aquarius Sun Pisces Moon

A more emotional Aquarian than some, you often hide your feelings away because you fear rejection. You give the impression of being open, friendly and rather rebellious but behind the scenes you are deeply sensitive and want a really romantic match. You are perhaps too prone to disappearing into your daydreams or acting out your life as a performance as a way of protecting your soft underbelly.

You want very Much to help people and are prepared to sacrifice yourself to that end but it can make you resentful and self pitying at times. Handling reality is not always easy for you which is why you often want to escape somewhere else. But your Aquarian Sun does give you at times the courage to make a determined stand. Being an air water personality you are pulled between thinking about life and feeling. This can be helpful because it gives depth to your ideas but it can also create problems since part of you fights shy of close one-to-one commitment. You need a lover who will give you a long rein yet be there for you when you are feeling timid and in need of sustenance. You like keeping up your own circle of friends. You also need a lover who can be firm with you when you are being too evasive and trying to duck out.

Pisces Sun Aries Moon
Emotional, excitable and wildly impulsive, you never sit still for long. You somehow manage to be deeply sensitive, refined and sympathetic at the same time as being fiery, upfront and self centred. You are a contradiction to yourself because your Sun and Moon signs are so different in type. Your mood swings are extreme as you veer between your feelings and your aspirations, your needs for security and your needs to be free. You rarely think matters through coolly and logically but leap to conclusions and then leap straight into action without engaging your brain first. Your courage (or foolhardiness) surprises even you at times. On your good days you are refreshing straightforward. On bad ones you become frustrated and resentful. But you have an enormously kind, helpful streak. It is just that your moods change so rapidly that others never quite know what to expect and sometimes find you unreliable. You need a lover who can anchor you a little more perhaps with a hint of earth about them. Not too much since practical people make you feel weighed down and suffocated. You certainly do not want highly emotional or reckless mates since that just pushes you into even more challenging situations. You need calming down.

Pisces Sun Taurus Moon
Charming, emotionally sensitive and warm, you love to demonstrate your affection. You want a great deal of physical comfort and cuddles in life and are not one to hide your needs away. Though change is not something you find easy especially at home and you cling onto the status quo fairly grimly. You are better grounded, more practical than most Pisces, able to balance all your wonderful daydreams and fantasies with a bit of action. You can turn your visions into reality so are less likely to be an escapist or addictive Pisces. Self protection comes high on your list of priorities and you are likely to work very hard to survive. Calamities and crises are not such a big deal for you since you have endurance and inner strength. But you can hang on too firmly to the past and your needs for security. You can also be quite manipulative when it comes to getting your own way, usually with great subtlety, but it can cause relationship problems. You need a mate who will share a beautiful, comfortable home with you and give you the support to do whatever you want in the outside world. You need a lover with a touch of air who can give you detachment and a sense of perspective about your life.

Pisces Sun Gemini Moon
Restless, changeable, never a one to settle to routine when you could be following more interesting roads, you can sometimes be too blown around by events or your own short lived enthusiasms. Your boredom threshold is very low indeed. Starting new projects is not easy for you, nor is staying the course over the long distance. But you are highly adaptable and will generally fit in amiably enough with what is going on around you. Being a water air personality you are pulled between your feelings and what you think. You are highly sensitive and prone to escaping into daydreams or even addictions as a way of getting out of harsh reality. You lack trust in life and at times sparkle. You need to become more grounded in your body to stay healthy and to develop your rather inadequate practical side. Getting better organised is tricky but crucial. Maybe a lover with a hint of earth about them might get you in touch more with the real world. Though you could not stand too earthy a

mate since you would feel weighed down and suffocated. You do need a lover who will cope with your unpredictable whims. Your head and your heart are often split about what you want. Desire and duty often pull you in two opposite directions. This is a lifelong battle for you but it can be won.

Pisces Sun Cancer Moon
Deeply emotional, very intuitive, and easily hurt, you sometimes clam up and hide away from emotional difficulties because they feel too much to handle. You are so impressionable to outside atmosphere you feel like a raft cast adrift on the high seas, blown hither and thither by the winds and the currents. You can escape into daydreams, even addictions, as a way of blocking out what is painful. At times you have real difficulty in facing up to situations which are beyond your past experience in life. The Cancer Moon is very rooted in the past in a sentimental way. You never like to look back and see the pain with the result that you cling firmly onto your childhood and old values but in a rather vague over-rosy way. You need to gain greater detachment and distance from your life. Once you see it more clearly then you are able to move ahead more freely. A happy home life is essential to your wellbeing and you love the idea, not just of an exclusive relationship, but of a whole tribe of family to whom you can belong. You need to overcome your self absorption which in a double water personality is almost inevitable. Then you can give unreservedly to others. But you will probably always go to great extremes because your feelings are so deep. You need a mate who is emotional enough to understand your fears and protect you from the rougher edges of life. But you also need one who can anchor you and not be distracted by your roller coaster emotional life.

Pisces Sun Leo Moon
A dreamer and an escapist, you want a life that is romantic, glamorous and very definitely five star. You are charmingly persuasive on the social scene and like to be admired. Your vanity is very easily wounded by criticism and you can at times appear arrogant. Though the truth is you are more timid than others imagine. You usually have a grand vision

about your life which is not always very practical. You lack grounding either in reality or in your body and could probably do with a lover who would anchor you a little more. Being a water fire personality you are emotional, excitable and wildly impulsive at times. Your mood swings can be fairly extreme as you veer between feeling and hoping, between your need to be attached and your need to be free. Having a solid, settled family base is exceptionally important to you. With a Leo Moon you need to be top dog at home with a den of your own and pride of place amongst your own tribe. You can express your feelings more directly than most Pisces, who on the whole are a timid breed, but at times you can be deeply frustrated at what is blocking your life. You give vent to unpredictable outburst of opinions or feelings which rather upsets your sensitive side when you look back. You desperately do not want to hurt others.

Pisces Sun Virgo Moon
An overly restless Full Moon baby you rarely sit still and often do not quite know what you want. Both emotional and practical, you can veer from being too sensitive to being too cool. You rarely feel totally satisfied with your life. When you settle with one partner, you promptly find someone across the fence who looks more fanciable and so it goes on. What you ought to stick with is never what you want. This desire duty dilemma stems from a childhood in which you saw your parents as being fairly incompatible. Since you inherit traits from both of them you cannot get together in your head but they could not get together in their lives together. You need to leave the past behind in order to rise above this conflict. You are one of the world's great worriers and if you ever clear your plate of problems you dream up a few more anxieties to burden yourself with. You can be escapist either into daydreams or addictions as a way of winding down your rather nervy state. But what gives you strength is your ability to survive through calamities and crises. You want a settled home and family life but you need a mate who can give you more sparkle and a little faith in life.

Pisces Sun Libra Moon
Rather refined, always good mannered, sympathetic

and eager to please, you are both emotional and rather thoughtful. You certainly want a "nice" lifestyle which is upwardly socially mobile and you do find facing the harsher side of life rather difficult. You loathe the idle, the unemployed and the great unwashed in almost equal measure. At times you space out into daydreams or even addictions to avoid reality which feels rough edged and painful. You need to protect your sensitivities always against difficult people and difficult situations. Beauty is hugely important to you either through well designed clothes, tasteful home decor or music. You are not always strong physically and need to keep stress at bay as best you can. A lover with a touch of earth can help to ground you and protect you from what you perceive to be outside dangers. Though you cannot cope with people who are too physical. They feel crude or too suffocating. You are less emotional than some Pisces but do certainly need another half in life. You like hard working mates who also have a feeling for harmony. You hate arguments and bad temper. You could perhaps do with more courage and a touch more faith in life to be there for you.

Pisces Sun Scorpio Moon

Deeply, intensely emotional you are driven to extremes of behaviour because your feelings can be so unpredictable. At times lovingly sympathetic and caring, you can sometimes shut other people out because you feel so swamped by feelings. You are too impressionable to the atmosphere around you and soak in everyone else's feelings. So you can feel like a raft cast adrift on the high sea, blown around by the winds and currents. At times you can come across as cool, very self absorbed and rather distant but that is only your way of trying to keep control of your deep yearnings and insecurities and your tendency to over react to the slightest pinprick in the outside world. You take pride in never letting it be seen that you are hurt. But you never forget those who have slighted you and never forgive. You can give a great deal to others since you have a fathomless depth of compassion but you need to have found your own balance before you are happy with a life of giving. Your Scorpio Moon can make you preoccupied with sex, seeking a transcendental union with the other which allows you to feel whole. You need a mate who is less emotional than you though sensitive enough to understand your anxieties and needs, someone who can provide an anchor for you.

Pisces Sun Sagittarius Moon

Restless, emotional, excitable and given to wild impulses, you never feel totally satisfied with anything you have in life. Your Sun and Moon are at gritty angles to one another so you constantly feel your head go one way and your heart go another. What you ought to do is never what you want to do. This desire/duty dilemma is rooted in a childhood where you saw your parents as being very different people. Since you inherit traits from both of them, you have become almost like two separate people inside yourself. You have to rise above the problems of childhood to find your own individual way of relating. Otherwise you will never settle, since every lover you find will promptly become less interesting than the one across the fence. Being a water fire type you are pulled between your feelings and your hopes, between your need to be secure and your need to be free. Your Sagittarian Moon wants to roam the wide open spaces and not be tied into heavy commitments. If it feels fenced in it will be off like a shot. Yet your watery Pisces Sun really wants a sensitive emotional connection and a protected family base into which you can escape. On good days you are direct, very honest. On bad days you can be explosively frustrated with life. You need a mate who can anchor your mood swings and give you some grounding, though not too much. You do lack staying power but you can be highly adaptable.

Pisces Sun Capricorn Moon

Deeply sensitive, you worry constantly that you are not good enough. Sadly you grew up believing you would not be loved if you did not achieve so you push yourself too hard. Often you miss out on the full satisfaction of relationships because you are working so hard to prove yourself acceptable. But on the other hand you are more practical, better grounded, than some Pisceans and less likely to escape into daydreams and addictions. You can turn your dreams and visions into reality. You tend to be too self protective and rather serious in your approach to life. But you do have strength, endurance and the stamina to walk through any catastrophe or crises. You hang firmly onto the old traditional values in life and very much want to be accepted by the respectable members of your society. Socially upwardly mobile is one of your aims. What you lack is sparkle, chutzpah and the courage to trust in life. You need to loosen up and be more reckless. A mate with a tiny hint of fire about them would help to lift you up and improve your sense of humour. Not too much since fiery people seem unrealistic and foolhardy to you but a little would help. You will mellow through your middle years anyway because any Capricorn influence improves with age. But you do need to learn to stand back from your life and see your actions with more perspective.

Pisces Sun Aquarius Moon
Emotional and up in your head at the same time, you are an enigma to yourself, never mind to companions. You are insecure, deeply sensitive and need a loving relationship, yet you are also scared of close one-to-one commitment. You frankly prefer being one of the crowd rather than being in a passionate, sexy clinch all the time. You would rather think about life at times than feel it. Your emotions are often put on hold since you immediately distance yourself from them and start analysing. You can be an observer rather than a wholehearted game player in life. At times you can be rebellious just to see the effect. You love startling or shocking others in a mild way to make them sit up. But you are an escapist at heart either into daydreams and fantasies or even into addictions. The harsher realities of life seem too tough, painful and hard edged for you. What you need to work on is developing your sparkle, courage and chutzpah. A lover who can bring you out of yourself and make you trust in life more would be a great asset. You are deeply creative and love to help others which can be outlets for your impressionable feelings.

Pisces Sun Pisces Moon

Highly emotional and impressionable, at times you feel too timid for the world though you have an enormous amount to give in the way of sympathy and creative talents. Like an oyster without its shell out in the world, you try to shut out anything which is too rough edged, painful or means facing harsh reality. Being a double water personality you over react to the slightest stimulus and can feel like a raft adrift on the high seas, being pushed hither and thither by the winds and currents. Since you were born at the time of the New Moon you feel less need to relate outside of yourself than some. You can be quite self absorbed perhaps because it feels safer that way than establishing emotional commitments on the outside. But at the end of the day you are a water person and need emotional security, warmth and protection. Your behaviour can sometimes go to great extremes just because you find it difficult to control the storm filled tempest that rages inside you. You need to find an ideal or a vision to dedicate yourself to and then it becomes easier to venture forth into the world of people. Otherwise you are in danger of becoming an escapist either through day dreams or even addictions. You need a lover who can provide an anchor for you, perhaps one with a hint of earth. But you also need some fire to give you faith in life, and some air to give you a sense of distance and perspective on your actions.

Chapter Three

AND SUN SIGN
SHALL SPEAK
UNTO SUN SIGN

Your Sun to their Sun

Having pulled your self together, identified your contradictory needs, lusts, dislikes and desires you can get to work on finding your perfect mate who has to be out there somewhere. At that first contact across a crowded pub/party/baseball game all you are likely to find out is their birthday sign. But it will tell you a great deal about them and what your interface is likely to be - smooth, gritty, explosive or defensive. Only later will you plunge into the depths of the complexities of Sun and Moon compatibilities. (Chapters four and five).

You are Aries
You are straightforward to a fault and are a joy to have around when a straight opinion is needed. Normally you have no side, no devious strategy, and will not try to please by telling others what you think they want to hear. Giving way is not inherently your strong point especially early in life since you like to go straight ahead and do your own thing. You do have a strong sex drive and can be highly romantic, adoring the adventure, the intrigue, the excitement and the thrill of the chase and the seduction in love. Your passions flare up quickly and must be indulged. Staying power, however, is not your strong point. You bore easily and sometimes want to wander off to find a new love interest to keep your adrenalin flowing.

As the first sign of the zodiac, you are often referred to as the baby of the star signs and you can be almost as noisy! You want attention no matter how many feet you have to stamp. What you want, you want NOW. Patience is sometimes in short supply. You have an infant's refreshing sense of being the most important person in the world. No false modesty or delicate anguish about the feelings of others gets in the way of your main aim. Number One is organised first, the rest can follow.

You thrive on arguments and confrontations. You hate wimps who will not stand up to you but on the other hand you do not like being dominated either. You need a good clean fight with preferably you as the victor at the end. Diplomacy and tact are added to your repertoire through life as you discover ultimately that you can win easier and more often with a modicum of charm. Male Aries can be incredibly sweet on the surface and resist growing up but underneath there still lurks that Knight in Shining Armour. Lady Aries tend to be upfront, none too domesticated, preferring to be out in the world shaking it up.

Your Aries Sun to their Aries Sun

Imagine the flash, crackle, pop of a rock concert on a boiling summer's day or of Scud missiles whistling on target for a direct hit - that is Aries on Aries. Very noisy, very explosive, very hot but not necessarily designed to last for a lifetime though oddly enough quite a few pairings of this sort do. One problem is that burnout can happen since both of you are speed freaks, adrenalin junkies and fairly ungrounded. Together you will egg each other on to greater risks, upping the stakes and ultimately falling out since neither of you is willing to step aside for the sake of peace and quiet. As geriatrics, mellowed by the passing years and softened by life's catastrophes you might just manage it - but not before 80 at the very youngest.

Your Aries Sun to Their Taurus Sun

You fire, them earth. You soar, they stand rooted. You enthuse, they point out practical flaws. You fantasise, they scoff. You get into trouble, they sort it out. You careless, they have common sense. There is merit in this combination though it is not exactly designer compatibility. You are almost complete opposites - the hare and the tortoise. You have initiative and starting power but are not a great finisher. They are achingly slow to get moving but have the stamina of a marathon runner. You dislike being trapped, they are possessive. You are not wildly physical, they are terribly tactile. Can opposites survive together? Initially they attract but really in the long term you do not truly understand what makes the other tick. You do have much to offer that the other lacks but you will need other good cross overs in your chart to make this one work.

Your Aries Sun to Their Gemini Sun
A sparkling combination where your wit, intelligence, fire and imagination strike a chord immediately with their fun loving, communicative, devil-may-care outlook on life. You will certainly never be bored, nor be silent for very long together. You both thrive on gossip, new ideas and an intense curiosity about life. What may lack a little from your relationship is common sense, practicality or great depth of feeling. Neither of you is good at staying down in your passions for long. Aries soars up into romantic fantasies where Gemini stands back to be fairly clinical. Neither of you is hugely physical except in the first flush of love. Both of you have notoriously short enthusiasm and attention spans. You could fly away together into the stratosphere or fizzle out like a spent firework. Give it time before you commit. If you have anchoring from your Moon connections it might just be what you are looking for. But banish jealousy from your mind. It is not helpful.

Your Aries Sun to Their Cancer Sun
Put fire and water together and the water may boil or the fire may go out. Your rather upfront style gets under Cancer's thin skin and threatens their security. All that soggy emotion of Cancer slightly frightens you, makes you feel you will be trapped for ever, pulled under water by hidden currents. Both of you are brimful of initiative and rather restless so as a working combination it can sometimes work. But Cancer is the most emotionally sensitive (hyper sensitive) sign in the zodiac and especially afraid of letting go. You hate being fenced in. You do not share the same fantasies. You want glorious adventure, knights on white chargers rescuing Princesses, Indiana Jones etc. They want rose covered cottages (large ones) full of children, grandchildren,

aunts, uncles, cousins. You would clash over who is boss.

Your Aries Sun to Their Leo Sun

Wow!! What a connection. All that fire, fantasy, heat and passion coming together in one glorious conflagration. Leo's solidity and stubbornness is a useful anchor to your zippy, never sit still, flyaway streak but there is still a fair danger of burnout since neither of you is practical, grounded or that interested in reality. Who would empty the rubbish? Or clean the bath? Leo would at least read the bank statements which is more than you do. This is a combination that often attracts. You share a refreshingly direct approach to life, love and danger. Both of you thrive on risk (Leo slightly less so than you), revel in romantic fantasy and adore the good life. The downside (apart from exhaustion) is that both of you in different ways not only like to win, you absolutely need to win. Egos will grind loudly and long. You cannot bear Leo's tendency to sulk and their surprisingly fragile vanity does not always take kindly to your trenchant honesty or sometimes overly direct sense of humour.

Your Aries Sun to Their Virgo Sun

Bit of a chalk and cheese mix this. You thrive on fight, flight and constant excitement. You have a gloriously insane faith in life and your good luck. Virgo can be timid, slightly over sensitive to too much stimulus and have an inbuilt suspicion about life's ability to be there for them. They nag out of insecurity and worry endlessly over a million nit picking details. You do not basically understand their anxieties and they resent deeply your lack of sympathy, empathy and mother hen qualities. What this combination does have going for it is Virgo's common sense and ability to keep everyday life ticking over with great precision which Aries almost totally lack. You can also add sparkle and courage to Virgo's tendency to dullness. But at the end of the day it is not designed in heaven for eternity unless the Moons give a hint of other deeper connections.

Your Aries Sun to Their Libra Sun

You lead and they follow - suits everyone! It works best

if Aries lady, Libra man since the male Libra tends to be a softer, sweeter person who does not mind being bossed around. The other way is slightly more problematic since Libra Ladies can have a fairly masculine approach to life which can clash horribly with an Aries warrior though they might make it better with an Aries Peter Pan. Not all signs get on with their opposites but this is a match often seen. Communication is good between you since both of you have bright, sparkling minds. Your fire sits happily with their airy approach to life though their slightly fastidious, sometimes snobbish outlook can cringe with embarrassment at your more direct outlook. You could not care less what others think and always do precisely what suits your purposes. You will cut corners to win. Neither of you is jealous though Libra is more faithful than Aries which could cause problems.

Your Aries Sun to Their Scorpio Sun
Not to be recommended unless there are major advantages coming from other quarters. Aries is like Icarus who wanted to fly to the Sun. Scorpio is more connected to Pluto, god of the underworld. Scorpio is deeply determined, power hungry and possessive - all of which sounds like a day in hell for you. You like winning, racing around at high speed, being free to do whatever suits you and with whom (no matter what your long term commitments are). Scorpio takes over control early on and has the tenacity of a scorpion when roused. Which is not to say that the early passions could not be wild, way out and quite transcendental but the long term outlook could be a rough, stormy road. You are basically wary of too much emotion where Scorpio thrives on turbulent, teeming, throbbing feelings. You are honest to the point of naivety. They are secret to the point of paranoia. There would come a time when you got tired living down in the depths and blocked them out. They could not live with that.

Your Aries Sun to Their Sagittarius Sun
Wonderful, happy go lucky, devil may care, feckless combination this which works surprisingly well. You are both fire so prone to wild fantasies, taking huge risks and

treating life as a bit of a practical joke. But since both of you are overloaded with luck even when you do not deserve it, you do better than most at pulling gambles off. You do both lack practicality and common sense so need an anchor from somewhere, hopefully more earthy Moon signs. Otherwise the boring domestic tasks never get done. Luckily Sagittarius though just as fiery and manic as you does have more adaptability so they will let you win more happily. Burnout and exhaustion could be hazards since neither of you know how to slow down. Pacing yourselves is a real problem. Sagittarius ladies are not remotely domestic and hate being fenced in and you are not always great at keeping your enthusiasm up for long term commitments so 45 year marriages could run into the odd problem.

Your Aries Sun to Their Capricorn Sun

This can work wonders as a good business combination. Both of you have initiative and drive. Aries has flair and imagination where Capricorn has earthy practicality. You both like the better things of life. Aries likes winning and Capricorn adores status, social acceptability and luxuries. It does however lack something in the way of deeper feeling for an emotional match. Capricorn can be a touch lofty about Aries rather more adventurous ideas about life and can be deeply embarrassed by Aries's lack of social sensitivity. The last thing in the world Aries cares about is respectability whereas with Capricorn it is the first. On first meeting Capricorn often comes across as cold and could be written off as repressed, prudish or just too serious. Their hidden fires sometimes take a while to break free. Whereas with Aries what you see is what you get - it is all out front. Timing could be a problem and a lack of mutual rhythm. What Aries wants it wants NOW. Capricorn has a much more ordered set of priorities.

Your Aries Sun to Their Aquarius Sun

This is a wild, whacky, way out and fairly frequent pairing. Everyone knows you are not like other couples and they secretly envy your madcap approach. Neither of you cares a hoot what other people think. You know what you do has to be right for you. But both of you are such individualists that you sometimes find it difficult to find the flexibility needed for a relationship. Give and take is a problem. Aries in a tight corner picks up its jacket and moves on. Aquarius just sits tight and waits for life/partners to come round to their way of thinking. If they don't? Well Aquarius knows it is hugely self sufficient. Total dependency is not part of this relationship and indeed this bond could wither away at some point just because both sides drift off after their own interests. But on the upside you do communicate well, laugh a great deal together. Neither of you is overly physical, nor too possessive though sometimes Aquarius can be so spacey you wonder if they want too relate at all.

Your Aries Sun to Their Pisces Sun
This should not work well as a pairing but I suspect it sometimes does because you both want the same things though you come from very different places. Both of you are hugely imaginative so much so you can spend a great deal of time wrapped up in your daydreams which is hardly a bother if both of you are at it. Both of you are fairly spaced out from the physical realm so you would not worry about being shut in a claustrophobic, too earthy relationship. Aries loves to win. Pisces will fit in fairly sweetly to whatever the prevailing order is. But it is an offbeat coupling. Aries brash, dynamic outlook does not always fit well with vague, super sensitive, emotional Pisces. The odd Pisces can also be a voracious, devouring sea monster. All that watery feeling could completely submerge your fiery spirit. Basically you fear all that chaos inside Pisces which threatens to dismember you if you get sucked into it. You are in this respect very opposite. You are about getting your ego together and standing rock solid for yourself. Pisces is about self sacrifice, giving up the ego altogether and dissolving into the cosmos. The mix is not a natural one.

<u>You are Taurus</u>
Second sign in the zodiac ,you are earthy, stubborn, practical and pleasure seeking. You are one of life's slow starters but once you get going you are impossible to shift. Think of an oak tree or a enormous bull that is Taurean strength at its best. You can be determined in your

approach especially to relationships. Me first, or at least my pleasure first is what you think. Other's wants and needs come distinctly second. Which is not to say that it is not a highly pleasureable experience being around you since good food, hugely comfortable, luxurious surroundings and good company are the stuff of your life.

Sensation is what you love, especially touching. It need not necessarily be with sexual intent. You just love that warm, animal feel of being in contact with another human being. But all the senses are important to you. Thus you love music for the ear; nature or art for the eye - colour is crucial; perfume to savour; the feel of fabric like velvet, satin, silk; and of course taste for almost anything indulgent to eat and drink.

Possessiveness can sometimes be a problem. You hate letting go. You like to control, to dominate and you can get rather blocked and bloated. The positive side of that is your ability to hold on through thick and thin and your loyalty. You make an excellent friend and can be extremely faithful as a partner if a little jealous at times. Relationships can be tricky since - dare I say it? - a touch stubborn. Giving and taking does not come easily to you. But you can make the most marvellous foundation for a happy home life since you can be warm hearted, affectionate, physically demonstrative and very down to earth.

Your Taurus Sun to Their Aries Sun
Can you tie a firefly down or chain a hummingbird? What you want is security, warmth, human contact. What Aries wants is freedom, adventure and the high road to places unknown. They bring out quite the worst of your controlling, possessive instincts and you make them feel a little like Cio-Cio San in Puccini's opera - a butterfly pinned to a board. Not the most ideal pairing this one. It does have its merits because you can give ballast, common sense and practicality to Aries's flyaway tendencies. If you do not mind being the anchor at home while they flit around off the leash, then it could work though it would stretch your jealousy to breaking point at times. They also give you a little zip, sparkle and chutzpah which is healthy since you are a very solid earth sign and inclined to get too stodgy if

left to your own devices. But direct opposites do not often make ideal long term living relationships. Sex could be a problem since you are very physical and they are not.

Your Taurus Sun to Their Taurus Sun
Solid, so solid this combination that you might get glued to the spot and never move again. You certainly both need security, both hate change, both enjoy the good life and a good cuddle. So there are strong pluses. But both of you tend to lack imagination and your vision might narrow and narrow down until you turned into vegetables. Too much practicality in a relationship is certainly better than too little. But an overdose can kill feeling, spirit, fire, passion and communication. Neither of you would question the whys and wherefores of life, love and your togetherness so you would never sort the problems out as they came along. You would expect to live your lives in the same unchanging pattern that your families have lived for generations. Constipation would probably clog romance up eventually. You would only survive together with maybe a fiery Moon connection to bring an element of danger or an airy Moon link which gave you more objectivity and dilute all that earth.

Your Taurus Sun to Their Gemini Sun
In astrological lore you are supposed to fear the sign before you and regard the one ahead as somehow having developed qualities that you lack. You come first in the zodiac so Gemini with its flighty, flyaway qualities fears your solidity, need for security and deep rooted-ness. You secretly envy their agile, quick witted mind and ability to reflect on life. But while opposites sometimes are initially attracted it is always a questionable basis for a long term commitment. You need more common ground. You are highly tactile, very physical in your expression of love. Gemini is spacey, often likes to think about sex rather than get too deeply involved. Not that some Geminis are not highly promiscuous but it tends to be of the here-today gone-tomorrow variety. Where you like the unchangingness of the same partner. They find you a little stodgy and lacking in courage, where you think them foolhardy and lacking in depth. You would

get very jealous of their wandering feet, always wondering where their thoughts were even when their body was within your grasp.

Your Taurus Sun to Their Cancer Sun

This can be a happy combination since you both adore security, happy family homes, the better things of life and living in luxurious style. You are practical and determined while they are full of initiative and great at starting new schemes. It works differently depending on gender. Taurus men are strong on the whole and Cancer women can be positively matriarchal as they age so there could be a fight for control especially on home territory. Cancer men are softer, sweeter souls who could quite happily be mothered by a Taurean earth mother who did not want her power base eroded though he could also be eaten alive. You are both jealous to a quite destructive degree if you do not keep a firm grip on your insecurities. Together you could also be a tiny touch over materialistic putting too much of a stress on the indulgences and outer appearances of life. Sex could be one area where negotiation is required since you are very demonstrative at a physical level. Cancer likes cuddles but of a fairly generalised nature and is not always too drawn by prolonged physical intimacy.

Your Taurus Sun to Their Leo Sun

A stubborn, very heavyweight pairing, where the high points at least early on could be very elevated indeed. But as the highs are high so are the sulks likely to be dark clouds over the long term. Neither of you gives way easily. Both of you approach life and relationships as events which will eventually have to adapt to your way if you just stand still long enough. It is a game that could go on for ever and ever with both of you playing it. You like to control, to hold the power and have immense stamina. Leo thrives on attention and only needs to appear to have the power. They will happily delegate the boring tasks of life to someone else so you can win if you just play to their vanity. You do offer them a practical anchor to reality while they offer you sparkle, fire and a sense of fun. But it will work better (not perfectly but better) with Taurus Man and Leo Lady. Leo ladies are marginally more able to flex, bend and give in than their counterparts. A Leo man would be too much the autocrat for a Taurus lady who is not given to suffering ego trips or foolish vanities too well. If it works then you'll have an indulgent, rather extravagant lifestyle.

Your Taurus Sun to Their Virgo Sun
Wonderfully sympatico combination this with all the earthy warmth coming together and Virgo will adapt where you stand solid. Indeed they will positively bless your rock steadiness as an anchor for their jittery nervy sensitivity. You can be amazingly stubborn but they are good at wending their way round oak trees. Both of you appreciate a practically well ordered life, love small animals, nature, gardening, the better things of life. Virgo being the sign of service will race around to see to your every need and you can turn a deaf ear to their nagging, nit picking and endless worrying. You would need a touch of sparkle from your Moon connections though otherwise life could become terribly earthy, sensible and lack fun.

Your Taurus Sun to Their Libra Sun
This pairing is not supposed to match but you both share the same ruler in Venus so it can work surprisingly well. Venus was the goddess of parties, loved the good life, dressed well, ate, drank, flirted and was wonderfully elegant. So you can share a love of the luxurious life and both of you have a real sense of style and taste. But there are also wide differences. You can find them a little too chilly and detached, not very physical, rather fastidious to the point of snobbishness and sometimes lacking in depth. In fact Libra is not superficial but they do tend to try to please too much which can comes across as lacking in integrity. However their thoughtfulness can be a positive advantage where your stubbornness is concerned. They will give in! You would need to watch that it did not become a little dry since neither of you have the sparkle from fire nor the emotional depth of water unless supplied by the Moon signs. You can be jealous which they will neither understand nor appreciate. You may also be made to feel rather too earthy at times since they are fairly detached from the body and all matters physical.

Your Taurus Sun to Their Scorpio Sun

The powerhouse of all combinations, this could start in earth shaking ecstasy but where it might end up is quite another matter. You are both hugely stubborn, very passionate, possessive, power hungry, determined personalities. Not much exists in the way of adaptability. It could be a fight to the bittern end with a great deal of bad feeling swept under the carpet as you struggle for supremacy. When the resentments break cover they could be very destructive indeed. On the other hand both of you like being in the depths of a very tangible relationship. Neither of you is designed for a wispy, here-today gone-tomorrow affair. What could be a real problem is you need a degree of unchangingess to give you security while Scorpio is never happy unless life is going through a massive sea change of an upheaval every so often. Both of you are highly sexual though in different ways. You are highly physical. Scorpio knows you need the body as the vehicle to move into more transcendental realms. It could be overwhelmingly wonderful or quite the reverse - probably both.

Your Taurus Sun to Their Sagittarian sun

You will adore their light, fiery spirit, their fun loving approach to life. They make you feel less stodgy, more alive. They adapt to your needs and make you laugh. That is in week one. What happens in week four hundred and fifty is quite another matter. You now begin to dislike everything you envied before. They are impractical gamblers never going to settle to steady a routine or carry responsibility. They joke where they should be working or worrying. Even worse they fly away when you want to pin them to the spot. They loathe being fenced in and you are possessive by nature so you have picked yourself a hair shirt to start with. You are highly physical and they are unhappy about being too intimate. They fantasise wonderfully romantic dreams. You want to live them out in the flesh. You can provide the gaps in the other's armour since you are opposites but in the end it is not a happy combination unless there are good Moon connections.

Your Taurus Sun to Their Capricorn Sun

Happy as bunnies in the field, your earthy qualities draw you together. You adore Capricorn's way of making things happen and getting new projects started though you may worry about their defensiveness initially. You thrive together eating, drinking, home making and cuddling as long as you have not picked yourself a cold souled, workaholic Capricorn in which case you will probably not get together in the first place. But there are pitfalls here. All the world's major dictators (and heavyweight boxers) are either Taurus or Capricorn so some power struggles are almost inevitable though they need not be physical (but they could be). You will not be allowed to sulk as much around a Capricorn which will help and they have a way of pushing you onto new tracks that are helpful. Both of you are very physical in the expression of your love though it can take Capricorn longer to find that out. You are more possessive and jealous so they can put a restraining hand on you. But both of you are loyal once you settle.

Your Taurus Sun to Their Aquarius Sun

This is earthlings trying to mate with Martians. You do not inhabit the same planet, speak the same language, or approach life with similar thoughts. You live for your body, pamper your senses, are jealous, feel attached to nature and can never see any point in thinking about things which are not practical. Aquarius tries to distance itself from the biological at every opportunity, loathes anything that smells like possessiveness and loves nothing better than a wonderfully abstract discussion about life, philosophy and the cosmos. You inhabit the physical realm. They inhabit the mind. You would not find what they describe as a relationship suits you at all. They think that touching fingertips or blowing a kiss across a crowded room full of friends is passion. You expect that from your postman. If you do not get full body contact - forget it unless both of you have rafts of other planets in the other's Sun sign.

Your Taurus Sun to Their Pisces Sun

This can be a felicitous combination since their sensitive adaptability can smooth away your cares and wend its way skilfully round your more obstinate points. You adore being pleased and looked after and Pisces can be deeply intuitive. Though they can also be so spaced out they hardly know you exist which would not please you abundantly. It slightly depends on which gender is which sign and what kind of Pisces you have. There are little fish Pisces who are sweet and accommodating and large fish Pisces who are voracious, man eating monsters. If it is the latter they have picked quite the wrong person since you have a core of solid oak and have no intention of being swallowed alive. Taurus men and Pisces ladies are the better combination or at least a more old fashioned - he walks in front, she walks behind - kind of mating. Taurus ladies and Pisces men could be trickier. She strong and the master of the art of passive resistance. He timid to the point of evaporation or octopus fighting for control. Either way not quite as easy. But on the whole it is a combination which offers both of you a great deal. You give practical, common sense to a creative but ungrounded Pisces. They offer you vision and hope. Sex might be a problem since you like it and they sometimes would rather daydream it than experience it in reality. Pisceans can either be platonic or very orgiastic. It depends again whether it be little minnow or large whale variety you land.

You are Gemini
As third sign in the zodiac and first of the airy ones you are flighty, restless, communicative and curious. Your mind and your tongue are always active. Your adaptable nature finds it difficult to settle down or commit itself for long to any one situation. But behind a great deal of your restlessness is a fear that you may never find your other half in life. You feel split and yearn for that perfect match which will make you feel whole. You hate that sense of a dry desert inside where your emotions ought to be.

But it is your strength to be detached, to be able to stand back and observe, to gain perspective. You do need to be fairly free in spirit to fulfil your needs.   Your favourite occupations are reading to pick up information, thinking and most importantly talking. Nothing is more attractive than a stimulating chat where your knowledge is paraded and titbits collected for future use. You are not desperately intellectual because you never stand still long enough to become a specialist but you have an amazing breadth of knowledge.

Unless sunk in the glooms of your dark side you make a great party guest - witty, bright, full of jokes. By the end of the evening you will have chatted to the entire guest list. You are happiest when doing three jobs and when flitting around an active social life. You perhaps need to learn the virtues of being a little more straightforward.

Your Gemini Sun to Their Aries Sun

You talk, they act. You never sit still, neither do they. You are not remotely practical, neither are they. Neither of you is especially jealous, possessive, over emotional, hyper sensitive or given to long sulks. This combination is good news. You love constant excitement and stimulation and they provide you with a running adventure story. You are reasonably adaptable so will not fall over if they insist on having their own way and winning (which they will). You adore their capacity for making life work, their courage at bouncing back, which you share. Where you lack a touch as a pair is in being able to connect with deeper emotions. Your lives move so fast that you have little time to settle down to find out what you really feel. At some point in life you may discover that running thrills, spills and adventures are not enough for your heart to flourish on. But then again you may not. Fidelity does not come naturally to either of you. That has to be worked on. Your enthusiasm span is fairly short.

Your Gemini Sun to Their Taurus sun

You know you need to be anchored, to have someone who can control your flyaway tendencies. But will you like it when you get it? That is quite a different question. Taurus certainly supply much of what you lack but they are such opposites to you that you really never feel spontaneous, light hearted and alive around them. All that earthy solidity makes you feel suffocated, trapped and over burdened. Both of you share an interest in the fun side of life but from very different perspectives. You like variety, stimulation and excitement. They adore to pleasure the body which after a while you find rather off putting. You live in your head, your ideas and your wit. They live in their body, in nature and the very practical realms of life. Sex might be a problem after a while since you are not keen on prolonged physical intimacy. They are fiendishly jealous and possessive which you are not at all. But you can adapt well to their stubbornness which in the right setting can give you a solid core to your life.

Your Gemini sun to Their Gemini Sun
Very heady, up in the air, communicative, but does it have much feeling going for it? Both of you are rather restless wanderers, who can lack deep connection to your bodies, your emotions or indeed a sense of sparkle in life. There will be an initial attraction because you have no difficulty conversing endlessly, about every subject under the sun. Both of you are butterflies, jack of all trades, who know a mite about a million different things so boredom is unlikely to settle in. The male of the species is a little inclined to wander and the female is not hugely domestic so you could drift apart unless there is a dedicated effort to hold together. There is a dark side to Gemini so it is possible for there to be a wildly, way out, seamy affair but not for long. If you stay on the light side then you could have a superficial social marriage where it looked fine on the surface but once you hit the stormy spots when you had to come down to face darker feelings and harsher realities there could be problems. Your coolness and tendency to analyze feelings before you have had time to experience them can result in a relationship that is lacking in passion.

Your Gemini Sun to Their Cancer Sun
This is a rather chalk and cheese mix, or rather air and water. On the upside you are both restless, get up and go types out in the world so there is much of general interest to hold you together. Cancer is by no means just a stay at home and read-the-knitting-patterns-and-recipes kind of person. But they are home and family loving, deeply possessive and inclined to make you feel uncomfortable with all their fluctuating feelings. You like to think difficulties

through. They react with their emotions and can be quite contrary because of that. Their mood swings will exasperate you, their sympathy sometimes feel smothering. You love to escape and they will not want to let go. You adore having a wide circle of friends and are never that happy about what you regard as claustrophobic commitment. They adore friends as well but want to turn life into one big, happy family which is not always your scene. You need to have a watery Moon or them an airy or fiery one before this will even have a hope of working.

Your Gemini Sun to Their Leo Sun

You adore the fire signs for their verve, vigour, courage and sparkle. You spark off each other in a stimulating way and boredom is never a problem. But Leo is possibly the least your type of the three fire signs (Aries and Sagittarius). They can be a touch pompous, have a dreadfully fragile vanity which your incisive wit sometimes ruffles, and can sulk which you cannot abide. They absolutely need to be centre of attention which your flexibility can cope with though it probably works better as Leo lady and Gemini man than the other way round. Neither of you is practical which can be a problem round the house, taking care of domestic business, looking after long term planning and where matters physical are concerned. But both of you can passionate in a fairly detached kind of way. You may not take kindly to being put down by Leo's innate sense of superiority, nor of being ticked off for social gaffes since they want to be accepted as the creme de la creme and you basically do not give a hoot. But it is a fair match and could work well.

Your Gemini Sun to Their Virgo Sun

A restless but amiable combination since Virgo is the lightest and most adaptable of the earth signs. They give you practical help without smothering you, warmth without too much possessiveness, and great communication. You can both talk the hind legs off a donkey, are interested in people, curious about life and enjoy swapping titbits of information. Boredom is not usually a problem. Both of you are adaptable which means there are no week long sulks and obstinate silences, though you do not always find it easy as a couple to make major decisions. One constantly defers to the other. On the downside you may not always take kindly to their nagging and constant worrying. You are much less fussed about the everyday details of life. Though neither of you is especially good at calming the other down. Both of you tend to be over highly strung. With a Gemini lady and a Virgo man the combination could become a little dry, unemotional, and wither away eventually for lack of sparkle. The other way round has more chance of staying alive, lively and breathing. Your Virgo other half will need to not become too fastidious since you live life exactly the way you want which does not always pay attention to convention.

Your Gemini Sun To Their Libra Sun

If you do not communicate you do not exist so Libra, another air sign, is made in heaven for you at least across the dining table. Both of you share the same detached, slightly unemotional, chatty approach to life. You are more of a flibberty gibbet, slightly less respectable sign than Libra who has been known to exhibit snobbish traits and be a touch superior. But really you do resonate along the same wave length. They will bring taste, elegance and charm into your life and put themselves out for your convenience. They are restless like you but probably better at starting new projects and keeping life moving. Though their indecisiveness at times will drive you potty. Neither of you is jealous though they may not take kindly, if you are a wandering Gemini, to your flights from the straight and narrow since they worry endlessly about what the neighbours/boss/friends will think. Neither of you is practical, nor terribly physical so your relationship may lack grounding and over a prolonged period physical intimacy unless you have warmer Moons.

Your Gemini Sun To Their Scorpio Sun

This should not work but oddly it sometimes can. You are airy, detached, chatty and rather unemotional while Scorpio are deep, secretive and highly turbulent. But because you are a split sign with one half bright, the other half dark you can be attracted to all that depth and blackness in

Scorpio who fight their own endless inner battle between the forces of light and dark, good and evil. But in the long term you are very different types and you would begin to find the abyss between your outlooks on life rather wide. The undertow from Scorpio's emotional life is very strong. They may look strong and rather impassive on the surface but the undercurrents could pull the unwary under. You are essentially distrustful of feelings. They are also hugely jealous while you are footloose, fancy free and dislike being tied in to one claustrophobic relationship for too long. You love crowds of friends. They want a hothouse affair that runs for a life time. Eventually you might find you need more space to breathe than they allow you.

Your Gemini Sun To Their Sagittarian Sun
An adorable match with all the zany lack of common sense you might expect from the liveliest of the air signs and the luckiest of the fire signs together. You are attracted to their sparkle, sense of fun, risk taking and general lack of concern for convention. Like you they are not stuffy. They hate being fenced in so will never question your whereabouts for fear you might retaliate. You just love their bright minds, spread of knowledge and way of thinking about everything in global terms. You are restless and they love to travel. No one will ever know where to find you since you are both constantly on the move. You are curious and they will fill you in with interesting facts. What you have to watch with all this movement, stimulating conversation and general busyness is that burnout is a possibility. You fly along at such speed that one day you wake up plain exhausted. Feelings need more of a look in, so does common sense. Earthy Moon signs would help.

Your Gemini Sun To Their Capricorn Sun
This is not supposed to fit together well but often it does, mainly due to your flexibility. It can be a rather dry, chilly or unemotional combination with work taking over too large a space. But if Capricorn can be persuaded to drop its workaholic tendencies and become more indulgent and you do not mind getting really physical then it can work well. You are airy and not very attuned to your body though you

like living well; where Capricorn can positively wallow in the flesh a la Elvis Presley. So it rather depends where on the spectrum you both exist within your own sign. In the long term it is not an instinctively good match since you have differing outlooks. You are a restless spirit who cares little for convention. Capricorn is easily embarrassed socially, is quite a snob and thrives on tradition. You can find them stick-in-the-muds at times. But they do have deep in their core a warmth that you probably could benefit from them if you can dig for it. It probably works better as Capricorn men and Gemini women rather than vice versa.

Your Gemini Sun To Their Aquarius Sun
You are instantly attracted to their wayward eccentricity, their uniquely one off personalities and their way of caring even less than you do for respectability.   They sparkle with wit, intelligence, rebelliousness and never give you a whiff of a feeling that they are going to trap you. Along the way you may even begin to wonder if you do mean much more than their other 93 friends but maybe that detached quality suits you just as well as it suits them. This is no claustrophobic, hot house affair.   They do seem to know everything there is to know about sex but practising it means getting into their bodies which is not their favourite habitation. Even you may feel the lack of physical intimacy which is odd since you are airy and rather shy clear of anything too continuously earthy. It probably works better as Gemini lady to Aquarian man - they are more of a cool, intellectual match. The other way round can be a problem since Gemini men are sometimes be real Don Juans and do not appreciate a dissertation on their favourite occupation rather than the real thing.

Your Gemini Sun To Their Pisces Sun
Air and Water are not supposed to mix but you are both mutable signs and therefore highly adaptable. Also Pisces's emotional nature is often channelled into their daydreams and fantasies so you will not be swept away by tidal waves of smothering feelings which can be the case with Cancer and Scorpio. You need to fill your life with multiple jobs, dozens of interests, friends and lines of inquiry whereas

Pisces have a more gentle, intuitive way of floating through life which intrigues you though you do not basically understand what makes them tick. You could co exist rather happily for years without ever getting into any great depth since Pisces tends to hold their inner world fairly private. But whether it is a good relationship is quite another matter. You may find them cringing and withdrawing from your rather abrasive approach to life, love and romance. You may find their sensitivities rather silly or neurotic. It works best with Gemini men and Pisces women though you need earthy moons to keep contact with reality.

You are Cancer
As number four in the zodiac and first of the water babies you are the most emotionally sensitive sign of all, terrified of letting the past go. You cringe at the prospect of separation or of being hurt by the actions of those brasher souls who surround you. The security of a happy domestic and family life is vital to your well being. But you have a driving spirit which also takes you out into the big, wide world. You have buckets of initiative, are great at starting new projects and thrive on enthusiasm. Because of your emotional sensitivity you can suss out what is in the public fashion at any given moment. Your love life is always a matter of great seriousness for you and rarely do you joke about romance. Once threatened either with ridicule or rejection you retreat at high speed and snap your shell shut. Although wonderfully charming when it suits, you can also be sulky, withdrawn and very stubborn. Like the crab, your symbol, you can dig yourself firmly into the sand and refuse to budge.

Passion does not run deep in your nature for intimate one-to-one relationships and over the years you add partners onto the brood as just another member of the family. Close physical intimacy is fine as long as it is cuddles but anything too sexual is not exactly your scene. Sometimes you have a way of trying to create perfect children, little works of art, which is not accepting of their spontaneity but on the whole you are an attentive parent though never good at letting go. You are wonderfully adept at setting up a beautiful home life since your have a highly creative sense in interior decor as well as clothes. You cook well and certainly you like entertaining at home.

Your Cancer Sun To Their Aries Sun

As a working combination this could be rather productive. Both of you have flair, get up and go, ability, and drive. As an emotional combination it does not have a lot going for it. You need warmth, security, tenderness, sensitivity and a certain attention to your needs. Aries, bless them, are rather brash, can be self centred, overly honest, loathe being fenced in, are not always faithful, and are certainly not well designed to think about the needs of others without a fair amount of forcing. Have you a masochistic streak? It could just work as a mother hen Cancerian lady taking on board a Peter Pan Aries man who refuses to grow up. But it is a certain disaster the other way round with a rather sensitive Cancerian male faced with a dismissive, tough minded Aries lady who wants a mate who is her equal especially when it comes to fighting. You hear criticism where none exists and magnify slights out of all proportion. Aries puts its foot in its mouth with great regularity since they rarely stop to engage their brain before uttering what may well be true but could very well have been left unsaid. Your nerves will end up in tatters.

Your Cancer Sun To Their Taurus Sun

This is a sweetly designed pairing which should do well. You love security, a happy home life and minor luxuries around. Taurus hates change, needs to be rooted, wallows in pleasureable sensations and usually has good taste. You are both jealous and possessive but once settled both of you are reasonably faithful so it should not matter. Though you can both sulk monumentally. You have the drive and determination to keep your lives together moving in exciting directions where Taurus has the hang-on-in-there ability which keeps you on track when you might become distracted. You are a great starter, not so hot finisher. They are achingly slow to get on track but unshiftable once there. It can be a very complementary mating. You lend emotional sensitivity and creativity to the mix. They add practical common sense and an anchor for your tearful, tantrum prone days when the emotional storms overtake you. They are more physical than you in their affections which could prove a problem in the long term unless you have an earthy Moon. It is better as Cancer lady and Taurus male though there could be power struggles since both of you like to be in charge. Cancer men might get pushed around a little by tougher Taurean ladies.

Your Cancer Sun To Their Gemini Sun
The astrological rule of thumb which says you fear the sign before yours would indicate rightly that this is not a totally in tune mix. Unless you are a very untypical Cancerian you fear all that icy detachment, that cool, dispassionate, unemotional, slightly dry Gemini approach to life. You thrive on feelings, empathies, sympathies and togetherness. They thrive on thoughts, ideas, space and distance. You adore the notion of a family tied together by bonds of affection. They want a circle of friends held loosely together by common interests. What you find nurturing, they find smothering. What you think is natural interest in the affairs of those close, they find claustrophobic, invasive or controlling. Water and air are in many ways a worse mix than water and fire. Fiery signs (Aries, Leo, Sagittarius) may be brash, insensitive and self centred at times but they can also be amazingly warm. Gemini can cut you to the quick by being so cold, so unfeeling. If they have warmth in their Moon it could work better. Indeed a good earthy connection here could save your bacon.

Your Cancer Sun To Their Cancer Sun
More signs than you might imagine get on well with their own kind. Here you could imagine a cosy scenario of all happy families together since you both adore the domestic scene and the larger extended tribe of relatives. All your attention would be focussed on establishing roots and a beautiful home. Certainly you understand each other's emotional sensitivities and weak spots and could provide a cushion for each other. Your interests are wide, both of you are restless, successful personalities. But over the course of time Cancerian ladies get stronger, more matriarchal and

there is a real danger of the slightly sweeter Cancerian men getting sucked into the vortex ending up as just another mini in the brood. Also one problem of both being the same is that you undergo upheavals at the same time which can be wearing. There is never one partner relatively stable to act as an anchor. Full Moons once a month would be a double hazard since both of you will be hyper-manic at the same time. You could end up feeling like a raft on the ocean blown hither and thither by the winds and currents unable to hold yourselves steady. You need more detachment from an airy moon connection to stop you swilling so much in feelings. Or you need an earthy Moon to give you stability on dry land and anchor in reality.

Your Cancer Sun To Their Leo Sun
Signs which lie side by side in the zodiac are never supposed to get on but you could do worse. Both of you have flair, colour, creativity and drive. Certainly you both revel in the better things of life along the luxury line and adore entertaining a wide ranging of interesting and elevated friends. You want security, warmth, comfort and a happy home life. Leos are known as the sign of passion or the burning heart, adore children, and being a fixed sign really want to have roots. Of all the fire signs they suit you best. They can certainly be insensitive to anyone's needs but their own at times but they can be generous in their own way as well. The downside is that both of you want to be top dog at home. Leos certainly need to be the one on the throne domestically. Cancerian ladies get matriarchal more with the passing years so that could become a long term headache. Cancerian men are more likely to fit themselves meekly in with the rest of the brood and lean happily on a stronger mother/ mate. Both of you are jealous but both are faithful and loyal once settled so that is no problem.

Your Cancer Sun To Their Virgo Sun
This mix offers a great deal in the way of contentment, security and affection. You want a sensitive mate who understands your knots and wrinkles and can adapt on your stormy or hyper sensitive Full Moon days. They are the sign of service and very adaptable to the needs of others.

Your Sun to their Sun

You dislike sudden changes or separations at home and they are for ever trying to keep chaos at bay by being ordered and routine so you should coincide over keeping excitement and upsets at bay. You are affectionate and sympathetic and respond well to their warmth and refinement. Both of you have good taste in decor, clothes, friends and the minor luxuries of life. Virgo is not likely to embarrass you socially or indeed outshine you. They work exceptionally hard and will be helpful at home in a highly practical way so if it is a long term commitment you will be able to put together a rather solid, elegant home. Their nagging and worrying may bother you at times. They can be critical which ruffles your feathers unduly since you loathe anything that sounds like a slight. Sometimes they analyse emotions too much rather than feel them which makes you feel edgy. But the pluses undoubtedly outweigh the minuses.

Your Cancer Sun To Their Libra Sun
You share a similar approach to life, are sympathetic to each other's taste in clothes, design, friends and life style. Both of you have initiative, are great at keeping new projects rolling along and want to be out there in the world succeeding. This can be a sympathetic match though you do find their rather airy, detached approach to life can feel unemotional to you. You thrive on feelings, on the intangible atmosphere around and can feel nourished in the silences. They thrive on thoughts, ideas and conversation. But they are the most relationship oriented of the air signs and very definitely like another half through life. So they need security as much as you albeit for different reasons. Neither of you is in to overwhelming physical passion. You like kisses and cuddles from everyone in the extended family so they will not feel rejected if you concentrate on others beside them. They will never understand your over reactions to emotional situations especially around the Full Moon but on the other hand you hardly want two of you swept around in the turmoil of your feelings. They can anchor you and cool the tantrums. It is not an ideal match but with compatible Moons it could just work.

Your Cancer Sun To His Scorpio Sun

This has depth, passion, an ocean of feeling, tremendous sensitivity and a potential for quite extraordinary telepathic communication. You just know what they are feeling without having to ask a question. But it also does have one or two drawbacks. Both of you are so emotionally hypersensitive that tiny slights can blow up into three week long sulks with neither of you willing to give way. Neither of you has much detachment or the ability to analyse a situation logically to bring a sense of perspective into arguments. "I feel this.. You feel that ..." can run into endless stalemates because there is no common sense prevailing or rationale for finding a settlement. You are also both too open to the atmosphere and over impressionable. As a relationship you swing high and you swing low but you rarely feel you can sit still. Like a raft blown around on the high seas you often feel rudderless and out of control. Still you do have an innate understanding of each other's difficulties with a cruel, hard world out there. Though you may want a more generalised family relationship. Scorpio wants an exclusive one-to-one no holds barred passionate clinch lasting to eternity. This can be a problem since Cancerian ladies get matriarchal with the passing years and do not like being controlled. Cancerian men can sometimes soften and not feel up to the constant Scorpio turmoil. But with an earthy Moon amongst you and a hint of air to give you an overview it could be marvellous.

Your Cancer Sun To Their Sagittarian Sun

You want security, warmth, affection, a mate to cuddle and one who will help you set up home. They want adventure, freedom and as little responsibility on the domestic scene as they can get away with. On the face of it there are not too many similarities there. Initial attractions can exist because you are both zippy, colourful, fun loving personalities but Sagittarius has a reputation for excoriating honesty which will leave your tender sensitivities wincing. They say Sagittarians need friends with the skins of rhinoceros hide - you are notoriously fragile when it comes to unintentional slights or brutal criticism. They never mean harm but they do blunder around. They also thrive on fantasy, foreign travel and abstract conversations about philosophy, world politics and the future of the cosmos. You want more immediate connections, warmer feelings and more family ties. They are flexible as a general rule but they will never adapt to jealousy, possessiveness and a sense of being trapped which is how they see your idea of commitment. Cross over Moon in the other's Sun sign will definitely help.

Your Cancer Sun To Their Capricorn Moon
Opposites attract initially though they sometimes the partnership wither s away eventually because you truly do not understand each other's approach to life. But this pairing can and does work not badly at times. Both of you have initiative, flair, creativity and work hard. Both of you admire traditional values, like the luxuries of life, like rising up to the social ladder and will never embarrass one another on the dinner party circuit. But you can find them cold, workaholic, judgemental and decidely unsympathetic. They have an opportunistic streak which cuts across feelings at times which you cannot stand. They can put practicality before love and affection. On the other hand they do provide an anchor for your tumultuous feelings especially around Full Moons when you feel a tidal wave threatening to engulf you. If they are out of their repressive phase and into feeling full bloodied and passionate which does happen you can find them very exciting. Capricorns can go years celibate if they are in their ambitious phase then all of a sudden passion strikes. Both of you can be fairly diffuse for different reasons when it comes to relating which suits both of you. You put the family as first priority, they put work so neither of you feel deeply rejected not being the exclusive object of the other's interest.

Your Cancer Sun To Their Aquarian Sun
Could not be worse. It would need a mountain of support from Moon signs to get and keep this together. You walk in opposite directions down the road of life. You head for home, family, security and clutch firmly onto the past while they head for the great unknown adventure of exciting new possibilities, freedom, few ties and as few commitments as possible. You would feel at times as if you were trying

to form a relationship with a computer which is what an Aquarian really wants to be - all high charged electrical energy, a super brain and no body, or messy feelings. They would regard you as a strangely unstable creature with quite irrational reactions. They like a logical life. Both of you are highly changeable but in different ways. You are always emotional sometimes outgoing, sometimes withdrawn. They switch on and off like a light bulb but like an absentminded boffins - it is all a thinking process. Feelings are rigorously suppressed. They are not too happy in their bodies either so prolonged cuddles make them nervous. They shy away from jealousy and possessiveness. You might as well be mating with an alien. You'd need much support from the rest of the chart for this to be a soul match.

Your Cancer Sun To Their Pisces Sun
What a dream you make together - all love and light, affectionate sympathy and telepathic awareness of the other's needs. They are blissfully emotionally sensitive and highly adaptable. So they will float round you like a cloud of ectoplasm ready to fit in with your wishes, needs, desires and lusts. You want security, a home, family and a luxurious lifestyle. They have taste, elegance, usually a creative flair to match your own, and need an anchor in life. Together you can be too impressionable to emotional atmosphere so Full Moon days can be a horror as both of you float around adrift on an ocean of feeling. But both of you innately understand the other's fear of rejection, humiliation and abandonment so you will not wilfully hurt them. Both of you can be quite vague in the application of your love. You spread it right round the family. They disappear into their inner world of dreams and fantasies or relate to the entire universe. But neither of you wants totally exclusive calls on each other's time and feelings once you are settled together. Pisces can be an orgiastic sign so you may fight for control at times as you feel swallowed up. But that is a small price to pay.

You Are Leo
As fifth sign in the zodiac, a fixed fire sign you are outgoing, obstinate, warm hearted and like to think of yourself as

generous. You love being the centre of attention in any situation. You are a born entertainer or boss. Authority sits well on your shoulders. Though you will settle for the throne leaving the power to others if it means less work. Practical you are not.

But what only those close see is that underneath your confident exterior lies a highly insecure personality. You can crumple remarkably quickly, deflate like a punctured balloon. Criticism hurts, wounds your vanity and makes you bridle. You need an audience around to tell you who you are and you are at times over dependent on other people's praise. Humility is not your strong point and you need to watch a tendency to being pompous, or to sulking when everything does not go your way. Failure sits more unhappily on your shoulders than any other sign in the zodiac. Apart from anything else failure is not nearly dramatic enough. You adore a life full of colour, pageantry and fantasy. They call you the sign of the burning heart though it can be half way through life before you acquire the compassion needed to make relationships work really well. Being self centred can get in the way. You have a very steady sexuality and need to keep it working. You thrive around children, love, laughter, parties, sport and entertainment.

Your Leo Sun To Their Aries Sun
A volatile, fun loving, risk taking, flamboyant pair you make. Life is all romance, glamour, excitement and rather noisy. There is little time or inclination for peace, quiet, calm and soothing balms. The noise comes from clashing egos since you want all the attention and they like to win. That can cause conflict and probably works better as Aries man and Leo lady since culturally women are better designed to step aside. Though the other way round is not a disaster since Aries ladies are all too competent at standing up for what they want. Both of you thrive on fantasies of life being a thrilling adventure movie which you want to be starring in. The problems can begin when reality creeps in since neither of you is practical or good at stepping back to analyse what the real meaning of the situation is. Common sense can be lacking in large measure. Both of you rely heavily on luck to pull you through because you know you are the

special people who get better fortune. That sometimes holds good but when it does not you can be left disgruntled and resentful. Burnout can happen since neither of you slows the other down. Quite the reverse. It could be a great passion which flares, then flicker and dies but with no hard feelings left.

Your Leo Sun To Their Taurus Sun

This is a solid, heavyweight pairing but very stubborn. Neither of you budges an inch in an argument. Both of you stand rooted, firm in the assumption that eventually the other will give way. Taurus is more than a match for your obstinacy. You are not inherently in tune with each other's energy. You are fire, enthusiastic, imaginative, sociable and high flying. They are earth, cautious, slow moving, rooted and sometimes quite narrow in vision. They can give you an anchor and a grounding in reality. They cope with the practicalities of life while you dream the dreams and throw the parties. You give them sparkle and a sense that life has more to offer than chopping logs and drawing water. But they can be scornful of your brighter ideas, pointing out all the flaws which makes your teeth grind and your ego wince in agony. You find them at times a touch tough even with their very earthy approach. Both of you can be warmly affectionate but they are more physical and this can be a hazard eventually. You have a steady sexuality but theirs can seem gross at times because they need everything to be so tangible. You need lighter, adaptable earth or water Moons to leaven the mix.

Your Leo Sun To Their Gemini Sun

A delightful combination since your fire resonates with their air providing a communicative, lively, fun loving and rather reckless relationship. They are adaptable by nature so will not argue everything endlessly like Taurus, Scorpio or Aquarius. They could be a touch honest for you and are certainly no diplomats so your ego or your vanity will no doubt scream in agony at points. But you do egg each other on to great excitements so difficulties pass by quickly. Both of you approach life head on with the idea that it should be lived to the hilt for enjoyment. You are probably more

Your Sun to their Sun
straightforward, certainly more naive than they are. Gemini can be like a barrow load of monkeys at times and not easy to pin down. But they amuse you so they sooth away your irritation in laughter and their constantly changing antics certainly keep boredom at bay. You need to be boss at home which suits them since they rarely stand still long enough to claim territory. But you may find them a little chilly at times since they dislike getting too close to feelings and can be extremely detached. Fidelity is not their strongest point especially amongst the males where you are loyal and steadfast once settled. But across the board is makes a good match for you.

Your Leo Sun To Their Cancer Sun
Cancer ladies can be very strong indeed as they mature and Leo men are equally so which could create a real power struggle since both of you like to dominate at home. Cancer men can be softer, sweeter creatures more inclined to lean so that way round might not be such a problem. But you are not really in tune. You always fear the sign before and you are rather wary of getting sucked into Cancer's emotional web. They really want to make you just another of the extended family whereas you know your place is on the throne - as the only really special person around. They are water and you are fire. But you do have attitudes in common. Both of you want security and a happy home life. For different reasons both of you adore children. You especially because you remain a child at heart. Cancer because they are basically a mother at heart, no matter which gender they are. Both of you are loyal and steadfast once settled. You are the most emotional of all the fire signs and you adore being looked after which Cancer does to perfection. You are more passionate than them and could find them evasive when it came to intimate cuddles. They much prefer having a family group to throw their arms round. This could make you feel rejected and flee for more exclusive companionship.

Your Leo Sun To Their Leo Sun
Both of you fight for all the attention and spotlight. This pairing can sometimes happen but it creates constant

tension, acrimony and bickering. Inevitably one half ends up pushed out of the limelight and becomes resentful. Two Leos cannot easily be spontaneous in the same space. The passions may have flared instantly initially and you seem to share so many interests that for a while it seems like a great idea. But you cannot both be top dog at home. One will ultimately end up the courtier and have to be servile which will not sit happily. Wounded vanities will ultimately erode the initial attraction. Competitiveness about who is doing better at work will also create areas of friction. There will be no soothing hand for moments of failure or inadequacy because they other will be so pleased to get the success spotlight all to themselves. Eventually you would find that envy was the real passion killer. Moons and Venus in Air signs might help.

Your Leo Sun To Their Virgo Sun
An astrological rule of thumb says that you do not get on with the sign before you. Virgo, which is a fairly adaptable sign therefore, should not take kindly to your healthy ego centredness but it is a combination that often works. Virgo bends round circumstances well and is good at serving so you feel your pride of place is not being eroded. They are refined enough to suit your grand ways though not so flamboyant they will detract attention. They cope with all the practical details you find so boring and you give their lives sparkle and excitement. They do nag and criticise which is your biggest complaint since your vanity does not like being ruffled. You much prefer mates who treat you as being perfect while racing around to sort out all the loose ends. Virgos will look after your health being great experts on all matters medical because of their own hypochondriac streak. You can usually persuade them to be more outgoing. They are good at organising parties which suits you but never very good at simply enjoying at them. Courtship can be tricky since they hate relaxing and always want to be working. Even later their workaholic tendencies can get in the way. But this is a 7 out of 10 pairing.

Your Leo Sun To Their Libra Sun
This can be a dream mating, though best with Libra male

and Leo lady. Libras are relationship oriented usually good at thinking of partner's needs and not too stubborn which suits you down to the ground. Not too many ego conflicts here. They are light, sociable, colourful, charming, highly refined, will not embarrass you at parties and will provide you with a suitably well bred escort worthy of your status. Their tact will gloss over your shortcomings. What more could you ask? At times they may seem a little cool or detached but that is what air signs are all about. At times they seem to lack courage just when you want to take a flying risk but that may be a positive help if they slow you down. They are generally a wise sign though indecisive which will irritate you as they agonise their way round situations. Neither of you is practical which could provide a problem where the business aspects of life are concerned though less so than with any other fire air combination. And there is less danger of burnout since Libra will strive to bring an element of balance into your life. Libra ladies can be a little fierce which is why they sometimes rub abrasively against Leo men. Arguments about who is right can be heated.

Your Leo Sun To Their Scorpio Sun
A tough, stubborn, chalk and cheese combination. Both of you will fight for control and Scorpio will probably win being more underhand than you. You also like to live life on the outside, shining in the spotlight at parties or playing games. They thrive on secrecy, manipulation, power games and like to live life in depth which makes you nervous. All those hidden undercurrents and black passions are not your cup of tea at all. Their watery turmoil will threaten to extinguish your fire while your happy-go-lucky, rather arrogant approach to life will drive them to boiling point. Both of you certainly share a passionate approach to life but you come out of your heart and your spirit and aim for the heavens. They are much more sexual and inclined to view relationships as an intense struggle where the agonies are as important as the ecstasies. You would wilt after a while and feel suffocated by all this angst. They are also jealous and possessive more so than you might like. Both of you are fixed signs and therefore assume if you stand firmly rooted long enough the other will adapt round to your way.

It could be a long wait.

Your Leo Sun To Their Sagittarian Sun

What a glorious couple - wild, feckless, carefree, irresponsible, imaginative, mad cap and extremely funny. They are highly adaptable so will not dig their heels in when you are being obstinate. They are fiery like you so you share similar fantasies and a sense of the ridiculous. They do not stand on their dignity as you are inclined to which is a help. There would be no shortage of jokes except when Sagittarius decided to let rip with their famed honesty. They tell it like it is - without pulling their punches. You do not have a rhinoceros hide and much prefer tactful souls who edge their way round the minefield of your ego's vanities. That could be one problem. Also they hate being fenced in and shy away from domestic responsibilities and commitments when they can. You are more fixed, loyal and steadfast. Jealousy on your part could be a problem. Neither of you is practical so burnout could be a problem as you listen to neither common sense nor your bodies as you rush around all the time at top speed. Watery or earthy Moon could help to give you a better balance though your natural energies are certainly in tune.

Your Leo Sun To Their Capricorn Sun

Both of you are top people, share traditional values in life, love social climbing, luxuries and dining in the right places. You are not supposed to be a good match and yet you share such similar approaches to life it is not surprising you click. On the face of it you are more passionate, more heart centred, but scratch a Capricorn and in time you find a depth of sensuality and passion which might surprise you. They work too hard and can appear chilly, standoffish and rather judgemental. They can go for years celibate, then all of a sudden they fall madly, deeply, truly in love in a hugely physical way. Their rather saturnine approach to life which is basically pessimistic, cautious, defensive and self doubting does not always sit well with your sunny, trusting outlook. But you could complement each other. They give you practical support and you lift their glooms. Capricorns are usually geriatric youngsters and become mellower with the passing years. By fifty they have positively developed a sense of humour so they are like good wine, better with age. Both of you like and are good with money.

Your Leo Sun To Their Aquarian Sun
Opposites in this case do not usually attract or complement. You are both hugely stubborn, unwilling to bend, give in or be flexible which is not good news for close relationships. Also you face different ways down the road of life. You want attention, warmth, parties, the grand life and social status. Aquarians would embarrass you with their zany eccentricities. They do not give a hoot what any else or social convention thinks. Indeed they are born rebels at heart where you are a traditionalist. You want to be a monarch. They want to be Che Guevara, a trade union strike leader, or an unreconstructed hippie. You are prickly when it comes to criticism. They are notoriously straight shooters when it comes to the truth. You come out of your heart. They are creatures of their head and shy clear of anything that smells remotely like a feeling. They think brilliantly and you could certainly have stimulating conversations. But would it be enough? They are not good in their bodies and regard too much cuddling with distaste. If you do strike up an affinity you have to watch that you do not live life in overdrive. Neither of you has any sense of pace. Neither of you listens to common sense advice or your bodies which often want to go slower.

Your Leo Sun To Their Pisces Sun
This can work better than it is supposed to since adaptable Pisces will wend its way gently round your need for attention and top billing. They fulfil many of their emotional needs in their daydreams so will not swamp you with too much feeling. Though at times you may get a disquieting sense that they are not relating to you at all which would be a worry since you like an attentive audience. Your fiery courage and faith in life will be good for their timidity. Their subtlety and artistic taste will appeal to your own creative flair. Both of you are great romantics at heart in different ways so the courtship stage will be gloriously seductive. Pisces can submerge their identities and melt into the other

which suits you down to the ground. No messy ego conflicts or power struggles about who is most important. There could be worries with large fish Pisces who can be rather voracious as opposed to small fish Pisces who are vague, amenable creatures on the whole. But they are refined, thoughtful, tasteful and on the whole sweet natured. You are not inherently the same kind of people but you can sink your differences better than most.

You Are Virgo.

As sixth sign in the zodiac, adaptable and earthy, you are practical, restless, bright, observant, and communicative but one of the world's great worriers. You like to be of service to others but often end up feeling martyred and resentful. You can be workaholic and end up dull because of it. What you need to develop is a sense of humour and a connection to the messier side of life. Fastidiousness taken to extreme can turn you into an old maid, whatever your gender or marital status. Underneath your prudish, modest exterior lie hidden, sensual depths if you can get at them. Your observant and analytical mind along with your conscientiousness make you a solid and usually successful citizen but that same trait in a negative sense makes you a nark, a nag and a critic. You can drown in details and be so obsessed with the flaws or minor drawbacks of a person or situation you lose sight of the whole. You are a great perfectionist and often lose relationships because you cannot bear to settle for second best. You need to learn to accept people warts and all without turning yourself into a doormat. Emotions should not be constantly analysed. They can be killed stone dead by your tendency to think not feel. You are deeply interested in all matters medical to the point of hypochondria. Let your warmth show.

Your Virgo Sun To Their Aries Sun

Fiery signs do lift your spirits up and give you courage but Aries? – a touch brash at times or too careless of your tender sensitivities. You are not concerned with your vanities but you do not understand their driving, competitive need to be first all the time. You certainly object to the way they tramp straight across anyone or thing that gets in their way.

Your more refined approach to life requires a gentler mate. Having a bright, agile mind you never quite understand their headlong rush to act often before engaging their brains. They never seem to consider the consequences of their actions whereas you endlessly do. Opposites can often help to give the other what they lack. So you do give them a practical grounding and can sort out a great many domestic and administrative tangles for them. They push you out of your cowardice insisting you get into life in a more wholehearted way. You should be a perfect foil for their "me first" approach to life considering your need to be of service but really you are very different. You also object to their upfront honesty. A critic you may be but you are never keen on the spotlight being put on you. You need a Fire Moon to make this work.

Your Virgo Sun To Their Taurus Sun
Cosy, cuddly, warm and rather sensual, this is undoubtedly one of the better combinations for you. Taurus are wonderfully tactile and refuse to let you disappear up into your head. They are a rock and an anchor for your excessive worrying and nit picking. They stand solid while you race round in ever decreasing circles. Your flexibility is a help because their obstinacy makes them almost unbudgeable at times. But that very dislike of change in them offers you security. You could together be perhaps a shade lacking in fun, fire and spirit. You could work too hard, be too practical together or too unimaginative. The warmer side of earth is life giving but its colder end is workaholic, overly materialistic or lacking in imagination. Taurus can be fairly keen on having control which eventually could unsettle you since you never like fighting for supremacy. They also need very tangible gestures of affection. Their approach to love is more physical than some Virgos. But you do share a common outlook in life because you are both earthy and you share a myriad of similar interests in nature, plants, small animals, medicine.

Your Virgo Sun To Their Gemini Sun
No one else will get a word in edgeways here since you are both the great communicators of the zodiac. A highly

restless pair of real jitterbugs, you will never be at peace together but you will never be bored either. Your practicality will be a help to airy Gemini and their sense of fun and adventure will haul you out of your timidity and natural defensiveness. But you may not always appreciate their rather cavalier way of cutting corners emotionally and professionally. Honesty is not always a strong point with Gemini, nor is fidelity amongst the males. You are not supernaturally jealous but you are straightforward usually and dislike subterfuge and betrayal. You could end up feeling door-matted since Geminis will tend to leave you with the heavy end of the responsibilities. Since you have never been known to say no to work and are a bad delegator this could be a problem. It is a mix which slightly lacks feeling and could cool itself away to withering point with you nagging and them evaporating into thin air. Both of you talk about feelings rather than feel them. After the initial flurry they are not always interested in too much physical intimacy which is a problem since you are earthy and in need of a constant cuddle. They are social butterflies when it suits them which may not suit your more reclusive tendencies.

Your Virgo Sun To Their Cancer Sun
A steady combination this with much resonance, similar interests and a sensitivity to the other's needs. You are practical, earthy, refined, highly strung and hard working while they are emotional, protective, highly domesticated but with a strong drive to succeed as well. It probably works better with Virgo lady to Cancer man since you are more evenly matched though you would probably nag them too much. Cancerian ladies tend to mature into stalwart matriarchs as the years progress and Virgo men, never the most courageous, can feel a little dominated along the way. Both of you will be interested in setting up a happy home life. You are excellent at domestic details and Cancer have a genuine flair for home making that is second to none. Neither of you are brash, upfront personalities so you can protect each other's tender spots well. Both of you are rather jittery though in different ways. You get wound up in a nervy sense over trivia. They get over emotional about

tiny hurts and slights. But you can probably balance each other's anxieties out though they may find you a little chilly with your analytic approach to emotions. What is perhaps lacking is a strong sense of humour between you or an adventurous streak. You need a fiery Moon to lift you up to greater heights.

Your Virgo Sun To Their Leo Sun
Astrological lore has it that you dislike the sign before you or fear it. Leo is just prior to you and their ego centredness is not your way in life but curiously your self effacing need to be of service does mean you can survive them better than most. Secretly you may even envy that barefaced grabbing for attention which you would never allow yourself. They are fire so come intact with a basic trust in life, a lively imagination and not much common sense. Your earthiness offers them practical guidance, a way of handling daily life with all its boring details which they loathe. They will certainly drag you out into life and especially onto the party scene which they adore and you normally try to avoid. There is a basic incompatibility in your outlook in life which will tell at some point though along the way you are both warm hearted and very straightforward. They can offer you security and an anchor for your endless, constant worries. Leos rarely bother to worry about the major things in life never mind the trivia which so obsesses you. They have a steady sexuality and your earthiness responds well to that if you are not too put off by their selfishness. They hate your tendency to criticise.

Your Virgo Sun To Their Virgo Sun
Some signs do and some don't - get on with their clones. You would find yourselves worked and worried to a frazzle if you tried to coexist with another Virgo. You need someone to pull you away from your anxieties not find you a few more you had not already thought of. Your already workaholic tendencies would be emphasised and both of you would be constantly nit picking over the other's flaws. Feelings would freeze before they had a chance to breathe with both of you pouncing to analyse them. You work exceptionally well together, respect each other's conscientious approach,

make good friends but unless your Moons fizz you are not designed for the grander passions of life together. You need more fire, more faith, more adventure. Life would grind to a halt since both of you are nose deep in trivia and the tiny minutiae of everyday living and cannot see to the broad scale. You would need a Sagittarian Moon at least amongst you and that would just add to the generally restless feel. Initially you might feel that your refined earthiness gave you a chance of a good physical relationship but you need to be continually pulled out of yourself into a more wholehearted approach to life. With another Virgo you would end up constantly on the sidelines, spectating on life and commentating on it - but never really living it.

Your Virgo Sun To Their Libra Sun
Sweet, refined, good natured pairing, both of you are determined to suit the needs of the others. Virgo likes to serve and Libra always thinks of the other. You share similarly good tastes in friends, furnishings, clothes and cultural pursuits. They are more sociable so good for your reclusive streak. You are warmer and more practical so good for their rather detached way of handling love, life and relationships. It works less well as Libra lady with Virgo male since she can be coolly straightforward wounding his pride and make him retreat from full blooded involvement which is always the death knell for Virgo men since they end up parchment dry and rather resentful. There can be slight problems but only minor because of Libra's indecisive streak and Virgo's highly strung tendency to worry about everything in sight and a few imaginary things as well. At the end of the day it can be a slightly dry combination unless both halves work hard to keep the passion alive. Libra prefers to stay on the surface and Virgo withdraws onto the sidelines. It could all too easily become non physical.

Your Virgo Sun To Their Scorpio Sun
This depends fairly and squarely on what kind of a Virgo you are. If you are fastidious, hygiene obsessed and rather prudish - forget it! Instantly! You will loathe Scorpio's muck raking tendencies, their compulsion to drag everything down into the depths, their need to live life as a constant

passionate power struggle. But if you are a Virgo who like your mythological counterpart Persephone has descended into the underworld and found your inner depths then it can work well together. But you need to find a fairly worked out Scorpio. The only ones who can cope with a raw, intensely determined Scorpio is another one. Best leave them to it. They understand each other. So with all the ifs and buts it can work with a passionate Virgo and a refined Scorpio who is willing not to indulge in too many underhand tactics to win control. You bring them a light earthy warmth while they bring you a glimpse of the ecstasies beyond everyday life.

Your Virgo Sun To Their Sagittarian Sun
A restless, talkative combination but one that works often very well indeed. You adore their cheerful optimism and envy their courage at taking risks in life and having faith that good luck is always on their side. They will teach you eventually to worry less unless you land with a real gambling Sagittarius which would be a disaster. You anchor them to the ground offering stability, practical common sense which they lack and a basic tact which they also lack. You may not always appreciate their blunt speaking which can prick your sensitivities but they are not malicious and never really mean harm. They just call a spade a spade and have an accident proneness about putting their foot firmly in their mouth, mainly because they rush so much. Together you rarely sit still and are not wonderfully good at relaxing. Both of you are rather over adaptive, finding it difficult to hold your ground. But long running sulks are at least not a problem as long as you manage not to nag too much especially about their impractical side. Though if you do keep on you may find one day they just fly away. They hate being fenced in.

Your Virgo Sun To Their Capricorn Sun
With only one real drawback, this can be the most marvellous combination. There is a natural affinity. Both of you are earthy, practical, hard working, well mannered, fairly traditional in outlook and rather reserved. Neither of you will embarrass the other or make waves when duty

calls. What can be a headache is the workaholic tendencies of both of you which can often pull you away from romance. Both of you feel slightly guilty about indulgences, relaxation and light hearted fun. Both of you can be slightly tunnel visioned about the practical affairs of life. You need to keep the flames of passion alight by giving yourself (or forcing yourself to make) time for love. It works marginally better as Virgo lady to Capricorn man since the energies are more evenly matched though he is even more likely than his counterpart to spend too many hours in the office. Since Virgo is fairly self sufficient this in itself is not an instant disaster. The other way round of Capricorn lady to Virgo man can make for a slightly less warm mating with her in executive control and him rather hen pecked.

Your Virgo Sun To Their Aquarius Sun
On a compatibility range of one to ten this is about five. You are warm, practical, good at helping people, sensitive to criticism, rather prudish socially and not keen on making a spectacle of yourself. They are cool, airy, rather eccentric, hideously honest since they always tell the truth no matter the consequences, and not very interested in close relationships. You can communicate well together since both of you have active, intelligent minds. But you just approach life from such different standpoints. It can appear to work at times because Virgo is fairly self sufficient and does not come across as over emotional, jealous or possessive but ultimately you would find it a little trying. Aquarius want friends, preferably en masse, not lovers in quiet moments. You like your own company and moments of peaceful romance as well. They know all about sex - in their heads - but prefer not too much physical contact. You like a good cuddle. But worst you will never settle to their way of totally disregarding convention and doing absolutely what suits them. You will cringe with embarrassment at what you see as social gaffes. Matching Moons may help.

Your Virgo Sun To Their Pisces Sun
You fit easily into each other's lives with few ripples. Not all opposite signs attract. But both of you are naturally sympathetic, sensitive, adaptable, restless and share

cultural interests. You are the more practical so can help Pisces a great deal in their everyday life. They have vision so can drag your nose out of the minutiae of life to see the broad scale and maybe the inspiration as well. Neither of you is good at holding your ground so sulks are not long lasting though you can as a pair do with more anchoring. You will find it difficult to institute changes together because both of you are natural followers not leaders. Pisces brings you romance since they have wonderful dream like imaginations and you bring them physical warmth but of a light enough character not to make them feel weighed down. You are self sufficient so will not mind them drifting off constantly into their inner worlds. Together with your earth and their water you make a highly creative couple.

You Are Libra

As seventh in the zodiac, a cardinal air sign, you are full of initiative, bright chat and rather wise. Always known as the relationship sign, you are curiously emotionally quite detached. This cool quality fools others into thinking you do not care but really you need another half in life whether at work or at home. You do not feel whole without it. Highly sociable you thrive on parties, friends and social gatherings. You adore living life at a rather superficial level where all relationships and friendly and there are no nasty rough edges. Your tactful, diplomatic approach (sometimes) makes you popular and an asset to most groups. Your drawback is a tendency always to find balance by putting the opposite point of view which makes you sound argumentative. Lady Libras, it would have to be said, are much sharper than their male counterparts. Not all signs vary so much between the genders but you do. The female of the species has a clear masculine mind and no nonsense approach to life while the males have a more feminine, sweet natured outlook and can be real softies. But both sexes can seem to be dithery and indecisive because you like to think your way right round subjects. Sometimes by the time you have made up your mind the opportunity for decision has long passed. But at the end of the day you can be extremely wise. You are afflicted with extravagant spending habits, an expensive and expansive taste in good food, clothes, furnishings and lifestyle. You can be lazy but your career usually gets together after the age of 29 and you cannot stand a lazy mate. Balance is your ideal and something for which you strive but rarely attain. Your mental balance is sometimes more precarious than your sophisticated image would suggest.

Your Libra Sun To Their Aries Sun

You admire their drive, chutzpah, courage, barefaced cheek and loathe their brash straightforwardness which tramps undiplomatically through everyone else's sensitivities. It can work though you need to be extremely clear about what you can cope with and what you cannot. Aries often do not change until well into their fifties. That's when some of them grow up! Some never do. So do not expect your harmonious approach to instantly smooth over their rougher edges. They have romance, fire and excitement in mega-doses so may appeal to you initially just because they can be highly appealing. But they can also be highly irritating and you do not take kindly to social gaffes, embarrassments their tendency not to engage their brains before they leap into speech or action. Be warned. It works better as Libra man to Aries lady though the masculinity is all on the wrong foot. The other way round could be war!

Your Libra Sun To Their Taurus Sun

Sharing a ruler in Venus, you know you share similar tastes in good living, food, drink, beautiful clothes and wonderful homes. You are adaptable where they stand solid and firm so they can provide you with an anchor. They can be hugely stubborn but that is sometimes an advantage in a sticky corner since they do not blow over easily. Always being the one who thinks about the other half in relationships you do not mind a more self centred partner which they can be. As long as you fit in with their pleasures you will do fine. But woe betide you if you try to go against their wishes! Even better than Cancer they are masters at the art of passive resistance. They do not budge. They are earthier than you which can provide problems since they undoubtedly want more cuddles, kisses and tangible signs of affection than most. Whereas you can be cool, detached and fairly up in your head. Communication is not always instinctive since they are not inward looking and write off many intriguing aspects of life as being not practical thus not worth considering.

Your Libra Sun To Their Gemini Sun
Light, bright, chatty you make the most sociable pair in the neighbourhood. Both of you thrive on friends, parties, reading books and swapping interesting facts. You are both air signs so live in your heads, your ideas and your opinions. Not inherently at home in your bodies the more physical side of love may slacken off fairly fast. You could find Gemini a little gauche at times, or social embarrassing because they do not have your innate diplomacy and need to keep the peace. They can also take short cuts which upsets your sense of natural justice. You are on balance more moral than them. It probably works best as Libra male and Gemini lady because he will be sweet natured and she infinitely adaptable. With the stronger Libra lady pitted against a wily Gemini Don Juan it could be a stormy match. One problem with all the air is a tendency to coolness which ultimately freezes feelings. The fires have to be kept alive.

Your Libra Sun To Their Cancer Sun
Air and water do not always mix well but you have more hope than some combinations. You can work in business well together since both of you have initiative, zip and vitality. You both adore large groups of interesting, well bred and cultural friends. Both want a beautiful, settled home. You need a partner in life and they need a family. But you are more detached, airy and rather cool at times. You think rather than feel whereas they approach life totally from an emotional standpoint and can threaten to upset the balance which you so strive to maintain. They live life like a raft on the ocean's surface, rising and falling with their moods - one moment outgoing and the next moment withdrawn. You also can veer from extreme to extreme which makes you a pair on see saws trying to find an anchor in the other. They are jealous. You are not. A six out of ten match. Cross over Air and Water Moons will help.

Your Libra Sun To Their Leo Sun

Air and fire make a heady combination. Think of a helium balloon taking off. That's you as a couple - full of enthusiasms, bright ideas and romantic fantasies. Hugely sociable both of you and revelling in the better side of life. Parties, the bigger the better, friends by the yard and an approach to life which always looks on the light side of life. Relationships are what make your world go round and they are known as the sign of the burning heart. Leos are hugely ego centred which could create problems though you can cope better than most. They want to do what they want and you to do what they want as well! But they will bring you a flamboyant life style and a colourful spontaneity which sometimes your airy coolness lacks. You could be just a tiny touch superficial together since neither of you is grounded. Neither of you wants to look into the watery, emotional depths or into the dark side of life. Nor are you very practical together. But a 7 out of 10 match all the same. The right Moons could make it 10 out of 10.

Your Libra Sun To Their Virgo Sun

Astrological lore has it that the sign before yours, which Virgo is, frightens or repels you. This may be the exception which proves the rule since you rather like Virgo's refined warmth and sensitivity. They go out of their way to be helpful, are generous, usually honest, hard working and share your fairly light approach to life. As an adaptable sign they will leave major decisions to you and generally fit in rather than get too stubborn about their dislikes. They can nark on rather continuously which is a bore. But their way of analysing feelings does not bother your airy detachedness. They are the least heavy of the earth signs and good at bringing you down to face reality in a tactful way. Where you part company is over parties. You adore them and they do not. But if you can persuade them to organise the social events, run round with the canapes and do the dishes, all of which they adore, then you can get on with enjoying yourself chatting, charming and flirting with your guests.

Your Libra Sun To Their Libra Sun
How will you ever decide anything together? Each keeps deferring to the other and asking for their advice. Both of you want to put the other first which is wonderfully altruistic but it could stop life in its tracks altogether if you are not able to say what you want for yourself. Despite your reputation for balance you know in your heart you are the most extreme of creatures forever wobbling from one end of the see saw to the other which is precisely what your other half here does as well. So it could be a fairly unsettled existence together. Being both air you could also be so detached and cool that the feelings would cool altogether eventually. You would be great party goers together since both of you are highly sociable but your lives might tend to run along the surface rather than penetrate to any great depth. You need warmth from earthy Moons or empathy from water Moons to give you a feeding source.

Your Libra Sun To Their Scorpio Sun
You like living life on the surface, keeping everyone peaceful and harmonious and generally speaking steering clear of anything too messy or uncomfortable. Scorpio compulsively plunges into the depths, loathes superficialities, and thrives on relationships where the agonies and the ecstasies are inextricably mixed. How are you ever to agree? You are cool, airy, detached and think feelings through carefully before expressing them. You exude light, cheerful, colourful vibrations. Scorpio broods, is strong, dark, silent and fairly power hungry. They express themselves through their turbulent and intensely felt emotions. You would constantly be pulling each other in the opposite direction. You are indecisive but well balanced and interested in natural justice at the end of the day. Scorpio are hugely determined , keener on gaining control than worrying about the finer points of what is fair. With a Scorpio Moon yourself you might just find a link but even then you are oddly matched.

Your Libra Sun To Their Sagittarius Sun
Light, bright, breezy, fun combination this which will keep you whistling cheerfully. You adore socialising, chatting, being part of a larger society. So does Sagittarius. They have

sharp, intelligent, wide ranging minds once you can get their comedy act shut down. Both of you are interested in matters social, political and philosophical. Being air and fire you are a heady couple always on the go. They fire you with enthusiasm and a slightly more devil-may-care attitude to life. You add a little wisdom to their madcap schemes. What can positively put you off them is their disastrously honest approach. They need truly thick skinned friends because they tell it like it is in triplicate. You being the soul of tact and diplomacy are not always used to the direct truth delivered unvarnished. That apart all is well. You have bags of initiative. They adapt happily to whatever you suggest. Both of you are spendthrift and extravagant but since they are lucky the books should always balance. You are not jealous so will not worry about their need to roam freely. They hate being fenced in.

Your Libra Sun To Their Capricorn Sun
A vital, zippy combination for business with both of you full of drive, bright ideas and initiative. Neither of you is a slouch and you respect each others strong sense of duty. It is a politically correct match socially but can be a little lacking in the deeper passions. Your mother will adore it but you may wish at times for slightly more excitement. Both of you are traditionalists at heart (snobs if one is to be truthful) and adore mixing in the best company. Your social life will be top notch and always busy. But they can be workaholics and difficult to prise away from business meetings which does not suit your need for an ever present partner. Curiously Capricorn can veer from a rather austere almost celibate extreme to one of rather decadent sensuality. They are at heart an earth sign which you could find a little too physical at times though they can also switch off for long periods as they become work obsessed. But it is a good pairing with helpful Moons.

Your Libra Sun To Their Aquarian Sun
Wonderfully light, bright, airy and chatty pairing. Both of you are air signs and adore a good natter about almost everything under the sun. Both of you are interested in society as a whole and its future. But, but, but ..... there

are drawbacks. You are sociable, refined, well bred, squirm with embarrassment over social gaffes, and love a mate in life. They are certainly friendly, adore group functions but are born rebels and anarchists at heart. Give them a status quo and they will upset it. They can be wildly eccentric, do not give a hoot what anyone thinks as long as they are able to express their individuality. On the whole they do not like close relationships and will run a mile at the first sniff of jealousy, possessiveness or too close ties. They need space. If you do settle with them you need to watch that the entire relationship is not conducted at a head level - all thinking, talking and no feeling. Neither of you is well grounded in your body. You need solid earthy Moons to give you a sensible link.

Your Libra Sun To Their Pisces Sun
Signs five removed from each other in the zodiac are not supposed to be complementary but you are both sensitive, cultured, creative, sympathetic souls who care about people, the world and making a better life for yourselves. Pisces are adaptable so they will follow your lead which is wonderful when you are being decisive and not so great when you are dithering. Your airy, detached rather cool approach may not seem custom built for a water sign but they can be rather spaced out into their daydreams so will probably not notice and you will not be swamped with too many troublesome feelings. You have a fairly aesthetic feel for the better aspects of life and luxury which Pisces share though neither of you is wonderfully practical. You will be better at coping with the harsher realities of life than them but they will give you inspiration and vision. They will also romance you wonderfully in the early stages. Pisces are the most seductive (not to say orgiastic) of the signs but not so physical that you would be turned off.

You Are Scorpio
Number eight in the zodiac, you are fixed and watery, a powerhouse of emotional intensity. Deep, dark, determined and challenging, you know exactly where you are going in life though you rarely let anyone else know. Wilfully stubborn at times and deviously secretive, you never take

no for an answer or listen to those who say something is impossible. It is not for nothing that you are known as a miracle maker. Power is what you really want in life. You are content to leave the glory and spotlight to others if you can just hold the whip hand and the reins. More than anything in the world you loathe being controlled by others. You are excellent at handling confidential information and secrets though you rarely reveal yourself. Relationships to you are about being plunged into the heart of your feelings which can be fairly stormy. You need a similarly intense partner who does not mind a gut wrenching partnership. The agonies are to you just as much a part of love as are the ecstasies and it is not everyone who can stand life lived at this level. For all that you are surprisingly sentimental in affairs of the heart and often are quite hurt by people close to you in the family. Your great drawbacks are a tendency to sulk endlessly and even worse to plot revenge when you have been attacked.

Your Scorpio Sun To Their Aries Sun

Never in a million years will you understand what this restless, flyaway firebird is all about. It's like trying to mate an octopus with an eagle. You want passionate clinches that last a lifetime or at least a decade while they are happy to land lightly in one place for a milli-second then flee for pastures new. Your thresholds of enthusiasm are very far apart. They are sprinters over a short distance. Boredom sets in fairly easily and they are never entirely happy in anything too physical. You are a steady marathon runner, secure in the knowledge that lust grows in time into deeper, more blissful states. The body for you is crucial to the love experience and the vehicle which carries you into transcendent places. You are jealous, possessive and driven by your emotional undercurrents. They hate being fenced in and if trapped will disappear into their daydreams to evade you. This can only work if one or other of you is suppressing your essential nature. Or if you have Moons which create such a strong link that you can over ride the Sun. But it will still be an uneasy match.

Your Scorpio Sun To Their Taurus Sun
This is a heavyweight match. Two hugely stubborn signs together but what is in your favour is that you both approach life with certain central objectives the same. You are both jealous, possessive and capable of living with great passion though you slightly more than Taurus who ever yearns for a peaceful existence. You can never be doing with wishy washy, milksop signs who want to live life on the surface. But you have to accept that sulks can be weeks long, that Taurus is never going to budge easily, and that their prime interest in life is generally pleasuring themselves. They can be immensely sweet, cuddly and sensual but they will not shift off base to fit in with your plans, at least not without a hurricane force wind behind them. They can make your life run more sensibly because they are earthy and practical. You force them to look beyond the surface to the greater dimensions of life. It is not an ideal match but it can survive better than some.

Your Scorpio Sun To Their Gemini Sun
Curiously this can work not badly for a while. Your watery depths are not supposed to dovetail with Gemini's restless, airy nature and they can be brightly superficial which is hardly your scene but they do have a very dark side as well which has an attraction. Both of you like to walk on the wild side of life, to explore the miseries as well as the joys, the agonies as well as the ecstasies. That can hold you together for a while. Though at the end of the day Gemini's are grasshoppers and will move on rapidly when their interest fades which does not suit your jealous nature. You have staying power and fidelity. They do not. You are deeply emotional and exist in your feelings where they live in their heads, their ideas and their theories. They can be tantalisingly split or to put it more bluntly two faced at times. So you never quite know who you are relating to which certainly does not suit your passionate nature which likes to possess body, soul and heart. Ultimately they will become scared of being swamped by your feelings and pulled under by the hidden currents.

Your Scorpio Sun To Their Cancer Sun
This can purr along very smoothly in the early stages. Both of you are watery, emotionally sensitive creatures so you understand each other's needs intuitively. There is no danger of either of you becoming scared of the hidden undercurrents or tidal waves of feelings which sweep over you. But you will at times feel like a raft cast adrift on a stormy sea with no anchor unless one or both of you have earthy or airy Moons to calm you down and detach you from all those turbulent feelings. The passions will rage but ultimately it could run into problems. Scorpios are always strong personalities but Cancer men tend not to be which can prove an uneven match. The reverse of a Scorpio man and an increasingly matriarchal Cancerian lady could turn into a battle royal for supremacy at home. Scorpio really wants one intense exclusive relationship. Cancer really wants a family and partners can end up feeling relegated to being just another of the tribe at some point which would never suit you. But it is still better than most matches.

Your Scorpio Sun To Their Leo Sun
Not a match made in heaven or really suited to an existence on earth unless there are overwhelmingly compatible Moon connections. You deep, dark, secretive, power hungry. They light, bright, attention seeking and basically frightened of the emptiness in their depths. They would freak out at having to live life at the level where you feel satisfied. Both of you are hugely stubborn so the sulks would be endless and no one would want to give way first. They for fear of losing face. You for fear of losing power. Certainly both of you are highly sexual but in different ways. You because you want to move into the ecstasies beyond the body. They being fiery are more into the fantasies of a true love, knights on white chargers etc. They may sound as if they would merge and possibly could do for a while but the gritty side would have to be ironed out. Both of you are certainly faithful once settled and home loving though Leos want to be top dog in the family and you never lightly relinquish control. Water and fire are a strange mix. You would be on a roller coaster of emotions from one end of the spectrum to the other.

Your Scorpio Sun To Their Virgo Sun

You have to pick your Virgo carefully for this to work. Select an old maidish (of either sex), dried up, parchmenty, nagging, nit picking, over fastidious Virgo and you would feel desperate within a day. Every feeling you had would be dissected, analysed and freeze dried before you had a chance to sink into it. All your visions of the ecstasies beyond boring reality would be killed stone dead. But there are warm, earthy Virgos who have learned to live life to the full and have plunged into their depths. As long as you are willing to respect their refined sensitivities and fairly cautious approach, they can be a reasonably good match for you. You will not experience the intensity you would with another Scorpio but your Virgo will ground you, smooth out your practical problems and will adore a good cuddle. They will be faithful so not upset your jealous streak and will adapt to you so your obstinacy can reign unhindered. They will serve your needs since that is what they really like. They will also talk endlessly which will not always suit you and have a slightly unhappy habit of usually being right. But that is a small price to pay.

Your Scorpio Sun To Their Libra Sun

In the astrological rule book you are supposed to fear the sign before yours which Libra is. In this case it is not so much paralysing terror as rather contemptuous indifference. You cannot understand why anyone would want to live life at that superficial level. All sociable smiles, sweet pleasantries and an instant balm to smooth away any ruffles in the atmosphere before they turn into arguments. Libras hate discord while you thrive on turbulent feelings. They like light. You head like a homing pigeon for the darkness. To survive together one or other of you would have to be operating well outside the milieu which suits your essential nature. Although known as the relationship sign they are airy so are detached, cool and sophisticated. You would feel very unattached and unconnected to your watery depths. You feel. They think. You want passions and are willing to put up with agony to get them. Libra wants peace, sweetness, harmony and what you consider to be a wishy washy life where everyone agrees. You would feel you had nothing to grapple with, nothing to stretch you to your limits. With a heavy water Moon on the other side you might just make half a go of it.

Your Scorpio Sun To Their Scorpio Sun
Heaven! Another soul mate who understands your strong yearnings, is not scared of your deeper undercurrents and wants to live life to the full, plunged right down into the depths. You are both passionately jealous and possessive so any hint of infidelity will blow up a major tornado. The sulks will be long lasting since neither of you gives in easily. There will inevitably be a ping pong match of who won the last round and who is going to win this one. Both of you will fight for control and supremacy while understanding that the other has to win sometime. Vindictiveness in petty ways could eventually start to undermine the relationship since neither of you can resist the temptation to get back, nor indeed forgive very easily. More Scorpios marry other Scorpios than happens amongst the other signs. Family life will be surprisingly sentimental since both of you are slushy at heart when it comes to kids. Once settled you can stay very loyal since you understand the pain in separation and betrayal. Though if it comes to a break very destructive, vengeful feelings will spill out into the open.

Your Scorpio Sun To Their Sagittarian Sun
You are ruled by Pluto, king of the underworld. They are ruled by Jupiter who was King on Mount Olympus, highest point in the heavens. Nuff said? You thrive on deep, secret passions and want endlessly binding clinches. They fly off at the first whiff of possessiveness, are not emotional except in their fantasies which they are not happy to share, and they never stand still for long. Being a fire sign they are naturally attuned to the body and how are you to experience all those sexual ecstasies which are your life's blood if they cannot stay with you in the physical experience? Their restless feet and wandering eye would keep you in agonies as well. Water Fire mixes are very tempestuous but not in the sense you appreciate. They just represent two opposites trying to mate - an octopus with an eagle, a scorpion with

a firebird. Initially they may present you with reason for hope because they can be excitingly dramatic personalities and keen to take risks. But where you are hidden, they are bluntly honest and open to the point of naivety. You will frighten them off fairly quickly unless you are acting very out of character. It needs a very strong Moon combination to get this better balanced.

Your Scorpio Sun To Their Capricorn Sun
A strong workmanlike combination which has a real chance of working as long as you do not pick a workaholic celibate Capricorn (and they do exist). Though, naturally, you may be the road to their salvation as you reintroduce them to the joys of loving and the pleasures of the flesh. If you can get their minds off money, status and achievements, they are an earth sign and hugely indulgent. You just have to rebalance them. Then your highly sexed, deeply passionate nature can be satisfied. Not in total because they are earthy and therefore not intuitively emotional. They can be warm, though that is true more of the males than the females, but it is an earthy warmth not a deeply felt experience. You might miss the descent to the agonies and the underworld which are so much part of your fulfilment in life. But you do respect their initiative, their devotion to hard work and their ability to provide a good life style. They are also not too stubborn so would not clash that much. They are honest at least emotionally and faithful on the whole so would not cause you too much insecurity. If they had a Scorpio Moon that would definitely help.

Your Scorpio Sun To Their Aquarius Sun
You live life. They think about it. You feel. They theorise. You adore being close, in passionate clinches. They are spacey beyond your comprehension and want friends not lovers. You breathe jealousy and possessiveness. They exude tolerance, preach free love and frankly would prefer to keep relationships as platonic as possible. They know all about sex. Aquarians are the great sexperts. But they know it in their heads from the best books and sophisticated conversations not from the practice of it. You are both stubborn so would find compromises difficult but you are

on different planets when it comes to love. You are Mars Pluto - all fire, emotional depth, lust and longing. They are Saturn Uranus - cool, defensive, out of their bodies and so individualistic that anything which gets more intimate than a passing kiss feels like a violation of their selfhood. You would constantly be grasping at a partner who does not want to be there in spirit. It would need great Moon connections for this even to make a stab at working.

Your Scorpio Sun To Their Pisces Sun
A blissful pair of intuitive watery types, you thrive together. Pisces is highly sensitive so you need to be wary of grasping them too tightly or you could find them reversing off into their daydreams and fantasies. But play them right and this can be a match made in heaven. You are fixed and stubborn where they are flexible and adaptable so the sulks will not last long. Pisces gives in. They prefer to merge into their partners unless, of course, you find the odd large fish Pisces who can be a trifle whale or octopus like in their approach to love, life and lust. But even their voracious, rather orgiastic appetites can suit your depth of passion. At times you may feel like a raft adrift on the ocean, rudderless and at the mercy of the winds and currents since neither of you has an anchor once the emotional temperature heats up. Pisces can sometimes be maddeningly evasive and even feel cool which is strange for a water sign. But that is because they have such a yearning to merge with the cosmos and all of mankind that they sometimes lose their sense of relating on a one-to-one basis. But the pluses undoubtedly outweigh the minuses.

You Are Sagittarius
Ninth sign in the zodiac you are fiery, restless and flexible. Energetic, impractical, cheerful and wildly communicative, you are usually highly popular because of your eternal optimism. You always look for the silver lining in any black cloud and 'never say die' is your motto. But as a rainbow chaser you dislike being made to stand still. Facing up to responsibilities and commitments in relationships makes you feel fenced in. Running off to roam the open plains is your best defence. Avoiding jealous, possessive partners is

your first aim. Finding one who is a strong individual in their own right comes next, then at least you know they will be self sufficient enough not to lean on you. Doing things on the small scale is not your style. You always take the broad view. Some critics might call you over the top. You loathe being forced to pay attention to practical details and minutiae.   Flamboyance is the name of your game. Distinctly over the top at times.   You are always up front with your opinions but not always too sensitive. Friends of Sagittarians, they always say, need rhinoceros hides because of your brutal frankness. Malice is not in your nature but you do lack tact. You are sociable, outgoing, usually good hearted, almost always naive. Interests in life include foreign travel, books, knowledge. You can be a real armchair philosopher when you are not exploring the four corners of the globe.

Your Sagittarian Sun To Their Aries Sun
Not quiet, not peaceful, not practical but what an amazing amount of fun - while it lasts.   Burnout is all too likely since both of you go at life wholeheartedly and in overdrive all the time. Both of you run on fire energy which acts first, thinks later if at all, and finds feelings a little tricky. So you race around taking risks, looking for glamour, romance, excitement and adventure. Life according to your creeds should be out of a thriller. Neither of you is jealous or possessive - quite the reverse - though Aries does not like to be a loser so infidelity is likely to be regarded as an aggressive act. Your marvellously adaptable nature allows you to fit in with your Aries' mate most of the time though you will insist on the freedom to roam as you please when the mood suits. Neither of you are tuned into the body so long lasting physical passion may not be so easy to maintain. Indeed the boredom threshold on both sides is likely to be very low indeed. Honesty sessions could also wear the relationship thin at times since both of you are bluntly honest to a startling degree. But whatever happens you are likely to remember the encounter with glee.

Your Sagittarius Sun To Their Taurus Sun
You need a practical mate who can put your feet on the

ground occasionally but do you need buried under a ton of earth? You like to fly free where Taurus needs to stand still. You loathe restrictions while they hate change with a vengeance. You are the most restless fire sign while Taurus is the most solid of the earth signs. It is a gritty, rather ill matched mix. In early adult life often opposites attract each other to fill in for what they lack in themselves. But as maturity rounds you out so do you discover you really have very little in common. Being out of sync at an essential level means you inevitably grow apart with different interests, different outlooks. Jealousy would be a problem in the relationship since you cannot stand it and Taurus hangs firmly on to what is regards as its own possession. On the up side your sunny adaptable nature can cope with their stubborn stance but for what? Unless Moons are highly compatible you might have a struggle at times.

Your Sagittarian Sun To Their Gemini Sun
You are opposite signs in the zodiac but not so different in temperament. Both of you talk endlessly, wittily, across a wide range of topics. You are gregarious, sociable, interested in what others think. You are restless, rarely sit still. Both of you are flexible, perhaps lacking a little in initiative and staying power but definitely of a temperament to bend round difficult people and circumstances. You do fit together better than many polar opposites. But you are a flyaway pair together with not much common sense between you. You like taking risks and assuming your luck will always hold out. Gemini races around like a demented butterfly at times and thinks that quick wits will get them out of most holes. Both of you need more of an anchor and more connection feelings. It could just work if you had an earth moon connection or maybe even a water Moon. If you have fire or air Moons you will burn out like a spent firework at some point. Too much heat never lasts.

Your Sagittarius Sun To Their Cancer Sun
You are not ideally designed for each other since you need to be given a long rein to roam free. Domesticity is not your bag of tricks at all and anything that smells of jealousy or possessiveness really gives you shudders of horror.

Whereas Cancer is home oriented, devoted to the sink, the stove and the hearth and can be immensely jealous if it feels its security is being threatened. They do not let go easily. You are fire and they are water. Together you will veer from high to low. Fire can boil water up to a heated passion but at some point the water will put out the fire. Basically you distrust feelings and are suspicious of the manipulation and control that tends to go with them. Whereas Cancer will tear their hair out at your searing honesty. They hate criticism in any form and your lack of tact will feel like lack of empathy to them. You tend to approach life with your thoughts or your enthusiasms but rarely with your feelings. You'll need really strong cross over Moons to make this harmonious.

Your Sagittarius Sun To Their Leo Sun
Fire on fire is a very combustible combination. Both of you live life at high speed with little thought for reality, the practicalities of life or the state of your body. You like living high, full of passion, glamour, romance with a burning vision of what you want. All of this can create a warm and wonderful relationship but can it last? Without care it could burn out quickly. Of course, you are deeply attracted to each other. You are on the same wave length. You can adapt to Leos stubbornness relatively easily. They will adapt less well to your scorching honesty since their pride and vanity wound at anything which is not outright flattery. But you do need an earth Moon or even a water one between you to provide some ballast otherwise the relationship will be undermined by lack of real feeling and probably lack of organisation. One partner usually needs to be the practical one and neither of you are.

Sagittarius Sun Virgo Sun
Being both mutable signs you are highly adaptable, restless and energetic. Not necessarily good at starting new projects together - you need a kick start from outside - nor good at staying over the long distance - you could do with more anchoring. Virgo will certainly be more practical than you and sort out the everyday details of life, obsessively so to your irritation at times but they will bring organisation to

the chaos of your existence. They are earthy and warm but fairly refined so will not offend you with too much gross physicality in the relationship. You need to be allowed to roam free and they are amongst the less jealous signs in the zodiac since they like time to themselves. They will not appreciate your straight-from-the-hip comments because they are sensitive to attack. If you are together it is probably because you have an earthy Moon which will be a definite help.

Your Sagittarian Sun To Their Libra Sun

As long as you can keep a grip of your tongue, this is a heaven sent combination. You are fiery, enthusiastic, interested in broad ideas, and sociable. They are diplomatic, wise, communicative and also happy amongst crowds of people (who have to be well bred). Both of you like to slide across the surface and are not too happy being plunged into the depths of feelings or the harsher realities of life. At times this will make the relationship seem shallow or insincere but it is how you like to operate. Neither of you is hugely physical where passion is concerned so that is no worry. You need a tolerant mate who will let you roam free. Libra is not jealous, though they loathe social embarrassment and humiliation so you must watch your step at times. They can seem a little cool at times especially the Libra ladies which may bother your fiery soul but they will provide you with a beautiful harmonious home base from which to take off.

Your Sagittarius Sun To Their Scorpio Sun

You are not ideally well designed for each other. You find them frighteningly dark, manipulative, secret and controlling. They find you a flibberty gibbet who never settles down, who is unrealistically optimistic and will not come down to the level where real life exists. You basically distrust feelings and are suspicious of emotional types. None come more with more hidden undercurrents and storm filled tempests than Scorpio. They can be just as sharp as you with their opinions but there seems to be more than a touch of a sting in them that is entirely missing from your more gullible, naive approach to life. They know that through sex and intense unions they can reach to a really transcendental place beyond. You feel frightened of being pulled that close to any one person and are in any event not that physical. You fire, they water. It can flare into passion early on but it will not last unless you have strong Moon combos.

Your Sagittarian Sun To Their Sagittarian Sun
A wild, way out and not very realistic combination. You could have an amazing time together for a short period and then it would all fizzle out since both of you go like space rockets. You rarely sit still and would lead a life together of dizzying activity but you really need a mate who can ground you a little, put you in touch with your body and your feelings. Together you would endless swap ideas, philosophise and ponder on the future implications for society. But it would all be too up in your heads and in your hopes. Getting the practical loose ends of life tied together would be a major horror since both of you bore easily when it comes to details. Neither of you is particularly good at starting new projects or sticking to long distance plans. You much prefer instant excitement which is all very well but usually one partner needs to have common sense and grounding if the relationship is not to take off like a hot air balloon. A good short term prospect. Only long term if there are steadying compatible Moons.

Your Sagittarian Sun To Their Capricorn Sun
There are pros and cons to this match though in essence the differences between you are so clear that it is difficult to see how you could ever be totally compatible. The plus points are that Capricorn would bring you down to earth and sort out the practical details of your life, not all of which will please you but it would help in the long term. They have initiative, get up and go on the work front where you tend to adapt yourself to whatever is already happening. The downside is that they tend to view you as unreliable, over optimistic, unrealistic and a bit of a gambler - all of which in their book is bad news. And Capricorns do disapprove rather noticeably. They can be highly judgemental. Your brighter, livelier spirits would ultimately be weighed down by their very earthy approach. They do not share your

whacky sense of humour at all. They would not tie you down which would help but they work so hard you might find their absence eventually irksome. If they have a fire Moon it might just work.

Your Sagittarian Sun To Their Aquarius Sun

Gloriously exciting, not very stable or realistic combination this is one which could work because both of you have the same zany sense of humour. Both of you are scorchingly honest and truthful, interested in society and the broad scope of ideas. Neither of you is keen on being crowded or possessed and you both adore freedom. So you fit each other's foibles remarkably well. The only problem is that neither of you is very realistic so you can sometimes take off together like a hot air balloon. Fire fuelling the air into some rather reckless enterprises. But it is always fun and rarely does boredom set in. Physically there will not be great passion that lasts for ever since both of you are rather separated from your bodies. Aquarius lives up in its head and ideas while you live in your fantasies, ideals and hopes. You could find them a touch stubborn but their enduring fixed quality can be a help in giving you some stability.

Your Sagittarius Sun To Their Pisces Sun

A pair of fidgets together, you will never sit still but you are a better fire water mix than virtually any other. Partly because Pisces if they do not get all the emotional nourishment they need will quite happily space out into their daydreams and not make you feel as trapped as the other two water signs, Cancer and Scorpio. Your direct truth telling may, however, upset their delicate sensibilities. Pisces cringe more than most at the harsher realities which you love pointing out. But you do understand their need for fantasy since you have so many of your own visions, ideals and hopes for the future and for the world. There may be a clash since you are essentially courageous and they can be extremely timid. You will give them more sparkle and chutzpah but they may find you boisterous exuberance tiring to be around. You adore their rather passive, self sacrificing approach to life since it allows you to do more or less what you want.

You Are Capricorn

Practical, ambitious, and determined to rise socially and professionally through hard work, you can sometimes be a touch lacking in fun. You started life as an old child, feeling deprived emotionally or financially but you will mellow through your middle years, gaining a sense of humour and end up a thoroughly impish geriatric. You are renowned as having a hard head for business and can at times be a real workaholic who has not time for a romantic or a sex life. But then you fall madly, passionately and not always wisely in love in a highly physical, sensual way. Known as the one who stands on the threshold, between the conscious and the unconscious you can be enormously creative with ideas, either teaching in a broad sense or turning dreams into money in business. Security is the most important thing in life for you. Retirement cottages are in your mind in your mid 20s and you fully intend to have your nest egg stashed away with your fully paid up pension plan. A real traditionalist you can at times put too much stress on outer appearance and are quite class conscious. You can highly sensitive about your social reputation and the approval of the right people.

Your Capricorn Sun To Their Aries Sun

A robust combination but one made for work rather than romance. Both of you are bursting with energy, initiative, drive and the will to win. Aries because they need to be first. You because you want to climb up the social ladder and acquire wealth for security. You can thrive together but it will be gritty and competitive. Ego clashes are almost inevitable. You may not always find Aries' rather self centred approach to your liking. They have no embarrassment when heading for their goals, no worry about what anyone else thinks, social niceties tend to be swept aside. Whereas you are keen to be seen as respectable, wince with humiliation if you are seen to be out of line, and worry about not being quite the thing. Neither of you is especially emotional though you are more physical. Aries at the end of the day can be too out of touch with their body to suit you totally. You will frown on their unrealistic approach to life while they will feel weighed down by your ever practical attitude. You will judge them harshly. If you do get together you'll definitely be successful out in the world even if edgy at home. Though compatible Moons will make all the difference.

Your Capricorn Sun To Their Taurus Sun

An earthy combination this which promises much in the way of physical closeness, a shared interest in work or in gardening and a fairly practical approach to life. You tune into each other's energies though at times you can be perhaps a little too narrow in your vision of what life is all about together. You will have to haul yourself away from work more to make the relationship thrive. And at times you will find Taurus's stubbornness irksome. You are restless, energetic and more inclined to give life a shake and make it go. Where they sit rock steady and assume problems will go away in time. Both of you are sensual, sensuous people and great gourmets. Taurus especially is keen on physical comfort and your home life together will be luxurious. You will want to refine your mate's taste in almost everything since they can be a little basic at times but they will warm you up and stop you turning into a workaholic. A good mix.

Your Capricorn Sun To Their Gemini Sun

Not instantly recognisable as a good pairing this sometimes works very well indeed. Both of you are hard workers, keen on making money and very energetic. Neither of you is hugely emotional. You have a healthier interest in physical closeness but Gemini can have a wild way about them which could suit (though that is the male of the species rather than the female). You will not always appreciate their way of cutting corners. They can be a little devious which upsets your strait laced soul. At times you wince because you need social approval and a good reputation while they are born rebels at heart and could not care less what anyone else thinks. It could end up a rather cool relationship because you have workaholic tendencies and Gemini lives up in its head, in its ideas and thoughts. They tend to detach themselves from feelings before they have time to develop. Not an absolutely ideal match but a good Moon mix will make it zing.

Your Capricorn Sun To Their Cancer Sun
Opposites sometimes attract, sometimes repel. Your base in life is undoubtedly work while theirs is home. But both of you are energetic, hard working signs and Cancer can make their way in the world as well as setting up a happy family foundation for themselves. You are earthy, therefore more practical. They are watery, therefore highly emotional. You will seem cool and critical to them at times. Your practical, always purposive approach to life cuts through their more sentimental, empathetic approach. If it is a Capricorn man with a Cancer woman there can be power struggles as you age as she will become more matriarchal and you may retreat more and more into staying late at work. The other way round will definitely have Capricorn as the dominant partner. Whichever way round it is likely to be a busy partnership with both of you constantly dreaming up new ideas and starting new projects.

Your Capricorn Sun To Their Leo Sun
You are fairly opposite energies but strangely you like the same things. Both of you adore social respectability and the good life. Neither of you was designed to be poor, derelict or unwashed. Life needs to be five star, perhaps more discreet for you and more flamboyant for them but definitely socially upwardly mobile .They will irritate you at times not just because of their demanding egos but because of their basically impractical outlook on life. You will find yourself picking up the bits which they litter behind them. They may find you cooler than they like because you tend to take a stalwartly practical view on everything and they loathe being judged. But for all that you will prosper because you will fill your lives full of interesting, important friends. They will bring sparkle to your rather withdrawn personality and you will anchor them to the ground a little more which they need. A not bad at all match.

Your Capricorn Sun To Their Virgo Sun
If you can both drag yourself away from work and obligations this can be a very good match indeed but you do both have workaholic tendencies which need watching. You are both earthy so share a similarly practical, realistic

approach to life. You both like good food, gardening and a good cuddle. Virgo can be too nit picking at times, too much of a perfectionist and an anxious worrier, so you will get exasperated. But they will respect and tolerate your need to be working longer hours than most people and you will offer them a protection against the world. They are also fairly adaptable and will fit round your needs. Both of you can go through cool, almost celibate periods when deep passion and warmth is pushed to one side but both of you are capable of very physical love if you let yourselves go. It will be a relationship which should mellow nicely with the years.

Your Capricorn Sun To Their Libra Sun Different energies but similar interests can make this a good, if slightly detached, combination. You are both keen on knowing the right people, being approved of, and living a good social life. You both have oodles of initiative and rarely sit still. You very much appreciate Libra's good taste in decor, entertaining, clothes and their tactful way of keeping harmony wherever they go. They respect your hard working abilities and talents, adore your growing respectability and share your traditional values. They can seem a little shallow at times because they basically try to avoid their feelings and stay on the surface of life but you really do not mind that especially. They are airy, up in their heads most of the time. You are more earthy and in tune with your body than they are which could cause difficulties in your sex life. But you are capable of switching off desire if need be for reasons of work or advancement so it may be a hurdle that you can overcome. It will probably work better as Capricorn lady Libra male. The other way round could be a little too businesslike.

Your Capricorn Sun To Their Scorpio Sun
This is theoretically supposed to work well but I wonder? Scorpio is deep, dark, intense, highly passionate, secretive. They need relationships they can sink themselves into, intertwine themselves around. You certainly have an earthy, sensual side but you can also come across as rather cool because you put work first much of the time. They

would feel dismissed and brushed off by you, hurt because you will not sink to their depths. Scorpio adore being down in the murk and although you can be extremely physical you do not appreciate being emotionally exposed to that extent. You are also very straight and rather traditional, whereas their rather devious ways do upset you and make you suspicious. You always have a nasty feeling there is dirty linen that might one day be washed in public. That is a humiliation you would go to any lengths to avoid. Cross over Moons will help.

Your Capricorn Sun To Their Sagittarian Sun
One astrological rule of thumb says you fear or dislike the sign before yours in the zodiac which Sagittarius is. You exist in a world which is practical, straightforward, cautious, at times even pessimistic. They are harum scarum creatures who trust to luck, are quite unrealistic, have their head in the clouds most of the time and tend to say the first thing that comes into their heads, polite or not. They are born optimists and luckier than you which certainly makes you envious. Not a happy combination though over the short term you could have something to offer each other. You would anchor them to the ground while they would give you a little sparkle, prod you into taking more risks and give you more trust in life. But at the end of the day you are such different animals it will throw up the odd problem. You need physical affection. They are not well tuned into their body and need to roam free. You are hardly the jealous and possessive type but with your work schedule and their wandering feet you might meet only infrequently. If they have an Earth Moon and you a Fire Moon it will be a definite plus

Your Capricorn Sun To Their Capricorn Sun
This would be a rather practical work oriented combination which could gradually wither on the branch and die. Certainly both of you can be physical and sensual but both of you have to be prompted into it by livelier companions. Otherwise you fall back into staying at the office longer and longer hours. Both of you are so ambitious for security, achievement at work and social respectability you would

forget to have time for relaxation and sheer indulgence. As an older couple it might work since you warm, mellow and gain a stronger sense of humour through middle age but early on you are certainly both too serious, pessimistic and blinkered to be happy together. You need a mate who can awaken your sense of vision and fantasy, to let you see more is possible than the mere making of money. There are beautiful, worthwhile ideals to which you can aspire. Love is not just bodies meeting. It is also hearts and souls. The Moons will have to match to make this zing.

Your Capricorn Sun To Their Aquarius Sun
Essentially a chalk and cheese mix this has its problem side. You are traditionalist, cautious and rather anxious about social approval. They are individualists, eccentrics, rebels at heart. They hate fitting in and never see any point in worrying about other people's opinion of them. You would cringe with embarrassment at their startlingly direct way of speaking the truth. You are class conscious. They are tolerant of all human foibles and willingly embrace the great brotherhood and sisterhood of mankind whatever their class, creed or background. You are earthy, physical and can be quite sensual. They are airy, very spacey and not tuned into their bodies at all. They know things about sex you never even dreamt of but they rarely practice - it's all in the head. You would find them cool to the point of chilliness, very friendly just not keen on close relationship. Moon input will definitely to needed to bring a real connection.

Your Capricorn Sun To Their Pisces Sun
A sweet match this with you out in the world achieving and being protective, while Pisces wanders round in their daydreams but being always sympathetic to your needs. They are highly adaptable which suits you and will generally follow along behind. They are passive and can lack courage. You are on the other hand assertive, dynamic, full of initiative. Together you make a good business pair because Pisces has the dreams and you put them into action. You anchor them in reality and they pull you away from too narrow and practical an outlook. They give you imaginative flair and ideals to shoot for. You are more physical than

them but they are a highly emotional, seductive and seducible sign which needs companionship. They may exasperate you because of their vagueness and their tendency to disappear into outer space in their fantasies from time to time but this can be a positive advantage when you are away at the office for long hours. They will happily occupy themselves.

You Are Aquarius

You are an independent-minded individualist, with a witty, inventive mind and despite a really stubborn streak are often seen as amazingly tolerant. Because you see no need to be one of the common herd you can be a great pioneer, treading unknown paths and being truly unique. You have a real sense of the great brotherhood/sisterhood of mankind and want to make a better society in which independence and freedom are the keynotes. The truth is highly important to you. Rarely do you cover over unpalatable facts for the sake of politeness. You tell it like it is, tactless or no. Your airy, communicative approach to life at times makes you appear emotionally cool or detached. Close relationships do try your patience since you hate being shut in a claustrophobic atmosphere and you also resent the give and take, necessary compromises, that are part of one-to-one unions. What you need is an independent mate who gives you space. Though ultimately you have to watch that space does not turn into distance and everything just withers away from neglect eventually. Physical contact is not as necessary for you as for some signs. Although you know a great deal about sex (the great sexperts are almost all Aquarians) it is more of a head exercise than a frequent practice. You will keep your own friends after marriage.

Your Aquarian Sun To Their Aries Sun

Zippy, zany, very noisy combination but always a great deal of fun. Boredom is never likely. You will happily let Aries win which suits them and they in turn with their irrepressible bounce will keep you laughing, joking and sparkling. They do not care if you are shockingly direct and honest because they are too. Neither of you is jealous or possessive or indeed very physical. They live in their fantasies while you live in your thoughts and theories. Sometimes your stubbornness will irritate them because of their passion for keeping on the move. Sometimes their very self centred approach to life will irk you because you see the value in having an equal, happy society, which is friendly and democratic. You tend to be more selfless. They may help to focus your ambitions more strongly. You will help detach them from their obsessions and give them perspective on their actions.

Your Aquarian Sun To Their Taurus Sun

Not a wonderful match since you are spacey, friendly rather laid back emotionally and physically. They are close, cuddly, warm, jealous, tactile and quite sensual. Your sex life would cause problems after your early passion had worn off. Their constant need for physical attention and demonstrative affection would make you feel cornered and restricted. You hate claustrophobic relationships and much prefer to be one of a crowd. Both of you are stubborn, neither would give way easily in arguments. Taurus is a past master at passive resistance. It just digs its heels in and does not budge, stands rooted like an oak tree. You are more explosive but are equally good at standing your ground. You would find them too staid, too traditionalist, too concerned with the boring practicalities of life. They would find you too concerned with abstractions, zany ideas, and madcap schemes. They would pour cold water over you and try to control your more wayward tendencies. You need compatible Moons for this to work.

Your Aquarian Sun To Their Gemini Sun

A non stop talk show, where both of you try to outdo each other with wild ideas, crackpot schemes and weird jokes. You both share a rebellious, devil-may-care approach to life which says to hell with convention, respectability and boredom. You are possibly a little too much together since neither of you is going to restrain the other with practical words of advice or caution. Both of you live up in your heads, not in your feelings or your bodies so you might find it difficult to stay together in the long term once the initial hot flush of passion has worn off. You would gradually drift into such an airy relationship with so little connection to emotion that it would wither away and die. Your sex lives could become problematic since you prefer the theory to the practice, and a long rein to experiment as you please. Gemini especially the male of the species is not known for its fidelity so you might end up with a relationship so open that it does not hold together.

Your Aquarian Sun To Their Cancer Sun
Not a good idea at all. Really you are such polar opposites in almost everything. You loathe jealousy, possessiveness, being trapped and are deeply suspicious of highly emotional people. You feel swamped by all those untrustworthy swamps and hidden undercurrents. You need to be allowed to roam free no matter what. Cancer are home based, emotionally deeply sensitive and moody, clutch on to mates like drowning men to straws and can be desperately jealous. In essence you both represent what the other most dislikes and fears. You possibly could be friends since both of you enjoy having crowds of people around. But Cancer are traditionalists at heart and can be snobbish. You are direct, down to earth, and tolerant of all human souls no matter their condition or class. You would probably embarrass Cancer with your truth telling since they are hyper-allergic to anything which smells like criticism.

Your Aquarian Sun To Their Leo Sun
Opposite signs in the zodiac sometimes work together, sometimes do not. In this case your central characteristic of stubbornness is not wonderful together. Neither of you give way easily. You both assume if you stand still long enough the other will adapt to you. Also you are way out, laid back and a real ageing hippie at heart. While Leo can be slightly snobbish and a traditionalist. They are desperate for social approval which you care not one fig about. So you would clash as they felt you were undermining their social status and reputation by behaving the only way you know how .You would not mind giving them centre stage since your ego is not that important to you but you would begin eventually to ask yourself why. What are you getting back in return? You are not custom built as a slave or a courtier which is what Leo really needs. Neither of you is practical

and you would end up taking off like a hot air balloon getting further and further removed from the necessary routines and organisations of everyday living.

Your Aquarius Sun To Their Virgo Sun

Good for friendship but perhaps less good for 24/7 intimacy. You would feel hemmed in by their need to keep life in order. Virgo is precise, obsessively tidy, rather a perfectionist, especially about other people and much more practical than you. But there are plus factors. Like they are fairly self sufficient most of the time and would not make you feel too guilty for being off after your own interests. They are not hugely jealous either though they can be traditionalists at heart and would not appreciate an open marriage. Partly because it seems messy and partly because it could be humiliating and they are highly sensitive to social approval. Neither of you are ego centred so there would not be endless clashes. They are adaptable while you are stubborn so that would work well and they do like to be of service. But it is a cool, rather pinched combination which would not bring out the best in either of you. They need more warmth and you need someone more reckless and less tidy minded.

Your Aquarian Sun To Their Libra Sun

Airy, communicative, thoughtful people that you are, this should make a good combination but there are problems. For one, Libra is acutely sensitive about their social reputation and whether or not they are approved of. They are class conscious, a touch snobbish and for ever trying to keep the peace. You do not give a toss about anyone's opinion, insist on doing your own thing no matter how bizarre or eccentric it seems. You know it is more important to be yourself than to be one of the common herd. You adore heated controversies, debates and general argy bargy which they loathe. Also since both of you are air signs and rather up in your heads you are both detached from your feelings and your bodies so the relationship could eventually wither away and die for lack of nourishment. Your social lives would be great since Libra entertains like a dream but that might not be enough and anyway you would disagree about each others friends. Yours would be hip. Theirs would be oh so classy. Emotional water sign Moons will help.

Your Aquarian Sun To Their Scorpio Sun
Not a great combination this unless one or other of you is not living out your essential energy in which case it will suffer in the long run anyway. You need space, distance, detachment and much prefer friendships to close one-to-one commitments. Scorpio on the other hand adores being plunged into the murky depths of their feelings, is dark, secretive, passionate and needs to be closely intertwined in an exclusive relationship. You would distrust their hidden undercurrents, their rather devious way of proceeding in life and their jealousy would give you the claustrophobic horrors. They would find your friendly but decidedly laid back approach to relationships too cool, too airy. They need a body to clutch onto and a mate with their special kind of emotional courage which does not come naturally to you.

Your Aquarius Sun To Their Sagittarius Sun
A great deal of laughs, not much common sense and non stop activity. When you come together which may not be that often you will have a real firework display. Sagittarius needs a long rein and so do you which is why the relationship may founder in the long term. Too much space can lead to increasing distance and then no contact at all. But while it lasts it is great fun. You are the more stubborn and rooted of the pair while Sagittarius is adaptable as long as they do not feel hemmed in or tied down. They loathe domesticity as do you so practical everyday details of house running may become a bore. Neither of you like chores nor thinking too deeply about money. But on the plus side you are not overly physical or jealous either of you. On the whole it is a combination which can work exceptionally well but you do have to watch each other's tendency to stray too far from the nest.

Your Aquarius Sun To Their Capricorn Sun
One astrological rule of thumb says you dislike or fear the sign immediately before you in the zodiac which Capricorn is. Certainly you are highly different temperaments. You do not like their class conscious, traditionalist approach

since you are an unreconstructed hippie yourself. They also seem to lack a sense of humour, be far too materialistically inclined where you rather look down on money or indeed security as an aim in life. They seem narrow, blinkered, judgemental, pessimistic and far too earthbound. They see you as abstract, eccentric, a minor social embarrassment since you do not care about anyone's approval. If you have to get together or stay together the plus points are that they will anchor you and organise the practical side of your life which certainly needs doing. They can also be highly self sufficient and so work oriented that they are not going to make you feel crowded. You will liven their lives up though they may not want that. You'll need Moons that spoon to make this work well.

Your Aquarian Sun To Their Aquarian Sun

Some signs mate together, some destroy each other. You adore your own kind. Both of you need space, want to be friendly rather than deeply and continuously passionate, are prepared to give each other a long rein. You are both stubborn but that seems not to matter since you are tolerant at the same time and happy to let each other be their own person. You share an offbeat, oddball sense of humour so can be whacky together. You will never embarrass each other socially by dropping clangers and telling the truth too bluntly because both of you respect directness and have little time for social niceties or insincere compliments. What you do need to watch out for, since neither of you is well tuned in either to feelings or bodies, is that you do not become too disconnected. Eventually you could both drift off in opposite directions with your own interests and own friends. You could separate almost without noticing it.

Your Aquarius Sun To Their Pisces Sun

Not an ideal match though there are several things going for it. On the downside - you are airy, detached and really quite suspicious of feelings. You fear hidden undercurrents and all those swampy emotions which could undermine you. So you stay up in your head and your ideas. Pisces is an emotional, sensitive creature, wanting sympathy, empathy and kindness. What makes them easier for you than the other two water signs, Cancer and Scorpio, is that they are often content to disappear into their daydreams and fantasies and not to worry too much if they are not clutching on to a real live relationship twenty four hours a day. Both of you do have dreams for a better future and a better society so that interest could tie you together. They would exasperate you because they are timid, evasive and rather vague. You are none of these things. You would frighten them at times with your directness. Your cool, airy approach would feel very cold at times. But they are hugely adaptable and keen to sacrifice themselves for others so they would bend to your needs.

You Are Pisces
Twelfth and last sign of the zodiac you are watery, adaptable, refined, sensitive, creative, a dreamer, maddeningly vague, rather timid and usually compassionate. You feel for other people's pain and are willing to make large sacrifices to improve matters. Sometimes you feel so much for the suffering of the world that it pulls you down. Although emotional you do find it difficult to commit to long term one-to-one relationships. Your feelings are so diffuse you want to merge with the cosmos not just one individual. Your emotional longings are also quite spiritual in tone, so you really want a god or a goddess to relate to, not some ordinary human being with dandruff and in-growing toenails. There are two kinds of Pisces - little fishes and large fishes. The minnow variety can show a lack of courage makes them evasive and they prefer to take the round about way to avoid confrontations. They can be long-suffering and feel martyred because of the weight other people put on their shoulders. Self pity can hold them back in life. The larger variety can be positive whales - voracious, orgiastic monsters who like to take over other people, swallow them up. Whichever is your type you like to escape from the realities of life into day dreaming and fantasising, sometimes into addictions. What is need is a practical partner to help you make these dreams live for you in reality. Music and the movies also provide escapes for you which nourish your soul.

Your Pisces Sun To Their Aries Sun

Not a match made in heaven since you are sweet, timid and hugely sensitive. Aries are fiery, straightforward to a fault and inclined to fly ahead without thinking of the consequences. You can certainly adapt to their energetic, competitive spirits but do you need to? They can offer you much in the way of sparkle and courage which you can lack. They also tell the truth which you sometimes avoid. But at the end of the day they will be exasperated by your lack of direction, your over cautious approach to life, your vagueness and will not understand your unfulfilled visions. You will wince at their rather startling directness and hear their version of the truth as criticism which you hate. Their lifestyle will be constant activity and noise which reduces you to a nervous wreck. You must have a haven of peace to which you can retire. For a brief fling they might do you good and shake you up a little. Make you more outgoing. But over the long term you would withdraw into home and they would advance in the world so you would drift apart. Moons need to match before this will work.

Your Pisces Sun To Their Taurus Sun

Planets separated by only one other in the zodiac are supposed to get on well together, so you are amiably well disposed toward each other. You do share an interest in certain rather aesthetic aspects of life. Taurus adores the comforts of life - eats, drinks and dresses well and adores a good cuddle. Your interests are rather more ethereal but do like to create a dream world of comfort around you. Sometimes you can be quite addictive and are attracted to Taurean's generous lifestyle though you do not share their need for constant physical reassurance. That is probably the greatest drawback because for you love can be something spiritual, almost platonic. Where for Taurus it must be passionate, very tactile and you can sometimes find that rather gross. It is not that some Pisces do not have an orgiastic streak but it is fairly switch on switch off. If you do find a fairly refined Taurus with artistic tastes you will do very nicely and they will help ground you, attending to all the practical details of your everyday life. You will adapt round their stubbornness.

Your Pisces Sun To Their Gemini Sun

A restless pair together, you do get on reasonably well since both of you are adaptable, fairly flighty and hate boredom. They may seem a little cool to you at times being an air sign and prone to analysing feelings rather than experiencing them. But you sometimes like to be left to conduct a rather internal emotional life in your daydreams so they will not harass you too much. You will have to be self sufficient to cope with a Gemini since they are constantly on the move and (especially the male of the species) not renowned for their fidelity. Over the long term you might find your interests drifted apart since you are water and air which are very different animals. You represent for Gemini that emotional connection they feel they will never find in their lives. They yearn for another half but you must get them to open up first and not flit endlessly like butterflies or grasshoppers through life avoiding their emotional needs.

Your Pisces Sun To Their Cancer Sun

Both highly emotional creatures you get on a treat together. You understand each other's sensitivities so are less likely to crash into criticisms, or hurtful remarks. You are both highly self protective which can make it difficult for you to open up to each other initially but once you have made the breakthrough then you can create a cocoon for yourselves which shuts the world out. Cancer will take more initiative than you and, though a water sign, are energetically competitive in the outside world. They will make the home you always dreamed of come true. Moodiness and sulks can be a problem since both of you retreat into your shells suddenly and with little exterior reason. You are both highly impressionable to the atmosphere around you so you will feel at times as if you were being tossed around by the high seas without any controls. You must always watch the company you keep. Difficult, anxious, nervy friends will pull you both down. Air or Earth Moons will help.

Your Pisces Sun To Their Leo Sun

Very different animals, water and fire, you can sometimes make a match because you share a similarly creative outlook on life. Both of you like living well, like entertainment, music, movies, art. In different ways both of you are highly romantic. You are adaptable so can fit round the needs of Leo's rather overblown ego. They need to be centre of attention all the time, want an audience and constant admiration whereas one of your essential drives in life is to be self sacrificing. You do end up feel martyred and self pitying but you do genuinely like putting yourself out for others. So you have complementary needs. They are fixed, rather stubborn so can provide an anchor for your rather aimless, at times over timid progress through life. They are also fiery so have a trust that you lack that life will always be there for them. It sometimes comes across as arrogance but it is good for you to see someone who will push themselves forward. You need more of that energy. Not a superb match without harmonious Moons but workable.

Your Pisces Sun To Their Virgo Sun
This is a reasonably common match and can work well. Some opposites attract, some repel. You just seem to fit together. Virgo are the most refined of the earth signs so can give you a practical help in life without making you feel suffocated or weighed down weighed down. Both of you are sensitive so will not unnecessarily crash through the other's protective barriers. Virgo can be fairly self sufficient and since you like disappearing into your daydreams that can suit both of you. They do nark and nag on a bit which is a bore and your vagueness will exasperate them. But that really is because they fear sliding into the chaos in which you exist most of the time. Their response is to become obsessively neat and tidy. This combination has pluses and minuses. They will sort your life out but they can also run against your grain. If you can persuade Virgo not to be such a perfectionist they are warm and tactile. You can be exceptionally romantic and seductive so there could be quite a wonderful connection.

Your Pisces Sun To Their Libra Sun
An elegant, tasteful mix this, one which has a great deal going for it. You both love art, beautiful people, pleasant social occasions and nothing too abrasive. You are sensitive to an extreme degree about the harsher sides of reality and

Libra absolutely must have harmony and balance. They can seem a little cool being an air sign which will not always suit your sympathetic, emotional nature. But you can withdraw happily into your daydreams to compensate. You are highly adaptable where they have buckets of initiative so you will follow their lead happily. Both of you tend to be self sacrificing in relationships, wanting the other to be happy which can make for a caring long term commitment. It possibly works best as Libra man Pisces woman. The male of the species in Libra is softer, sweeter, almost feminine in outlook where the Libran ladies are quite sharp, cool, almost masculine in their thinking. It is not absolutely ideal since you are very different energies but it can work well with the right Moons.

Your Pisces Sun To Their Scorpio Sun
Two water signs together make an excellent match but you have to be a tougher minded Pisces than the norm to cope with Scorpio's intensity. Really they like to mate with their own kind who are happy to live in the depths of their feelings, with that kind of tortured anguish which also promises ecstasy. But it is not a pleasant trip for a vague, timid Pisces. You could feel yourself overwhelmed. Your sense of identity is not strong at the best of times. You are self sacrificing by nature but Scorpio will needle you until you stand up to them. They do like power but they also like a robust, substantial relationship. However, you are both emotionally, sensitive signs able to suss out each other's mood and you are certainly not given to treading on corns. You basically like peace and harmony. Scorpio's stinging responses can sometimes hurt you though your tendency to martyr yourself perhaps helps you hide it. This can be an invigorating match if you are up to it.

Your Pisces Sun To Their Sagittarius Sun
Totally different energies, you being water and they being fire, this is not an instant first choice. Water and fire together can sizzle and boil but it usually ends up a damp mess with Sagittarius flying off to sunnier climes. On the plus side what it does have going for it is your shared ability to bend in the breeze. When the going gets rough you do not

instantly dig your heels in but bend round the difficulties. You are both on the lighter end of the sun signs so will not instantly cause each other problems. But Sagittarius is notoriously outspoken and you can be extremely thin skinned. They mean no malicious harm but they are blunt. They are also allergic to the first whiff of jealousy or possessiveness. This may not matter as much with you as with most water signs because you can disappear into your daydreams and do not always like hugely committed relationships yourself. Both of you could do with cross over Moons to make this work.

Your Pisces Sun To Their Capricorn Sun

Signs separated by only one other in the zodiac do match well. You provide the inspiration here, the emotional sensitivity, the flexibility and the need to be helpful. Capricorn will provide the energy, the drive, determination and practical common sense, you sometimes lack. They will ground you and give you a lead to follow which suits you down to the ground. At times they may feel too work oriented, rather chilly, rather remote and weigh you down with judgemental comments about your vagueness. However you do need a mate who can help you turn your dreams into reality and you can offer them a safe haven from the rigours of the world. They are softer than they appear inside if you can actually get them to open up. Though they are noisy at home which may upset your need for peace, quiet and bliss. You do have shared interests in creativity and the arts which can help to cement a bond.

Your Pisces Sun To Their Aquarius Sun

Not an instant fit, since you are gentle water sign and they are a cool air sign, stubborn, idiosyncratic, argumentative and not at all keen on too much emotion or intimacy. They need to be allowed to go their own road in life. It may work just well enough if you are a very absorbed Pisces lost in your own inner world and not one to worry about absent partners who have completely different interests. In your own way you also sometimes shy away from claustrophobic one to one relationships. You will not appreciate their blunt truth telling or way of analysing emotions before they have experienced them. You will not persuade them to get lost in your romantic glow. You are seducible and seductive. They just like to talk about the theory of sex. If you have the Moon sign in the others sun sign it will work better.

Your Pisces Sun To Their Pisces Sun
You should be divinely happy with another of your own kind, sweet, sensitive, refined, always aware of the other's need for peace and protection. Yet you are both over restless, over adaptable, sometimes aimless creatures, who would drift around, as if blown by the winds and the currents. You really are too impressionable a sign to survive well in the world without an anchor, a practical mate who can give you help with the everyday details of life, who can give you more sparkle and courage. You would be like two orphan waifs in the storm. You are both moody, hyper reactive to atmosphere and can be self pitying. Two martyrs together are not good news. You need someone to jolt you out of your oyster shell into the world a bit. Certainly you would have the joy of someone who shared your obsession for music, the movies and art. But it would need earthy Moons to keep it on track.

Chapter Four

DO YOUR MOONS SPOON?

The Sun is the core of your identity but the sign your Moon was in at the exact moment you were born tells you about what emotionally nourishes you, what makes you feel comfortable and comforted, how you relate to your body, how you see your past, your childhood and your family. It is, if you like, the feminine half of the personality.

Even if Sun signs are compatible, if the Moon signs are out of sync you will have problems setting up a stable home together, will have wildly differing approaches to sex, children, eating, relaxing, cleanliness and home decor. You will also not have your moods in tune. You want sex when they want to cut the grass. You want to work when they want to be quiet together. The Moon changes sign every two and a quarter days and it's fickle nature is the reason why some Aries for example lean this way rather than that. The core identity is still the same for all Aries but the Moon sign shows up one facet of the personality more than others, and sometimes suppresses a vital element of it if the Sun and Moon signs are in real conflict.

Your Moon Is In Aries

A fire moon, you are excitable, impulsive, explosive, rarely stand still, loathe tranquillity, are constantly seeking challenges. You are also strongly independent, take criticism badly and can tend to dominate others emotionally. Underneath you can be quite insecure. Your moods never last long but others find your constantly changing reactions rather unreliable. What comforts you is ACTION, adventure, a bit of zizz and sparkle.

Your Aries Moon To Their Aries Moon

Earplugs are a must for neighbours as your eruptions can be spectacular if short-lived. You will have problems keeping track of each other since both of you leap around like grasshoppers on hot tarmac. Certainly you like the same things but that constant need for adventure and excitement is likely to pull you apart faster than it keeps you together. You both have a way of insisting on your own way and will tolerate no interference. Not much room for give and take. It could have a noisy ending.

Your Aries Moon To Their Taurus Moon
What nourishes you is the thrills, the spills, the drama of a high adventure, constantly changing life. That is their absolute horror. They are nourished by the unchangingness of a secure home base, the kind of regular physical contact you would find stifling, and worst of all they are deeply possessive. Certainly they will keep your feet anchored to the floor, will organise financial stability and give you constant affection and comfort you never dreamt of. But you will dislike their laziness, resistance to change and find their sensuality a little much to take. They can be achingly slow as far as you are concerned.

Your Aries Moon To Their Gemini Moon
Your comfort demands paradoxically that you keep on the move. So, even more so, does theirs. But are you ever going to meet as you both jitterbug about. These are the two Moons who most frequently change their minds. What you want ten minutes ago is not what you want now. How are agreements ever to hold together? You are the pushier of the pair, demanding your own way, irritably if necessary. They will adapt but one day they will also fly away. Neither of you are well tuned into the body so meals will be erratic. Sex will be fabulous and fiery initially but boredom will creep in rapidly.

Your Aries Moon To Their Cancer Moon
Not great news this really. You want space to fly around madly, chopping and changing your mind at whim, not really having tedious obligations or commitments. They want a cosy home and family set up with everyone tied in together. They feel the pain of separation more than most. Their emotional storms and insecurities will irritate you. Certainly they will provide you with a wonderful domestic set up, well decorated, good cooking, all the comforts. But it does come at a price. They brood, they smother, and have extreme sensitivity to criticism which your rather abrasive

approach would not improve.

Your Aries Moon To Their Leo Moon
Instant passion but will it last? Two fiery Moons together always make for higher noise levels but with one proviso this could work well. You want to generate a constant feeling of being alive at home, which means never sitting still. They are more fixed and stubborn but they adore the flamboyant life style and together you will set up a wonderful pad, throw great parties and rave it up all over town in the best places. The main problem is that you go your way, say your thing very bluntly . They have a fragile, if overblown vanity which dents very easily. You hate their sulks.

Your Aries Moon To Their Virgo Moon
Both of you are quite insecure but show it in entirely different ways. You zap around like a thing possessed. They sit and worry endlessly about trivia. You would never understand or sympathise with their phobias, fears and anxieties. They will certainly adapt to your need for no interference, would organise you a well run home with good food and keep the medicine cabinet stocked. But is it enough? Sex would become a problem as they can be prudish and you have short lived enthusiasms. Their nagging about tidiness will drive you to distraction at times.

Your Aries Moon To Their Libra Moon
They are thoughtful, sweet, generally considerate and will organise you a beautiful home with a collection of really classy friends. But it may all prove a touch pretentious or precious after a while. You have tastes for high excitement and will speak your mind no matter what, which will ruffle their feathers enormously. You could not care less about social niceties. They blush at the tiniest gaffe. You are fiery, they are cool. Sex would be a problem since you would lose interest and they basically dislike anything too sweaty or passionate.

Your Aries Moon To Their Scorpio Moon
You fly free, they cling on with the tenacity of an octopus. You want change, excitement and new thrills all the time.

You will not tolerate interference, they are possessive and manipulative. They are fixed, stubborn, more security conscious than you and certainly a great deal more jealous. Though they hide their hurts and feelings very well, until that is their need for revenge gets out to play. Initially the earth will move since your fiery passions can be hot and they certain are sensual but will it last?

Your Aries Moon To Their Sagittarius Moon
A spectacular firework display with all the bells and whistles going at the same time. That is the initial coming together. The downside is that neither of you stand still. Certainly neither of you is jealous which helps enormously. But you tend to hop around like a grasshopper and they take off across the open planes at the slightest provocation so you could drift apart rapidly. You need a joint scheme or joint hopes for the future strong enough to bond you together at the points where your notoriously short lived enthusiasm sags.

Your Aries Moon To Their Capricorn Moon
You have hot blood rushing through your veins and need a sense of aliveness. They are rather gloomy, self doubting, low self esteem types who need to work like maniacs to prove they are worthy of the love which they rarely find time for in their busy schedules. Their reserve would bother you. Your brashness would offend their social sensibilities. It could end up a cool, detached relationship indeed where business was the priority. Your moods would never coincide. You want sex. They want to read the accounts. They want a cuddle. You want to dash out.

Your Aries Moon To Their Aquarius Moon
An exciting, communicative, never dull match but it is difficult to make a real exclusive match with an Aquarius Moon because they fear one-to-one commitment. To some extent so do you fear loss of personal freedom so it could work though you would eventually have less and less time together. They love to startle and shock which bothers some but would enchant you. Sex could be a problem since they are spaced out from their bodies and you are not well

attached to yours. Eating would be erratic.

Your Aries Moon To Their Pisces Moon
They are supersensitive to emotional atmosphere and nuances and even at your most vain you would never describe yourself as that. You would endlessly be treading on corns you could not see and have watch them withdraw into their oyster shells to protect themselves. Their timidity would exasperate you. They always feel like martyrs and their self pity would pall. At a pinch they could making you gentler and you make them more courageous. But it is hardly made in heaven.

Your Moon Is In Taurus
An earth Moon and the most sensual, you are nourished by your senses. Whatever feels, smells, looks and tastes good makes you purr like a pussycat. You are affectionate, demonstrative very tactile and highly sensual. Love has to be expressed in tangible ways or you do not think it exists. Stability and security are more important to you than almost anything. Sudden change, especially at home, is difficult. Jealousy, possessiveness and obstinacy can create emotional problems.

Your Taurus Moon To Their Aries Moon
Your first reaction in an emotional crisis is to feed yourself and sit still. Theirs is to leap off into activity. You are placid, affectionate and possessive. They are highly insecure, outspoken and very independent. You certainly will offer them a comfortable, not to say luxurious base in life but you are highly different animals. They would find your passive resistance to anything which does not fit in with your needs impossibly irritating. Arguments over their wandering feet would run and run.

Your Taurus Moon To Their Taurus Moon
You would provide each other with every comfort under the sun. You share the same tastes in good food, luxuriously easy homes, wonderfully sensuous clothes and endless cuddles. You could certainly grow fat together! Both of you are practical but together you could do with a spark more

vision or imagination otherwise your world would become very narrow, even slightly gross. Obstinacy certainly would create a problem as neither of you would give way. Both of you are jealous but usually faithful.

Your Taurus Moon To Their Gemini Moon
A bull and a grasshopper may well have something to offer each other but as a settled relationship it leaves a lot to be desired. Your rooted-ness would drive their flyaway nature to distraction. You would feel unsettled because they never sit still for long. Although placid, you are possessive and they hate being fenced. You are into the body, are affectionate, cuddly, constant and sensual. They are into their heads and rather switch on switch off in their sexual needs.

Your Taurus Moon To Their Cancer Moon
This could run and run. Both of you are into comfort, security, luxurious homes, good food, and not too many upheavals. You might fight eventually over the children since Moon Cancer likes to smother and dominate, while you are possessive in your own way. But you are an excellent match. You can provide an anchor for their moodiness and hyper sensitivity but in a warm affectionate way. Your solidly physical approach to sex might in the long term prove problematic since they want an all family relationship not necessarily just an exclusively one-to-one commitment.

Your Taurus Moon To Their Leo Moon
The bull and the lion together make a mighty awesome pair. Obstinacy will be the greatest problem here since neither of you give way easily at home. But on the other hand both of you are loyal, faithful and good at staying put which is a major plus factor. You are practical, good at food, furnishings, garden, clothes. They are wonderful with children, parties, sport and fun. You will keep the domestic machine running smoothly. They will add sparkle. Their vanity and extravagance may irk you but both of you have a steady sex drive.

Your Taurus Moon To Their Virgo Moon
You will enjoy many happy hours together in the kitchen,

the garden, having a quiet cuddle or planning new decorations. Both of you are earthy and tuned into physical comforts. Moon Virgo's endless worries and anxieties will drive you slightly daft but you are patient and their tidiness if not carried to extreme counter-balances your laziness. Sex could be a minor problem since they have to be coaxed out of a prudishness that is sometimes (but not always) superficial.

Your Taurus Moon To Their Libra Moon

Aesthetic, cultural, elegant and luxurious, your home life will appear to be a dream of comfort and good taste. You need a solid, happy family base and Libra has a magic touch. They are slightly over sensitive to the approval of others and may find some of your basic ways a minor social embarrassment. Sex could be a barrier since you are in need of constant physical reassurance. They are an airy Moon, not well in tune with the body, and slightly fastidious. What nourishes you sexually will not fit their needs. But they are loyal.

Your Taurus Moon To Their Scorpio Moon

A seethingly, passionate, jealous combination this which will either provide endless arguments and real agony or it could with subtle handling provide real ecstasy as well. Neither of you like a home life in constant upheaval and both can be faithful. Both of you are fairly preoccupied with sex. You admittedly from a more physical viewpoint. They because they want to journey to nirvana through sex. You will not understand all their motivations but the trip will bring you pleasure. But it is a match which has the seeds of its own destruction buried deep inside. Neither of you are forgivers.

Your Taurus Moon To Their Sagittarian Moon

A difficult combination to make work unless the Suns are in the others Moon sign. You are nourished by clinging on firmly to a comfortable luxurious home with a highly cuddly relationship inside. They fly free at the first whiff of jealousy and hate being anchored. They are nourished by books, by conversations and by travel. Certainly they would adapt to you in some respects. You could also offer them much in the way of practical help in their domestic life. But sex would eventually throw up odd problems because you need such different things.

Your Taurus Moon To Their Capricorn Moon

Two earth Moons together normally suggest great physical comfort, a solid home, well run, good food and a luxuriant garden. An idyllic domestic base. But you might find your Capricorn Moon is rarely there. They sadly lack self esteem and feel that only by achieving in the big outside world will they be accepted. So the love they chase gets further away. They can seem cool, distant and over serious to you who basically want demonstrative affection, lots of cuddles, and a regular sex life. They can be indulgent sexually but they can also be celibate for periods. They would also want you to social climb which you would hate.

Your Taurus Moon To Their Aquarius Moon

You live on earth. They live in outer space. You are tuned into the body, domestic comforts, physical sex and a great many cuddles. They are nourished by erudite conversations, constant travel, not too much close contact and certainly no heavy one-to-one commitments. Their insistence on going their own way and filling your house with group meetings and friends would drive you spare eventually. Your jealousy would nag constantly. Both of you are also highly obstinate and would insist your way was the one to be followed.

Your Taurus Moon To Their Pisces Moon

A sweet, protective combination this with you providing a shell inside which they can feel more confident. You are good at the practical, physical life - making a solid, comfortable home, giving cuddles and demonstrating your affection openly. They appear wispy, frightened creatures but they do have an amazing emotional sensitivity if they feel safe enough to open up. Both of you need peace and bliss though for different reasons but it gets you to the same place. They are highly adaptable which helps because you like to dig your heels in.

Your Moon Is In Gemini

An air Moon you think first and try not to feel too deeply. A real butterfly, you hate sitting still. Your emotional reactions change constantly which upsets others who sometimes find you cool, too detached or fickle. Boredom is your great bugbear in life and being stuck in a rut is almost unbearable. Your enthusiasms are strong but are rarely long lived. You hate being pinned down and stability is never an attractive idea. Nourishment comes from reading, talking and knowing a lot. You are not well tuned into your body or your physical needs or at least do not stand still enough to comfort yourself on a constant basis.

Your Gemini Moon To Their Aries Moon

You talk endlessly, are quick witted, resourceful and have been known chop and change your mind and your feelings with great frequency. So you will have no problem keeping up with their antics, firework displays and excitements. You are adaptable where they leap in to take the initiative. You will not take offence at their brashness. But the match could lack depth of feeling or body connection. Both of you have dangerously low boredom thresholds.

Your Gemini Moon To Their Taurus Moon

On the upside they will give your endless fidgetiness some stability. They are placid, affectionate, good at organising the practical comforts of existence. You are adaptable and will bend happily round their obstinacy. But their jealousy and possessiveness will frighten you. Their constant need for sex and tangible affection will feel at times physical to you, certainly wearing. Their need for an unchanging lifestyle will give you nightmares. Ruts and routines make you feel ill. You are not wonderfully in tune unless Sun signs help.

Your Gemini Moon To Their Gemini Moon

You certainly have the same emotional reactions, will have no shortage of topics of conversation and will live in a library of a house, full of telephones! But will you ever get together? You are both so changeable, so fast moving you may just drift apart. You need a mate who will bring you into your feelings and body not join you up in your head. The relationship could be superficial. Both of you analyze feelings rather than experience them. You need more warmth, more anchoring. Anchoring Suns will help.

Your Gemini Moon To Their Cancer Moon
You with an adaptable air Moon want chat, ideas, and a great deal of variety. They having a watery emotional Moon want a settled home and family base, close ties, and life much as it has always been. You might feel stifled, bored even by the sameness which feeds them. Their jealousy would be sparked by your wandering eye and feet. Certainly they would provide you with a wonderful home, beautiful meals, all the comforts. But you would not understand their moodiness and hyper sensitivity. They would find your cool, analytic approach rather unsettling.

Your Gemini Moon To Their Leo Moon
You like variety. They like flamboyance. You want stimulating chat at home. As long as they get to be centre of attention they will converse with great style. They will provide an anchor for your wandering moods since they are more fixed. Your adaptability will come in handy with their tendency to be fixed. They adore the five star life style which is not necessarily your wish but you like the excitement that goes with it. Their extravagances may begin to pall and you will not suffer their need for constant reassurance well.

Your Gemini Moon To Their Virgo Moon
A lovely combination with just a few drawbacks. On the up side you are both adaptable so long drawn out arguments are less likely. They are practical and tidy so will organise the domestic set up to perfection, leaving you free to read and chat on the phone. They are reasonably self sufficient so will not fuss as you wander off after your own interests. What could be a problem is their constant worrying about everything under the sun for which you would have little sympathy. Their obsessive need to keep order might wear thin as well. But mainly the tendency you both have to analyze feelings before letting them develop could kill the relationship before it takes root.

Your Gemini Moon To Their Libra Moon

Airy Moons together certainly mean there will be no shortage of stimulating chat or books lying around the house. Both of you are nourished by ideas, thoughts, theories and looking at the meaning of life. But you do lack connection to your deeper feelings. You constantly analyze them before they can develop. Libra likes everything to be so harmonious that no difficult feelings are ever aired. You might find it a little dull eventually and you will not be understanding of their excessive sensitivity to other people's opinion of them.

Your Gemini Moon To Their Scorpio Moon

This should not work at all because you think and they feel. You fly around and they hold on tight. But despite your rather flibberty gibbet moods you do have a leaning for the wild side of life, at least for short periods. You hate being fenced in and loathe jealousy which are all Moon Scorpio traits but you have an attraction/revulsion for all those turbulent depths, that steamy passion, that preoccupation with sex. So for a time you will stay and love passionately. Then you will take fright and run. They will never forgive you.

Your Gemini Moon To Their Sagittarius Moon

Life will never be dull, never be the same two hours running, and eventually may never be together. Both of you are driven by a need not to be chained down emotionally and you will both fly off at the first whiff of possessiveness. Conversation will never be lacking since both of you have wide ranging interests and are nourished by books, travel and wild theories. But as a match it lacks an anchor, lack feeling depth and lacks commitment. Sex could be fiery then cool off. Neither of you has a high boredom threshold. Long reins can lead to increasing distance and eventually to no connection at all.

Your Gemini Moon To Their Capricorn Moon

This could be a little intellectual or too businesslike to make a real love match. You hardly sit still long enough to feel deeply while they work like maniacs to prove their worthiness to be loved. Both of you in different ways can be too cool. You need warmer mates all round who will give you affection without tying you down. They could certainly organise your home for you but they might hardly be there. They can be judgemental which would not suit your rather rebellious side. You do not care about social respectability. They do. This needs good Sun cross overs to work.

Your Gemini Moon To Their Aquarian Moon
You will pass like two spaceships out in the galaxy. Only remote contact is likely. You are restless beyond belief and they are positively scared of one-to-one commitment. You will have friends galore but passionate moments may get fewer and further between after the first flush has worn off. Intellectual interests will dominate your relationship but is a talking shop a good basis for a lifelong partnership? Feelings will find it difficult to get a look in and neither of you are good with too much physical intimacy. You would need grounding from earth or water suns to help you nourish the relationship when it threatened to dry up.

Your Gemini Moon To Their Pisces Moon
Both of you are adaptable, restless creatures so sulky, brooding silences are hardly likely if you argue. You never keep a feeling for long and in ten minutes will have forgotten your gripe anyway. This could work better than an air water mix suggests. Pisces Moon is deeply sensitive but often hides away in its daydreams as a protection so they would not swamp you with feelings. At times they might be hurt by your rather cool, analytical approach. They are sweet, sympathetic creatures and would look after you well, sacrificing themselves in the process.

Your Moon Is In Cancer
A water Moon you feel deeply, intensely and fear separation. You are home and family oriented, and deeply attached to the past. Your sentimentality often does not let you change old habit patterns or let childhood memories go. Domestic and emotional security are hugely important to you. You only let mother's apron strings go when you can set up an adult family for yourself. You are desperately sensitive to the pain of separation which can make you emotionally

manipulative, or smothering. You hate criticism and hear it even when not intended. If wounded by the slightest thing you withdraw into moody, broody silences, snapping your shell shut. You gain great comfort from creating a beautiful home, decorating in style, cooking well and entertaining rather elegant friends.

Your Cancer Moon To Their Aries Moon
Not an ideal match since their abrasive, rather self centred style will wound and irritate you. You need harmony at home within the bounds of your own emotional ups and downs. But they crash around, never sitting still, being fiery, noisy, explosive and none too considerate of your needs. You may sense they will embarrass you socially which you loathe since you need approval from significant people. You want a family. They want to be themselves. You are reasonably controlling and they hate interference.

Your Cancer Moon To Their Taurus Moon
You both aim straight for a solid, settled, luxuriously comfortable home life. For different reasons because Taurus is earthy and fixed so needs to be rooted. You hate letting childhood and the past go. But if you end up at the same place, who cares? Both of you are driven to organise a domestic machine which positively purrs along. They are more sexually oriented than you, always tactile and very affectionate. They will help anchor your emotional highs and lows. Both of you are jealous but equally both of you are faithful once settled.

Your Cancer Moon To Their Gemini Moon
Not a wonderful package since you feel and they think. You clutch and they hop out of your reach. You would never understand the way their feelings appear and disappear. You can be moody but they are a complete enigma. At times they feel cool, having been wonderfully enthusiastic ten minutes ago. Just as you are having an intimate smooch they start to analyze what the emotions are, which freeze dries them before they have had a chance to develop. They are quick witted and talk a very great deal. But you really want a sensitive, intuitive mate who can protect you. Not

one who can write a thesis on you.

Your Cancer Moon To Their Cancer Moon

Moody, magnificent, very deeply felt, and positively oceanic with all its storms, tempests, undercurrents and calm patches. But you might feel overwhelmed at times since you would have no one to hang on through the roller coasters of your feelings which do need either an anchor or some detachment to give you perspective on them. You certainly both want a settled, beautiful family home and would cook wonderful meals together. But you would be both trying to play top dog at home and two hyper sensitive souls together could be a little precious. the sulks would be very long. Full Moons would be a nightmare. An earthy Sun in here will help.

Your Cancer Moon To Their Leo Moon

Not a bad match since both of you basically want a happy, luxurious home life with rather upwardly mobile friends. You are nourished by security and the patterns of the past. They are fixed, hate upheavals and in their own way have their roots firmly attached to traditional values. They are marginally more extravagant than you, always wanting to live the five star way which could provoke arguments. But they can be good with domestic finances. Deciding who rules the household could eventually become a problem since both of you like to be in control of the family tribe.

Your Cancer Moon To Their Virgo Moon

This can be a sensitive, refined mating with you providing emotional comfort, a happy home environment, energy and determination. They provide practical expertise on the domestic front, know how about food, health and bodies. They love to be of service and you adore being looked after. They can nag, nark and worry overmuch which is a bore. Their obsessive tidiness is good up to a point since it allows you to be lazy. But beyond that is a bore. Both of you are affectionate but not exactly sensual so you will settle happily into your own sexual routine.

Your Cancer Moon To Their Libra Moon
What this has going for it is a shared liking for an elegant social life, for a beautiful, luxury home base and not too much emotional hassle. They want harmony above all else and while at times you may find that a little shallow they will keep the peace. Both of you need social approval so will not attract embarrassment by speaking or acting out of place. They may seem a little cool at times because they are an air Moon. You feel, they think. But they are thoughtful and do need a mate in life so they will move your way.

Your Cancer Moon To Their Scorpio Moon
On the outside no one will see the depths of intensity and feeling contained in this relationship. The sulks and agonies may be out of sight but the hidden ecstasies are there as well. With two water moons you have to expect overwhelming feelings at times but Scorpio Moons are tightly controlled and fixed so they will stabilise you a touch. Neither of you forgives lightly if at all but both of you are fairly faithful once settled. They are more preoccupied with sex than you which could be the major drawback. In time you like more generalised family cuddles than infinite endless exclusive passion.

Your Cancer Moon To Their Sagittarian Moon
You want a happy homestead with roses at the door, children in the garden . They want the open plains and as few obligations and commitments as they can manage. You would feel deeply wounded by their need to shoot like an arrow from a bow at a moment's notice. They are excitable, fiery, restless and not always considerate when it comes to other people's needs. While you are thin skinned and need protecting, being made to feel secure. Your jealousy would become a problem. Your aims are different and they might prove a social embarrassment. You want to look good. They could not care less.

Your Cancer Moon To Their Capricorn Moon
Opposite sign Moons often want totally different comforts in life. You want home. They want work. You hate being far from happy domesticity and the family while they stay

overlong at the office. Their self esteem is low so they think they have to earn being loved. You could do them a great deal of good by teaching them about their essential value and getting them connected to their feelings but it would be a long slow job. They can be cool and judgemental while you are deeply sensitive to slights, criticisms and disapproval. Your moods would never be in sync.

Your Cancer Moon To Their Aquarius Moon
Not a totally compatible combination this unless you have overwhelmingly positive Sun connections. You are emotional, needy, protective, possessive, a traditionalist at heart who is keen on social approval. They are wild, whacky eccentrics, who think more than they feel and back away from intimate one-to-one commitment. They love being one of the crowd which is fine because you like friends as well but you would miss having a real relationship at the centre of it. You need a settled family base while they would feel stifled by it. What nourishes you repels them. They like thinking, talking and travelling.

Your Cancer Moon To Their Pisces Moon
A dream of a match with both of you billing and cooing, protecting each other's hyper sensitivities, happy as an oyster sharing the same shell. You want a happy home. They just want somewhere to let their defences down. Basically very timid creatures, they often hide away their beautiful, sympathetic natures to avoid rejection or being hurt, which you understand totally. They are adaptable so would not rock the boat. Their slight air of self pity or constant martyrdom may irk you but it is a small price to pay.

Your Moon Is In Leo
A fire Moon you act first, think later. Entertaining, charmingly persuasive, rather grand with a great deal of personal magnetism, you certainly like to make an impression. A prima donna at heart you want your place in the spotlight, but you also love children, games and fun. You adore the luxuries and extravagances of life, always wanting to travel first class and stay only in five star hotels.

Criticism is not something you take at all kindly to being easily wounded. Indeed vanity and pride can be your downfall. Your stubborness is also a stumbling block to happiness at home unless your mate is flexible.

Your Leo Moon To Their Aries Moon
Fiery, fun-loving, passionate at least initially, this is a real snap, crackle and pop relationship. You may not always appreciate their blunt, rather tactless approach because your ego is fragile. But you will share similar interests in a thrill filled, adventurous life style. Boredom is not likely. They are less stubborn than you but do like to win which could cause the odd ruction. But neither of you are good at getting down into the depths of your feelings or facing the darker side of life. So the stormy passages may be difficult to negotiate.

Your Leo Moon To Their Taurus Moon
This could be a glorious indulgence in all that is decadently and expensively wicked in life. Comfort definitely comes first. But it could also be a tough struggle since neither of you give way easily if at all at home. They would want power, you would want all the attention. In good moments you would flirt, cuddle and adore every passion filled minute. In bad times you would sulk like crazy while they got slightly bitter. It could just work because both of you need constancy and security.

Your Leo Moon To Their Gemini Moon
This has real possibilities because they can adjust to your whims while you sail on rather grandly. You want limelight, admiration and a flamboyant lifestyle. They want fun, excitement, constant movement and stimulating chat. Though there might be a lack of feeling here. The highs would be wonderful but you would get lost in the low patches. They might even flit off because they are wanderers at heart. You could be exasperated by their lack of staying power. They would make fun of your puffed up grand ideas and take wicked delight in teasing you.

Your Leo Moon To Their Cancer Moon
Home would be magnificent as both of you adore a luxurious pad. You could get all the attention while they mothered you, cooked for you and kept the domestic organisation running. But both of you in different ways are slightly hyper sensitive, certainly to criticism, which could create very long sulks indeed. Your fire and their water could be a boiling combination or one which damps the flames fairly quickly. But you are both family oriented, domestic creatures who can be faithful once settled.

Your Leo Moon To Their Leo Moon
Who is going to be the star and who the audience? You would both be scrabbling for the limelight all the time. Both of you are stubborn, demanding and fairly determined to suit yourselves. Really you need a flexible Moon not another fixed one. Certainly both of you can be warm, persuasive and charming so the initial contacts could be delicious but in the long term you would find it an expensive relationship, not very practical, and given to explosive fights.

Your Leo Moon To Their Virgo Moon
Your need to be centre of attention and live flamboyantly will be happily complemented by their flexibility, common sense, and practical efficiency. Their tidiness and nagging may drive you to distraction but it is a small price to pay for being allowed to live like a monarch while they do the skivvying. They worry more than you so you help to give them confidence, courage and sparkle. But sometimes their anxieties are right and counter balance your lack of realism. They will not upset your vanity too much though they will not understand your need for grand living.

Your Leo Moon To Their Libra Moon
A wonderfully sociable match this. Together you will throw the best parties, in the most elegant house in the neighbourhood. They like to keep the peace so will not upset your vanity. You adore being admired and they are hugely tactful. Money could be a problem since both of you have expensive tastes, to put it mildly. What the relationship lacks is much depth of feeling or connection to the body.

You might drift apart just because of this superficiality. But if you do manage to stay the course neither of you are wanderers.

Your Leo Moon To Their Scorpio Moon
A steamy connection this which no doubt sometimes works but the struggles are long and awesome to behold. Both of you are fiercely stubborn. You want attention and admiration. They want control and are not above undermining you with a real stinging remark which will wound your vanity. They have a greater depth, indeed real turbulence of feelings which you slightly distrust. If you have compatible Suns you could make a go of it as long as you sort out the power struggles before they get too destructive.

Your Leo Moon To Their Sagittarius Moon
Two fire moons together are delighted with the thrills, adventures and fun of a high speed, non stop social life, sporting life. But what happens in the quiet moments in the months when you have to economise and life gets dull. You will sulk because you need luxuries to keep you happy. They will fly away because they hate being fenced in especially to tedious commitments. You need to have a more earthy connection through the Suns for this to work well long term.

Your Leo Moon To Their Capricorn Moon
You have both similar aims in terms of a good lifestyle - traditional, secure, rather grand. You adore being admired and they feel unworthy so they will not be grabbing your limelight. Their earthiness could be a help at home since you tend to be wildly impractical. But the one drawback is that they tend to work non stop so you may never see them. It is a fairly cool combination at the end of the day more concerned with outer appearance than inner warmth. You need to tap into their sensuality.

Your Leo Moon To Their Aquarius Moon
You want attention while they want freedom to roam which is going to cause friction. Basically they fear one-to-one commitment and insist on a life full of friends. You are

not deeply jealous but do like a settled home and family life which makes them claustrophobic. You might also be embarrassed by their rather startling behaviour at times. They put it on just to wind everyone else up, you included. They can be horribly honest which will not suit your fragile vanity.

Your Leo Moon To Their Pisces Moon
Quite a sweet combination because they are sympathetic and adaptable while you are flamboyant and attention seeking. They do need protecting since they deeply fear rejection but once they feel safe to trust you will make your life a haven of bliss. They are not so emotional they will make you feel swamped. They can disappear happily into their daydreams so not demand too much from you though they will always be happy to sacrifice themselves to your every whim. They can go on a martyr trip which is a minor bore.

Your Moon Is In Virgo
An earth Moon you need to be practical, close to the material world. You can worry more than anyone else under the sun and indeed invent anxieties to keep you going. At times your obsessive tidiness and fussing about details endlessly drives mates to distraction but you can keep home running efficiently and are conscientious.   Deep down inside you are rather frightened of your emotions. On the outside you can look prudish and rather critical but once you soften your rigid need to keep order everywhere you can be quite sensual. Learning to let you hair down is crucial.

Your Virgo Moon To Their Aries Moon
A schoolteacher marrying a circus acrobat! Not really a compatible pairing. You want a tidy, ordered existence while they want constant noise, excitement and challenges. They would worry you to death with the chaos they leave trailing behind them. Certainly you would help them to be more practical but is it worth it? They could show you what it is like to have more trust in life but at the end of the day you would write them off as hopeless gamblers. Their brashness would upset your tender sensitivities.

Your Virgo Moon To Their Taurus Moon

A happy coupling of two earthy, home loving souls. You do share common interests in comfort, good food, gardening, small animals. They are more demonstratively affectionate than you which will help to iron out your wrinkles. Also their solidity will wind your anxiety levels down. Their stubborness will not bother you excessively since you are adaptable by nature and happy to be of service. You work too hard which will suit their lazy nature but then you are not happy being idle. Between you, you do need a little more vision in your lives.

Your Virgo Moon To Their Gemini Moon

Restless, talkative (in the extreme) and rather highly strung together, this can work well because you both basically want to fit round each other. You worry too much while they flit around in a slightly unsettling fashion. But boredom will never be a problem. Your practical side will help to ground them while their airy intuition will teach you to see problems in a different light. Your home will be packed full of books. Sometimes Moon Geminis can be wild, wayward and none too faithful. You are not desperately jealous but you do get hurt if rejected.

Your Virgo Moon To Their Cancer Moon

Both of you have highly nourishing Moons. You connect to practical matters, the body, the garden and small animals. They connect to feelings, food and beautiful environments. They are moody but in a different way to your highly strung anxiety so you can cope with their Full Moon blues while they soothe your endless worries. Both of you are sensitive to emotional hurts so will not intentionally cause damage by wandering or abandoning each other without thought.

Your Virgo Moon To Their Leo Moon

You can certainly cope with them but do you need to? They love entertaining, being grand, looking flamboyant and travelling first class. You do not need all that show and although you can adapt to their stubborness at the end of the day you need to ask yourself why you are doing it all. Certainly they will bring sparkle, chutzpah and courage which is lacking in your life. You will organise the practical facts of life which they regard as beneath them. They are warm as long as they are being admired. You might grow to hate all the parties since you have to do all the work.

Your Virgo Moon To Their Virgo Moon
The nervous tension levels would be off the Richter Scale since both of you have an endless supply of anxious concerns. You would just give each other more to worry about. The nagging and obsessive tidiness would get to ridiculous levels. Both of you need a more amiable, laid back Moon or at the very least Sun to mate with. Then your better qualities of practicality and warmth can appear. You would both be too narrow minded together, only concerned with your shared hypochondria and with what is material in life. You need more vision.

Your Virgo Moon To Their Libra Moon
You like order and they like harmony. Both of you are refined, sensitive, easily embarrassed in public by social gaffes and want a beautiful home. You match well since your practical flair combines with their elegant taste. It could be a touch cool at times if you are standing on the sidelines and they are being snobbish, which happens. But neither of you would rock the boat too much. You might get tired of all the socialising and living on the outside which Moon Libra tends to do. You care less about appearances and social reputation.

Your Virgo Moon To Their Scorpio Moon
Could be hot, could be horrible. It depends on whether you are an over controlled, rigid Virgo Moon in which case it will not work with their torrid preoccupation with sex and living life in the depths. But if you are open to passion it could be earth moving. You would never quite get to the bottom of their feelings which are a highly private area but you would provide them with a solid practical base. They would not let you worry as much being a fixed Moon and very strong emotionally.

Your Virgo Moon To Their Sagittarian Moon

Restless, energetic, talkative combination this which would never stay bored for long. Neither of you are good at sitting still though they tend to fly further afield than you when the mood strikes. However your infinite capacity for worrying about everything under the sun would not meet with sympathy from their optimistic, unrealistic, rather reckless temperament. They would liven you up but you are fairly incompatible types. They hate being fenced in while you do like a semblance of order around. It could be fun while it lasts.

Your Virgo Moon To Their Capricorn Moon

Earthy common sense abounds between you but will it kill passion. Both of you can be a touch too practical, workaholic and sit on your feelings. If you can open up then both of you have depths of sensuality but it will take time. You worry endlessly while they feel unworthy of being loved if they do not achieve a great deal. They tend to work long hours at the office and you might find you never had the time or inclination to relax together which would eventually undermine the base of your warmth towards each other.

Your Virgo Moon To Their Aquarius Moon

This may not be too wonderful since you basically need someone to calm you down and ease your highly strung nerves while they take the greatest delight in stirring up the atmosphere. They love being bizarre and shocking mates just to see the effect. They are frightened of one-to-one commitment and you can over control your feelings so it might end up very spacey and cool. You will adapt to their rather stubborn ways but why would you want to? You are sensitive, and want a tidy life. They are disorganised hippies whose life style would make you shriek.

Your Virgo Moon To Their Pisces Moon

Happy as bunnies down a burrow you have a great deal to offer one another if you can keep your obsessive tidying and narking under control and they are not too wimpish. They retreat into daydreams because they fear rejection and living in hard reality. But you can provide a perfectly protective cocoon for them with your practical skills. They will teach you to soften down your workaholic tendencies and make you less rigid. Both of you are sympathetic, caring, adaptable types who would not intentionally hurt the other. You might find yourselves very indecisive at home.

Your Moon Is In Libra

An air Moon you think always before you feel. Life to you should be a graceful business with everyone being tactful, charming and kind all the time. You can come across as insincere because you agree too much just to keep the peace. You like your house to be elegant, your friends to be upwardly mobile, your mate to be hard working yet supportive. Your love of beautiful surroundings, good food and luxuries gives you expensive habits. Class matters more to you than it should and you are certainly over sensitive about the approval of those around. The idle, the unemployed and the great unwashed hold no fascination whatsoever for you.

Your Libra Moon To Their Aries Moon

You want peace while they want excitement. You are the soul of tact and are desperate for approval while they crash around, dropping clangers, tramping on sensitive corns and being generally over impulsive. They would make you wince from one end of the weekend to the other. You lack between you much connection to the harsher realities or deeper feelings in life and might eventually drift apart because there was little to nourish and recharge the relationship. This needs anchoring Suns to work well.

Your Libra Moon To Their Taurus Moon

A shared taste in elegant, comfortable, not to say luxurious living will draw you together. They are demonstratively affectionate which will warm your rather laid back soul. Sex might prove a problem because they want constant, tangible expressions of love while you can take it or leave it. You are more concerned with outer appearances and social approval than them. But they can help to ground you and keep life rolling along at a practical level. They can be stubborn but you rarely dig your heels in for long.

Your Libra Moon To Their Gemini Moon
Two airy Moons together are intellectually stimulating but leave a little to be desired emotionally and physically. You have a tendency to like life to be too nice. They do not but are uncomfortable around intense feelings. So you could end up gliding across the surface and drawing further apart. They might be a little wild for you socially since they have a quirky sense of humour and can embarrass you. But if you do make it match then your home will be full of books, visitors and a high level of interest.

Your Libra Moon To Their Cancer Moon
Two essentially different energies you can get along happily because both of you want an elegant, well organised home life. They can be emotionally more roller coaster than you understand but they are not sharp edged and vindictive. You like calm, harmony and peace above all else and might find their ups and downs wearing. They tend to retreat and sulk if misunderstood but on the whole you are supremely tactful. They will be exceptionally caring, cook well and love to mother you. What may cause problems is your rather cool, laid back approach to the emotional subtleties of life.

Your Libra Moon To Their Leo Moon
You suit each other like a dream, will strive hard to make yourself accepted by all the best people, will only eat in the best restaurants together, and will create a sumptious palace of a home. Both of you are traditionalists, keen to keep up appearances and are horribly extravagant. You do lack an emotional depth however in the relationship and need to work at ways to nourish yourself together that is not just all on the surface. You have to feel good together, emotionally and physically, as well as looking good.

Your Libra Moon To Their Virgo Moon
This is a quietly compatible pairing since they are adaptable and you resourceful. They are sensitive, refined and not prone to crashing into social gaffes. They may criticise more than you might like and certainly they worry obsessively which becomes a bore. But your airy way of spreading

harmony about the place will put them at their ease. They can help to keep the everyday running of the home ticking over nicely since they are practical and earthy. You add a touch of taste. It could at times by too cool and detached. You need to work to keep up the warmth.

Your Libra Moon To Their Libra Moon
You would spend all your time racing around to ask what the other one wanted! It sounds divine but really you need an anchor not an echo. Both of you would chat charmingly and intelligently, would entertain superbly and generally be an asset to the social scene. But you ultimately lack feeling together. The relationship needs deeper connections to body and heart before it will have the inner strength and stability to last long term. More nourishment needs to come from Sun signs.

Your Libra Moon To Their Scorpio Moon
You skate like a dragonfly across the surface of life, glittering colourfully, while they plunge into the murky depths. Their intensity and turbulence of feeling would frighten you. Your rather superficial need to keep up appearances and be socially acceptable would appal them. They control their feelings tightly so you would never quite know what was going on but would suspect (rightly) that they were always trying to control you and gain the upper hand. You have difficulty facing up to the harsher realities of life while they adore wallowing in the mire. Not really too in tune.

Your Libra Moon To Their Sagittarian Moon
This has promise as long as they are not too rough a diamond. You can put a veneer of good manners on them while they give you more courage, sparkle and spontaneity. You are a traditionalist and, dare it be said, a snob at heart. They are more devil-may-care, reckless, even gamblers in their souls. But they are warm and communicative while they stand still. You like intellectual stimulation and do not mind too much if they fly free which they will frequently. Neither of you is especially jealous though you do hate the humiliation of being seen to be rejected. You do need more depth in the relationship.

Your Libra Moon To Their Capricorn Moon

This can be cool, a touch too businesslike and hold together for the sake of status and reputation but it can also work well. You are both traditionalist, slight snobs, and want to be accepted. So home will be elegant, your entertaining impeccable and friends rather classy. They work too hard since they never feel worthy of love unless it is earned. You might find them never there though you can settle for the shell of a marriage if it looks good enough. If you can banish their workaholic tendencies they are warm, earthy and practical. You can soothe them, make them feel accepted. They can cuddle you.

Your Libra Moon To Their Aquarius Moon

Two airy Moons should have an initial attraction though you are ultimately too cool, too up in your heads to nourish the deeper levels of the relationship. Even the early attraction may falter because you are super sensitive to social embarrassments and they are bizarre, eccentric and given to slightly shocking displays. They love to see the effect they make on others. Your sensibilities might not stand it. Also you do really want a relationship. They really do not. They are scared of one-to-one commitment and much prefer to move in groups or with friends.

Your Libra Moon To Their Pisces Moon

Blissful, sensitive, refined, caring, creative - what more can you ask for. Air water mixes do not generally work but here it can. You want harmony and they want peace. You are tactful, charming and thoughtful. They are self sacrificing, sympathetic and caring. You would give a great deal to each other. You would never feel swamped by their emotions because they drift gently off into daydreams much of the time. They can be a touch self pitying , feeling themselves martyred but with a protective environment that will disappear.

<u>Your Moon Is In Scorpio</u>

A water Moon, you are deep, dark, intensely private, secretive and passionate, an enigma even to intimate lovers. As a matter of pride you never let anyone see the turbulent intensity of emotions churning inside you though you are extremely jealous and possessive. If you are hurt or betrayed you absolutely never let on but will never forgive. You plot and plan revenge for years afterwards. Your romantic life is never taken lightly or with a laugh - it is life or death, love or hate. There is no wishy washy in between stage. If lovers leave or are abandoned you absolutely never stay friends afterwards. Your feelings are always tightly controlled. In true Scorpionic fashion you are fairly preoccupied with sex. Through the sexual act you hope to achieve a higher union.

Your Scorpio Moon To Their Aries Moon
You exist in the subterranean depths of your emotions. They leap up agitatedly if as much as a sniff of a feeling gets remotely heavy. They are fireflies and speed merchants, where you want to be locked in an intense clinch most of the time. You would constantly be trying to grasp an untameable energy. Your jealousy and possessiveness would drive you and them crackers. Their insecure, over independent stance which pushes them into dominating others would soon fall foul of your need to be in control.

Your Scorpio Moon To Their Taurus Moon
Two mighty strong personalities coming together can either be an explosion of passion or end in a catastrophic bitterness. Both of you are jealous, stubborn, fairly power hungry and very immoveable. You more obviously fight for control but they are past masters at the art of passive resistance. They just smile lazily and dig their heels in deeper. Certainly they are cuddly, will surround you with every imaginable comfort, and are demonstratively affectionate. But you may find them too materialistic and lacking in your depth of vision. Not bad if you can stand the struggle.

Your Scorpio Moon To Their Gemini Moon
Better than it might appear but certainly not perfect. They are basically butterflies who never sit on one flower for long. They flit restlessly around which would raise your hackles instantly. You like to possess, to control, to sink into the depths with your mate. What is the positive note at least for short term flings is that they do have a leaning towards the

dark side of life which suits you admirably. In the long term though your turbulent feelings would threaten to envelope and frighten them. They like staying up in their heads, in their thoughts and ideas which you would find far too cool and unemotional.

Your Scorpio Moon To Their Cancer Moon

Wonderfully intuitive, empathetic connection between you since you are both water Moons. You would swirl, toss, roll and sink on the rise and fall of your feelings. Admittedly at times you would feel you were cast adrift together on a rudderless raft because both of you are highly impressionable. But you are more fixed and in control which is a help. The problems could come long term as you like to dominate and Cancer will gradually try to take over. You also want an exclusive, intense sexual/emotional relationship. They really prefer a more general family, all cuddles together type of contact.

Your Scorpio Moon To Their Leo Moon

Not too easy this one since they fly high and you like to sink low. They are fiery, scared of emotions, adore admiration while you do not care about appearances. You want to be in an intensely private, exclusive affair. Their extravagance and arrogance would irk you and your need to control would bother them. Certainly both of you have a fairly steady sexuality though it comes from different motives. They can be selfish but at best are heart centred. You are more loin and soul centred.

Your Scorpio Moon To Their Virgo Moon

This is supposed to be a gas but, but, but...you need to watch what kind of Virgo Moon you pick. Some can be ravers, highly sensual, earthily warm. But some can be dried up old prunes, fastidiously and obsessively tidy and supreme naggers. Guess which you would like? They will always be less emotionally intense than you but they can help to keep your home life running smoothly at a practical level. They will tend your medical needs, understand your diet and look after your pets. They will adapt where you are stubborn and you could help to loosen their rigid approach.

Your Scorpio Moon To Their Libra Moon

This is not inherently in tune this combination since they are fastidiously 'nice', rather class conscious, fairly cool, laid back and unemotional where you revel in the murky depths of your more intense passions. You want committed union, a real soul-mate, and ongoing good sex. They want a colourful social life, upwardly mobile friends and nothing that smells bad. You would frighten them with your stormy undercurrents and they would exasperate you with what looked like superficiality. You think the agonies are worth it for the ecstasies that come along as well. They want total harmony all the time.

Your Scorpio Moon To Their Scorpio Moon

Bliss. Both of you understand each other like a dream and nothing will ever be too emotionally stretching or too much of a challenge for either. Someone who can understand your most hidden desires, darkest yearnings and deepest passions. No other sign in the zodiac understands you like one of your own. The fights and sulks will certainly be long, could be bitter. You will both have to curb your instincts about getting back. Try to be more flexible and tolerant. Your sex lives would be the envy of the neighbourhood except you never tell.

Your Scorpio Moon To Their Sagittarian Moon

This is a tricky mating since you are basically opposite energies. They are fiery, freedom loving, over talkative, over optimistic, gamblers at heart, not well connected to their bodies. You are deep, dark, sexy and need an exclusive one-to-one commitment. They would start to feel suffocated and promptly escape. Your jealousy would be terribly out of control. They refuse to admit there is a dark side to life and hate facing the harsher realities. You have utter contempt for those who cannot live at your level. Sex would be an abyss between you.

Your Scorpio Moon To Their Capricorn Moon

Find the right Capricorn Moon and they can be earthy, sensual, rather decadent. But most feel so unworthy of love and admiration that they work 90 hour weeks to earn acceptance thereby never being available for the relationships they so desperately want. You are not one for a workaholic absent partner and you are too robust to enjoy supporting a fragile heart. If they are truly connected to their bodies and indulgent side then certainly you could operate well together though possibly over the long term you might find them too materialistic and lacking in your sense of vision. You can be quite spiritual as well as highly sexual.

Your Scorpio Moon To Their Aquarius Moon
Ooh, this one is really tricky. They are more scared of one-to-one commitment than almost any other Moon sign. Every time you wanted a twosome they would invite six friends along to brighten the atmosphere. You do not appreciate your romantic life as a permanent party or group meeting. You want sex, they want conversation. They love the theory of sex, you appreciate the practice. Both of you are hugely stubborn and would not give way to the other's quite contradictory needs. They fly away at the first whiff of jealousy while you really cannot help your tendency to possess.

Your Scorpio Moon To Their Pisces Moon
This could be bliss as long as you curb your octopus tendencies and you do not pick an over timid, wispy Pisces Moon. They can be such scary creatures they hardly emerge from their shells in case they get hurt. They can spend their lives daydreaming or indulging various addictions as an escape from relationship. You would feel chilled out and exasperated by them. They can be slippery, evasive souls when they do not want pinned down.   Certainly you are both water Moons so there should be a depth of emotional understanding. They are kind, caring and very self sacrificing and would adapt to your rather fixed ways.

<u>Your Moon Is In Sagittarius</u>
Fire is in your veins and the wander lust is in your feet. You need freedom and wide open spaces more than anything in your emotional life. Being fenced in or committed to long term relationships can make you panic. Lovers have to be

friends as well and you can sustain spacier relationships than most people. Your honesty is at times a touch direct since you rarely stop to think of the consequences on someone else's fragile ego. You need a robust mate. Honesty and naivety are your more beguiling character traits. What is most important is that you have strong beliefs by which to live your life.

Your Sagittarius Moon To Their Aries Moon
Noisy, volatile, impulsive, you would always be getting yourselves into impossible scrapes but boredom would never get a look in. The only problems come when life slows down or hits hurdles. Neither of you is well equipped to face the harsher realities of life or to connect with your feelings which always happens when you come to rest. Your similarities will provide an initial magnetic attraction but over the long term both of you need more of an anchor, a mate with common sense and emotional/physical warmth to contain you without making you feel trapped.

Your Sagittarius Moon To Their Taurus Moon
A firefly and a bull, you do not make an easy match. You are flyaway, freedom loving, scared of being possessed or pulled down too much into your body. They are solid, earthy, jealous, immoveable and need constant emotional and sexual reassurance about your love. Certainly they would provide you with every comfort but they would also expect you to share their needs and indulgences. They can be blinkered and they do loathe change. You adore constant movement even of houses which they would hate. This needs good Sun cross overs.

Your Sagittarius Moon To Their Gemini Moon
Not much stability or solidity or common sense between you but the conversations will sparkle. You are both grasshoppers who adore philosophising about life and can be romantic in short bursts in your own way. But fidelity can be a problem as neither of you has much staying power. Both of you avoid facing feelings so you lack ways of nourishing the relationship when it becomes dry. Difficult patches would be harder to overcome since both of you lack

the resources to do anything other than think or run. It will be fun but you need an anchor not a playmate. Earth or Water Suns will help.

Your Sagittarian Moon To Their Cancer Moon
You face down different roads in life. They want home, family, secure commitment and emotional empathy. You want freedom, excitement, bright conversation and not too much feeling. You distrust those hidden undercurrents which in Moon Cancer grow stronger with age. Certainly they would provide you with a wonderful home base but they would become more possessive as the years went by. They cannot stand separation. They quite like you as one of the family rather than as an exclusive couple but you would still feel fenced in.

Your Sagittarian Moon To Their Leo Moon
Two fire moons together are noisy, volatile, warm and passionate at least in the early stages. The main problem is how to keep the flames burning since neither of you is well connected to your feelings or your body. Moon Leos are more settled, home oriented and stubborn than you which would provide an anchor but their ego really requires a constant mate while you quite like to be flying free whenever it suits. Your strong, not always tactful, opinions would also ruffle their fragile if over blown egos. They desperately need to be admired which would irk you. Your extravagances together could get well out of hand.

Your Sagittarian Moon To Their Virgo Moon
Restless, energetic and very chatty together, you could do a great deal worse. Their obsessive tidiness and nagging might drive you spare but they would keep the boring practicalities of life ticking over for you. Your sunny, outgoing confidence would give them courage and maybe(!) stop them worrying. Both of you are adaptable so sulks would not be long lived though indecisiveness could be a drawback. They are not jealous and are fairly self sufficient so would not try to fence you in. But you need to soften down their rigid outlook.

Your Sagittarian Moon To Their Libra Moon

Fire to air Moon creates a lively atmosphere, excellent stimulating conversation and usually a great social life. They are a touch class conscious and too 'nice' for you which will irk eventually. You are prone to sailing into over honest, rather tactless, opinions which would have them wincing especially if you are out on the social circuit. They desperately want harmony and respectability. But they will bring a touch of grace, elegance and charm when you will bring them courage, fire and more directness. However neither of you are good at facing the practical realities of life. When the stormy times came you would fly off and they would politely look the other way. You need more depth from your Suns.

Your Sagittarian Moon To Their Scorpio Moon
You would feel as if you were trapped in a spider's web. What nourishes you is freedom, flying high in your ideas and staying friendly rather than feeling suffocated. They on the other hand need intense, passionate ongoing exclusive relationships. Your sexual needs are so different you would never either be wholly pleased. Their jealousy would be aroused by your escapist tactics and bother both of you. And never, never would you ever understand what is going on within them. They are private, secretive and manipulative where you are open, gullible, naive and staggeringly honest.

Your Sagittarian Moon To Their Sagittarian Moon
You light each other up with your ideas, your beliefs about life, your travel plans and your wide social circle of friends. But will it ever stay together? The flames of two fire Moons can burn out fairly fast so the early passion just suddenly is not there anymore. You both need so much freedom that you could drift apart without noticing it. Neither of you is good at commitment, nor setting up a practical home. Finances would always be in chaos. It feels a shame since both of you are ultimately so likeable but you'll need a more solid Sun match to make it work.

Your Sagittarian Moon To Their Capricorn Moon
Their judgemental side probably bothers you but this could be better than it looks. You dislike being fenced in

and need elbow room. They feel unworthy of being loved so have to work like maniacs to prove their value. You certainly do not object to a fairly absent partner and their practical streak would be an asset around the house when they are there. Realistic you are not, so they might keep a curb on spending and run the budget sensibly. You would always feel slightly weighed down by them because you are basically an optimist. They are born pessimists. But some of each might rub off on the other which would be no bad thing.

Your Sagittarian Moon To Their Aquarius Moon
Wild, whacky, way out and always on the go this could be an uproarious combination. Both of you are reckless in different ways so boredom is never going to be a problem. Both of you like being pals, adore friends and will have a house full of people. But what happens when life slows down, the parties stop and you have only each other to face across an echoing room? They are more wary if anything than you of one-to-one commitment. Neither of you are well connected to your feelings so when the rough times come you will be lost. You may find it difficult to sustain the relationship over the long term unless you have nourishing Suns.

Your Sagittarian Moon To Their Pisces Moon
Fire and water do not mix, they say, but you could almost make a go of this match. Both of you are adaptable, not very intense personalities. You like freedom and they are the least jealous of the emotional signs partly because they escape into their daydreams so might not even notice your absence. They are highly sensitive so might object to your rather blunt speaking. They can withdraw very fast into their shell. But they are basically kind, caring, sympathetic souls who will sacrifice their own needs to suit yours. Your outgoing optimism will be good for them as long as you keep them safe.

<u>Your Moon Is In Capricorn</u>
An earth Moon you are tuned into the material world. Emotionally life was tough for you in the beginning so

you have ended up feeling unworthy. Love for you has to be earned by achievements which is quite the wrong way round. You have to learn that you can be wanted for just being you. Certainly you can be successful but your ambitions often drive away the very relationships you need. In crisis you can be superb and you are always practical. When you can relax you are indulgent, earthy, almost decadent at times though it does not occur often. Luckily you mellow through the years, warming up as you age. You will sacrifice almost anything to achieve your ends in life and have been known to be ruthless. Others can see you as cool and too detached.

Your Capricorn Moon To Their Aries Moon
A rather gritty combination this you might find your moods never quite fitted in the same moment. You are cautious, rather pessimistic and approach emotions tentatively whereas they take the bull by the horns and charge. Neither of you are at home in your feelings. Your emotional self esteem is low while they appear to be over confident though their insecurity is all too evident. They never stand still and you rarely stop working so you might find making meaningful connections difficult. You are earthy and practical. They seem unrealistic and rather abrasive. With cross over Fire and Earth Suns it might work.

Your Capricorn Moon To Their Taurus Moon
You purr in each other's company, cuddle up close and you just adore their way of constantly demonstrating their affection. Both of you are earthy and indulgent though you try to hide your lazy side away. They will provide you with every comfort and make you enjoy it. Their stubborness will not bother you especially because you just flit off to work when the going gets stormy. They are possessive but that can feel like security and support to you as long as they do not start issuing orders. Both of you are manipulative in different ways which you need to watch.

Your Capricorn Moon To Their Gemini Moon
A rather cool combination because you work too hard and they think too much. Neither of you are into feeling in depth

which could be the stumbling block to long term intimacy. They are basic butterflies who never settle for long in one mood, in one place or with one face. They are not necessarily unfaithful just rather casual. You would find your earthy side needed more physical contact. Your judgemental streak would also come out rather destructively to point out their shortcomings. At the end of the day you need someone who can make you feel valued. Supportive Suns will help.

Your Capricorn Moon To Their Cancer Moon
Opposite Moon signs can be a blessing or a curse depending on which are involved. At best your moods will always be slightly out of sync. They want to make love when you want to sleep. You want to cut the grass when they want to go on the town. They will certainly provide you with a wonderful home base, great cooking, elegantly upmarket friends and lots of sympathetic support. In time they might even make you learn to value yourself more as a human being who can be loved. But they are jealous and might not take kindly to your long working hours or need to constantly keep doing. Your criticisms will wound them. Both of you need to mellow to make this work well.

Your Capricorn Moon To Their Leo Moon
Definitely an upwardly socially mobile pair, you would put great stress in being seen in all the right places, with the right friends. They are gloriously extravagant, needing to live life the five star way. You are a traditionalist, a tiny bit of a snob and constantly striving to prove you are acceptable. It could work but ultimately you both put more value on outer appearance than on how you feel. You always feel unwanted and unworthy which their rather ego centred approach might emphasise. As far as they are concerned you need to give them all the attention whereas you really need to give more to yourself. But it still could have its strong plus points.

Your Capricorn Moon To Their Virgo Moon
Cosy, cuddly, comfortable or cool, overworked, rather rigid. This combination could work either way. Both of you have the capacity to indulge, to be sensual but they need to

loosen up and forget about keeping life tidy. You need to stop trying to achieve to earn love. If you can get into your bodies, down into the depths of your feelings which might be painful at first you would find this match offers both of you a great deal. They are adaptable, rather highly strung. So will fit in with your ways and rely on your advice. They are helpful, keen to give service and generally kind when their perfectionist streak is kept under control.

Your Capricorn Moon To Their Libra Moon
Gritty though not impossible combination this. Your moods will never quite be in sync but you both have relatively similar aims in life. Both of you are sensitive to social approval, are snobbish, class conscious, want to know the right people and live in an elegant home. If this sounds a touch cool, it might end up that way. Ulterior motives of a material nature never suit the heart's intentions. They can come across as superficial because they are so determined to keep the peace and to please. But you are at times happy enough being left to work hard and not be embroiled in heavy emotional scenes. They are not jealous.

Your Capricorn Moon To Their Scorpio Moon
A heavyweight relationship which will only work long term if you are willing to get into your feelings, not easy when you have always felt slightly unwanted and unloved. They have turbulent, intense emotions which they need to live out in a close, exclusive twosome. Both of you in different ways are highly sexual though you often repress your physical needs for the sake of ambition. You might find their possessiveness a bore when you wanted to escape back to the office. Both of you have a way of cutting corners and manipulating for your own ends which could cause problems.

Your Capricorn Moon To Their Sagittarian Moon
Do pessimists and optimists cancel each other out? You are basically very different energies. They are reckless, impulsive, outspoken, outgoing, adventurers at heart. You are cautious, defensive, hard working and rather judgemental. They fly high on a Pollyanna trip with their heads in the clouds, you walk resolutely on the ground

facing reality in all its bleakness. You need to be nurtured more, taught to love yourself. They are undiplomatically blunt in their opinions. You might end up feeling worse at times. Certainly you would regard them as impractical at times. Highly compatible Sun signs would be needed.

Your Capricorn Moon To Their Capricorn Moon
A rather gloomy, over worked, pessimistic pair you would make with both of you feeling you had to out vie the other in achievements to earn acceptance. You would both spend so long in the office you might never meet. It could become very cool indeed. There is, however, a flip side to you which is earthy, sensual and quite decadent but whether you would bring that out with another over defensive Capricorn Moon is questionable. Your vision of life together would be too practical, too materialistic. You need more chutzpah, more sparkle and more optimism. Fire or Water Suns would help.

Your Capricorn Moon To Their Aquarian Moon
If you want a spacey, non relationship this has much to recommend it. Your workaholic tendencies keep you away from home a great deal and they positively fly scared of heavy one-to-one commitments. Neither of you is good with feelings and you distrust being swamped by emotions you cannot control. They might not always suit you socially because they adore startling or shocking others by doing or saying bizarre things just to see the effect it has. You would cringe with embarrassment. They would find your judgements stuffy and tedious. They are stubborn and would not give way easily. You'll need decent cross over Suns for this to be a vibrant match.

Your Capricorn Moon To Their Pisces Moon
You could do your strong, protective act providing them with a solid, secure home base while they would float around caring for your every need, making you feel loved and valued. They are the most adaptable, least jealous of the water signs. If your absences were prolonged at work they would just drift off into their daydreams. What you might have to watch is that both of you are slightly addictive by nature. That could get out of hand. You would need to

soften to make a good match of it. They could teach you in quiet ways to appreciate your feelings.

Your Moon Is In Aquarius
An air sign you think first, analyze your feelings next and then most often forget them. Emotional involvements make you nervous and you would much prefer to be one of a crowd of friends. You can be rebellious, idiosyncratic and downright eccentric at times, often just to make a point. Your sense of humour is always to hand and startling companions is one of your hobbies. Underneath your bravado, however, lurks a sense of insecurity about one to one relationships. Your connection to your feelings and your body can be lacking so you become too impersonal and detached. Sensuality is difficult for you. You need warm mates who do not cling too hard.

Your Aquarius Moon To Their Aries Moon
The wit will sparkle, the jokes be raw and fast, no punches pulled, no offence taken. Both of you are verbally robust and not overly sensitive about your feelings. But that could be a problem long term since you do not know what to do when life's stormy passages push you into your depths. You do live too high, too recklessly both of you and could burn out fast or in time just drift apart since neither of you will be fenced in. They do like to dominate which you will just ignore. You'll need an anchor from a solid Sun.

Your Aquarius Moon To Their Taurus Moon
Two hugely stubborn, entirely opposite personalities, you neither want the same things emotionally nor will you give way even marginally to suit the other. You want freedom, change, excitement and space. They want security, no change, a solid rooted existence with them firmly in control. Their possessiveness though often hidden behind a lazy smile would unnerve you. They certainly would provide you with all the comforts but you are less concerned with cuddles, indulgences and the like than most. You would feel suffocated by their very physical approach, fenced in by their need to be together, especially sexually. Both of you need to soften down slightly to hold this together.

Your Aquarius Moon To Their Gemini Moon
Bright, breezy, fast moving and highly talkative together, you would think life and love was made for you at the beginning. But you have more an intellectual contact than anything else. You fear close involvement and they rarely stand still. Their mood changes like the wind and what you agreed yesterday would be out of the window today. The amusement factor is high but the durability factor doubtful. When the going got tough both of you would be off like a shot. Neither of you is connected well enough to your body or your feelings. There is not enough to nourish the relationship long term or recharge its batteries so you'll need Sun input here.

Your Aquarius Moon To Their Cancer Moon
Hmm, tricky. You are scared of being trapped. They are crab-like in their attempts to hang onto mates for security and comfort. Certainly in time they will not want a totally exclusive relationship. You will be added in as just one more of the family but their jealousy will always be a problem. You basically distrust emotions and being a water Moon they have undercurrents which make your hair stand on end. You do not understand what makes them tick because they are not sensible thinking creatures like yourself. They feel! They will find you too detached, cool and evasive. More harmonious Suns will be needed to keep this flowing along.

Your Aquarius Moon To Their Leo Moon
Opposites do not necessarily attract. You are a slightly eccentric soul who loves to waken up parties with a shock or a bizarre happening. Apart from the fact that they loathe embarrassing exhibitions they also want all the admiration and attention going. They can be rather uppity and arrogant while you are gloriously un snobbish, highly tolerant and fond of the world's oddballs. Your friends would be very different.   Being an air and fire mix also you do lack a certain practical, grounding quality to the relationship and there is not enough feeling. You are not inherently suited but it you do get together watch for burn out.

Your Aquarius Moon To Their Virgo Moon
This could just work though it would be cool. They can be highly self sufficient, rather intact people so would not mind your tendency to wander off. They are more reclusive than you and might not appreciate all the friends you drag into their quiet space but they will provide you with a well run home life. They can be naggers and great critics and being a rather traditional type will not always appreciate your hippy attitudes. With helpful Sun matches it could amble along though not with great joy.

Your Aquarius Moon To Their Libra Moon
Two air Moons together can be too cool, too detached and rather up-in-the-head. On top of that you are quite different personalities. They are rather well bred, slightly snobbish, highly sensitive to other people's opinion. Where you are wild, way out, quite eccentric and do not give a toss about approval. Indeed you will positively seek to embarrass or startle others as a way of making them sit up. Certainly they are not jealous or possessive and would not seek to corral you. But they would try to turn you into a proper person which you would resist strenuously. Still it has its upside.

Your Aquarius Moon To Their Scorpio Moon
You will have a job making this work since you run a mile from the experiences they regard as essential. They want to plunge into the depths of intense, turbulent feelings, to intertwine passionately with a soul mate . Your hackles rise at the very thought. You are wary of close one-to-one commitment and would insist on bringing a few friends along to ease the atmosphere. They are secretive where you are open. They are jealous where you are tolerant. They want exclusive rights where you like open relationships. Sex would become an abyss as you fight to stay out of your body and they want to drag you firmly into it.

Your Aquarius Moon To Their Sagittarius Moon
No shortage of excitement here or instant fireworks. You both love thrills, spills and adventure. Neither of you appreciate tight, exclusive relationships but there is a

possibility that fairly soon you could drift apart as you pursue your separate interests. There might not be enough emotional or physical contact to keep the relationship fed, watered and nourished. Both of you live up in your heads, your ideas and your theories but it really is not enough. Certainly both of you can stand each other's savagely direct jokes. If it ends you will stay pals for ever. What you need a more sensible Suns.

Your Aquarius Moon To Their Capricorn Moon
Cool, maybe even workmanlike but is it what you want? They work like maniacs, longer hours than anyone you have ever seen which certainly would not make you feel trapped or fenced in. But what is there to hold you together? You are whacky while they are traditionalist. They like to fit in while you insist on being eccentric just to stand out. Their rather saturnine judgemental streak would exasperate you. Your friends would never mix. Yours are oddballs and hippies. Theirs are leaders in the community. Both of you need to be more middle of the road.

Your Aquarius Moon To Their Aquarius Moon
You can talk for several years non stop together with sparks flying and a high level of interest. But passion? Less likely. You are both so laid back you are practically computers and together you will devise theories that make sex obsolete. You will probably co author a book about it. Certainly neither of you like being fenced in and neither of you are jealous so that seems to work. But you need a mate who can warm you a little without making you feel overwhelmed, who can bring you just a touch more into your body.

Your Aquarius Moon To Their Pisces Moon
Not ideal on the face of it but this pairing can work, just. They are deeply sensitive, caring souls who will make sure you have every comfort. But they are not so emotional that they will make you feel trapped. If ignored, which they may feel as you zip off, they will just disappear into their daydreams. Both of you have a way of making partners feel they are not being exclusively related to which suits both of you. You will feel too cool and laid back to them at times so

you need to warm up. They will teach you gently to be more caring. Watch your shock tactics. That will unsettle them and make them withdraw in a hurry.

Your Moon In Pisces

A water Moon, you are deeply sensitive and often hesitate to speak your feelings in case you are rejected. Romantic opportunities often slide by as your timidity prevents you making a play. If you do find a protected space you are one of the world's beautiful people, calm, giving, caring and sympathetic. Taking on board the world's suffering sometimes brings you down but giving to others feels like your role in life. Sometimes you feel martyred and self pitying because your efforts are taken for granted. Then you escape into your daydreams, fantasies and often addictions as a way of escaping from a reality which feels too harsh for you.

Your Pisces Moon To Their Aries Moon

Will you ever venture out of your oyster shell with them crashing around, causing waves, voicing opinions so direct they go straight through your thin skin? No doubt they could give you more courage, sparkle and dynamism but you are great opposites. Your timid sensitivity in matters of home and heart really is not well suited to their rather inconsiderate way of behaving. You like peace apart from anything else while they live in a constant battlefield. You would never feel protected since they change so frequently you reckon they can never be relied on.

Your Pisces Moon To Their Taurus Moon

A good match this since both of you like security though for different reasons. You waft around in the breeze and never feel strong enough for the harsher realities of life. They will provide you with a comfortable emotional base and a sense of protection. Your adaptable nature will fit in with what they want. They are stubborn and not good about tolerating anyone else's needs but you are self sacrificing so that will hardly matter. Sex could be a problem since you can be fairly platonic while they like constant physical reassurance.

Your Pisces Moon To The Gemini Moon

You are a restless, flyaway pair who are not essentially on the same wavelength but it could work. They are chatty, changeable and never stand still, often come across as cool, rather unemotional. You are equally changeable but can get your emotional sustenance from daydreams so will not always notice if they are absent in body or in spirit. You will be fairly indecisive together and rather impractical at home which could be a problem. But the very fact that neither of you is stubborn and neither of you is really happy with a madly committed intimate relationship gives it hope.

Your Pisces Moon To Their Cancer Moon

This is blissful. Your emotional sensitivities match wonderfully well. You will feel safe enough to really open up and express your most tender feelings. They will give you a protective shell, a happy home base and settled family life. They are jealous but you probably will see that as positive because it means you will not be rejected. You can care for them, quite intuitively knowing what they need, which will make them happy. They are more decisive and energetic than you but you have a flexibility they lack.

Your Pisces Moon To Their Leo Moon

Self sacrificing, sensitive and adaptable as you are, you could be reasonably good at coping with their constant demands, stubborness and touchy pride. In return you would get an extravagant lifestyle, flamboyant parties and friends, and a lesson in how to be more outgoing and confident. They will warm your heart because they are so vibrant. You can cope with being ignored at times because you feed yourself on your daydreams though at the end of the day you need to ask yourself why you are settling for less than you want. Neither of you is practical.

Your Pisces Moon To Their Virgo Moon

This could click. Both of you are sensitive and unlikely to tramp on the other's vulnerable spots. They are more practical and can help to organise a smoothly run home, healthy eating habits and bring order to your chaos. They will worry endlessly, as you do, which is not helpful, and nag constantly which you will ignore as you disappear into your daydreams. Both of you are flexible, not especially jealous and rather restless so anger will not stay in the air for long.

Your Pisces Moon To Their Libra Moon
Could be cool but could be workable. You both share rather aesthetic, elegant tastes in clothes and home decor. Both want a life full of peace, harmony and no arguments. Neither of you is hugely physical so you will not feel too weighed down by their demands. They want a relationship but nothing too overwhelming since they are an air sign. You might at times find them unemotional, too cool and detached. But the pluses undoubtedly outweigh the minuses. They are quite snobbish, adore throwing parties full of upmarket people so you will be drawn out of your shell.

Your Pisces Moon To Their Scorpio Moon
You have to be robust to cope with this but the rewards could be high. Two water Moons together make for a highly intense emotional scenario. They adore being plunged into the turbulence of their deepest feelings which you understand though you are a more timid creature. They are fairly preoccupied with sex which on the whole you are not. But you have an intuitive understanding of each other which helps. Being the stronger, they will offer you protection which you need and a solid base in life. They may object as you disappear into your daydreams since they want on going exclusive one-to-one commitment. You may appear evasive to them.

Your Pisces Moon To Their Sagittarian Moon
Restless, flexible and always on the go, you are basically different types but it does sometimes hold together. They are fiery, sometimes brash, want freedom, hate being fenced in and are stimulating conversationalists. You are sensitive, timid, emotional, sympathetic and self sacrificing. Their directness may wound your sensitivities at times but curiously for a water Moon you do not mind if you do not have a totally exclusive relationship. You are never totally

satisfied with real human beings and often disappear into daydreams for emotional nourishment so you might not mind their absences. Neither of you is hugely jealous and you are very good at putting yourself out for others.

Your Pisces Moon To Their Capricorn Moon

This can be a cool, workmanlike, compromise which offers much of what you need. They are practical, energetic and decisive which helps prop up the chaos in your life. They sadly always think they are unworthy of love unless they earn it by achievements so they spend long hours at the office. You will help gently to give them more self esteem but not mind being left to your daydreams most of the time. As an earth sign they do have a sensual, indulgent side which is sometimes kept repressed since ambitions always come first. You are never too happy about too physical a relationship but you should not be overtaxed here.

Your Pisces Moon To Their Aquarius Moon

This does not sound custom built for an ideal match but oddly it can since neither of you mind having space. They are wary of intense one-to-one commitments and will always invite six friends along to ease the atmosphere. You can be quite happy to disappear into your fantasy world and have your own problems about coming down to earth to form a real live relationship. Dreams and the movies always provide much nicer mates! You can gently bring more feeling into their lives since they are very abrasive and airy, up in their heads. They think, they do not feel. They will give you more detachment on emotions, teach you to stand back a bit. They will at times be too sharp, or too honest which will hurt.

Your Pisces Moon To Their Pisces Moon

You are two deeply sensitive, indecisive souls who could offer each other much in the way of empathy but is not really a great idea when it comes to coping with the world. If you ever got together in the first place that is, which is questionable since both of you are so terrified of rejection that you hardly dare voice your feelings. Neither of you is practical, indeed you tend to live in a certain amount of chaos, which would be doubled. Highly impressionable you would both be swept around by the slightest stimulus both from outside the relationship and within. Both of you need an anchor and more solid Suns would definitely help.

Chapter Five

SUN TO MOON - YIN AND YANG

The sun sign (your birthday sign) is the essence of your personality, who you really are, your identity. It dictates career, talents - what you do and how you do it in the outside world. That is the masculine side of your personality, the inheritance from your father. Your feminine side comes from your Moon sign - it tells you what nourishes you, comforts you and makes you purr contentedly in your emotional life. That is the inheritance from your mother. In short hand your Sun sign tells you what you ought to do, what your responsibilities are, what your aims in life are about. Your Moon on the other hand is about what you want emotionally. Ideally in a perfect match your Moon sign should be in your mate's sun sign.

If your Moon is nourished by what kind of a personality your mate is, how they live their lives, not emotionally, but in reality at work, with friends, in their interests, then you have a really strong connection which gives you a foundation for a good relationship. If your Moon is not made comfortable by the essential being of your lover then you may adore them in bed, appreciate their goulash but you will not respect their talents, their career ambitions and their way of handling responsibility.

A partner with a compatible Moon will support their mate in everything they want to do in the outside world. An out of sync Moon will be continually undermining their lover by suggesting they need to be other than they are just to suit the needs of the Moon. The desires of one half need to match the sense of duty or ambition in the other for life to run smoothly and successfully.

Your Aries Moon To Their Aries Sun
Brilliant. You feel good about them being active, courageous, slightly foolhardy but glamorously reckless as you see it. It bothers you not at all that they are brash, abrasive, firecrackers. The truth is you cannot be happy without a life of adventure. You love their competitive streak and hard drive to win all the time. Others may wince at their lack of social niceties when it comes to getting their own way. You

praise it.

Your Aries Moon To Their Taurus Sun
Teeth achingly irritating. You cannot envisage how anyone can be that slow, that rooted, that security conscious and so unchanging! You want a fireball of a lover/mate who will make you glow with pride at their high flying exploits. Respecting someone who will happily work for results in ten years time is not the same. You are nourished by crazy schemes, wild gambles whereas they take pride in being practical. You would constantly be narking at them for being clodhoppers and dunderheads (quite unfairly). You just need different things. If you can relish difference then you might just do OK.

Your Aries Moon To Their Gemini Sun
You feel happiest around partners who move non-stop and there is none more fidgety than this short of an Aries. Your mate probably does three jobs on the trot, talks endlessly and wittily, thinks up magic schemes at the drop of a hat and is never to be found where they were yesterday. Boredom is not a problem. You do not even mind the way they have been known to take shortcuts at work. You adore opportunists.

Your Aries Moon To Their Cancer Sun
Surprisingly you do appreciate their initiative, their creative talents, their career drive and their flair. Cancer are not just stay-at-home and read the recipe book types. They are go getters in the world. You will not always understand their motivations or ways of handling inter personal relationships at work because they are emotionally moody. And your moods will not be in sync a lot of the time - when they want to work, you want to make love. When they are smoochy, you will be ready to rave. Not ideal but it could be worse.

Your Aries Moon To Their Leo Sun
You adore their flamboyant way of attacking the world, their talent for entertaining others, for getting positions of authority where they attract attention and admiration.

Though supporting their fragile egos when dented by unappreciative bosses or adverse criticism from workmates will not come easily to you. You like competitive people whereas Leo likes being on the winners' podium but does not necessarily see why they should go through the hassle of getting there. You will not respect their insecurity. They will not take kindly to your hard hitting opinions. If both of you can mellow it could be great.

Your Aries Moon To Their Virgo Sun
This is sticky. What you feel comfortable around is constant movement, excitement and challenge, and people who are hard driving go getters. Virgo is too neat, precise and self effacing to keep you happy. You would not see the point in their constant worrying and nit picking because you do not see the point of a meticulous job well done. You need an adventurer, a competitor, a winner.

Your Aries Moon To Their Libra Sun
Not a hopeful match since you appreciate a lively, combative mate while Libra is always trying to calm ruffled feathers. They are resourceful and energetic at work but their indecisiveness would drive you spare since they rarely make up their minds in less than a week. You do it in half a second. Male Libras are soft, sweet creatures whom you would secretly despair of because they do not have your courage. Lady Libras are clear cut, more masculine, certainly more argumentative but they can fuss too much about doing the socially acceptable thing for your liking.

Your Aries Moon To Their Scorpio Sun
If ambition makes you purr which it does then Scorpio should suit your book though they have a very different approach to your hash, crash and bash version. You have immense respect for their way of making miracles happen, of doing the impossible. You do not understand one smidgen about them and rather distrust what you fear are manipulative qualities hidden inside them
(you are right). At the end of the day they care less about winning the race than getting the upper hand, and wielding the power.

Your Sun to their Moon

Your Aries Moon To Their Sagittarius Sun
Their devil-may-care, reckless, optimistic approach to life suits you down to the ground. They are full of hope, vision and dreams of grand schemes to come. They never stand still so you will hardly be bored. They will not even notice when you call a spade a spade, because if anything their tongue is rougher than yours. They will certainly not feel fenced in because you will give them a long rein. All this presupposes a feckless Sagittarius. There are deeply intellectual, rather narrow minded ones who will deeply disapprove of you. Pick the right sort and you can't lose.

Your Aries Moon To Their Capricorn Sun
You appreciate their ambition, their will to win, their initiative. At times you do not entirely support their need to be always moving up in the world for class conscious reasons. Though since you like winners that is hardly a huge problem. You may find them a touch serious, self doubting and downright gloomy for your tastes and inclined to settle into fairly slow moving professions. They scale the peaks but with long term goals in mind. You only ever see three days ahead. Your moods could be constantly out of sync.

Your Aries Moon To Their Aquarius Moon
You do not mind their eccentricity, strongly independent streak nor even their need to take constant risks at work. But you may needle them occasionally because you are more competitive than them. You like winners. They want to be one of the crowd. They will provide you with excitement, good conversation and not too much in the way of restriction. You certainly will not possess them.

Your Aries Moon To Their Pisces Sun
This one needs handled with delicacy. You appreciate brave warriors who confront the world, who make it happen by force if necessary, who are adventurers and heroes. Pisces is a vague, sometimes timid creature who can certainly be highly successful but you just cannot see how they do it. They would slither away from you, disappear in a puff of smoke, if you tried to argue with them which is one of life's pleasures for you.

Your Taurus Moon To Their Aries Sun
Not a happy match since everything you not only appreciate but absolutely need they make great strides to avoid. They are fast moving, constantly changing, adventurers. Whereas you want a mate who will offer you security, comfort and constant cuddles. You would frequently point out the practical flaws in their schemes, missing the grand vision hidden in them. You would threaten to put their flame out. It'll need an extra input to even this one out.

Your Taurus Moon To Their Taurus Sun
What a dream. You would cuddle and smooch endlessly, live a life of unchanging comforts and probably grow a wonderful garden together for 45 years. You respect their practical skills and way of completing long term projects. They are no short distance sprinters but you do not mind. You can wait for results. Both of you appreciate the same luxuries which means you never have to argue or give way to the other.

Your Taurus Moon To Their Gemini Sun
Everything you appreciate, respect, admire and need is singularly lacking here. They are butterflies where you want an oxen. They are restless, short distance enthusiasts whereas you need a marathon runner who can pace their lives steadily with the long term in view. They react with horror to the unchangingess of your lifestyle, to your possessiveness and your sheer earthy solidity. They need speed, you need security. You'll need a matching Moon to keep this on an even keel.

Your Taurus Moon To Their Cancer Sun
A happy pairing since you like security, a rooted existence and all the home comforts while they adore a harmonious family life. You admire even if you do not quite understand their initiative, drive and resourcefulness out in the world and their creative flair. You can sometimes undermine them by pointing out the practical flaws in their schemes thereby killing the flame of inspiration. But on the whole you are good together.

Your Taurus Moon To Their Leo Sun
Their extravagant lifestyle to some extent feeds your needs for comfort. You certainly like eating, drinking and dressing well. But you do not understand their over obvious need for attention and their willingness to settle for a position in the world that gives a shiny outside appearance but may be fairly hollow inside. You certainly do not respect their unrealistic, impractical wish to be grand without putting in the necessary legwork to earn it. They need someone who would prop up their fragile ego better. If you have a Fire Sun it will definitely help.

Your Taurus Moon To Their Virgo Sun
Adorable. You love their way of working conscientiously, especially when the rewards come home to you. They slave self sacrificingly to be of service, are meticulous, practical and usually to the point. You are lazier than them so may not always support their need to go sixteen times over every tiny detail. They appreciate your efforts to provide comfort at the end of a long hard day.

Your Taurus Moon To Their Libra Sun
You are different energies but you do appreciate their initiative, flair, drive and ambition. You do not even mind their indecisiveness since you can be quite slow to make up your own mind. Their way of working to provide an elegantly tasteful home and indulgent lifestyle suits you down to the ground. Where it could come unstuck is in their need to be spacey, not physically intimate and their rather superior view of your more earthy habits.

Your Taurus Moon To Their Scorpio Sun
Your moods would not exactly be in sync - you want to cuddle, they want to plot a conspiracy. They want a deeply passionate encounter just when you want to trim the hedge. But you do have an appreciation for their incredible determination, drive and staying power. Their secrecy would worry you but on the other hand you are not invasive and are usually happy to leave them to do their thing. Both of you like a settled life style.

Your Taurus Moon To Their Sagittarian Sun
Unless you have a fiery sun this will never work. You only purr with a contented, rooted life full of home comforts, cuddles and reliable mates with pension schemes. These are great talkers, wonderfully inspirational but really fairly impractical at heart. You would constantly be pointing out the flaws in their schemes, calling them unrealistic, crushing their inspiration. They would fly away from your possessiveness.

Your Taurus Moon To Their Capricorn Sun
Happy as bunnies down a burrow this works well with one proviso. You admire their earthy initiative, practical ambitions and way of setting long term goals. You are equally a long distance runner though lazier at heart. What could be a problem is their over serious, rather judgemental approach to life which will keep them away from your cuddles too much and cause them to frown on your indulgences.

Your Taurus Moon To Their Aquarius Sun
This could be a constant seesaw or tug of war. Certainly you appreciate their ability to stand solid in the face of change but they are eccentric, oddball creatures where you are basically traditionalist at heart. They like to roam, to think, to talk endlessly and mull over madcap schemes. You would not understand their interests which are ultra modern, usually high tech. Your earthiness would eventually threaten to suffocate them. If you have an Air or even a Fire Sun it will help.

Your Taurus Moon To Their Pisces Sun
You might suit them better than they suit you but you could complement each other not badly. You would never understand their vague, unpractical way of floundering through work though they do seem to come up trumps more often than not. You would offer them a solid home base and all the physical comforts, though perhaps with a touch too much contact. You need to understand that they have the vision you lack slightly. So appreciate their creative flair and you could help them to turn it into reality.

Your Gemini Moon To Their Aries Sun

You are more weighed down by boredom, lack of excitement and routine than anything else in the world so they should suit you admirably. Their lives are a constant run of thrills, spills, adventures and noisy arguments. They have drive, ambition and real killer competitive instincts for which you have a sneaking admiration though you lack the edge yourself. They will adore your witty chat.

Your Gemini Moon To Their Taurus Sun

You will have to stretch your ingenuity to see how to admire such a slow, placid, earthy creature. They think long term, while you cannot think beyond the moment. You adore a constantly changing kaleidoscope of a life while they like it always the same. You would always be pouring scorn on their very solid virtues and talents while they would make you feel fenced in, weighed down and possessed. It will be a plus if you have an earth Sun.

Your Gemini Moon To Their Gemini Sun

Wonderfully compatible. You admire their ability to hold down three jobs at once, keep up a witty flow of chat, maintain a wide circle of intriguing friends and have so many different interests. You need a versatile mate and this is it. You even have a sneaking admiration for their way of cutting corners and being opportunistic. You will never stop talking together.

Your Gemini Moon To Their Cancer Sun

You certainly appreciate their way of making it in the world, with initiative, drive, creative flair and energy even if you do not totally understand their methods. They have an emotional approach to work as well as home life and can be moody which does not sit well with you. They will also make you feel fenced in. Their sense of security demands that they keep you close. If you have a Water Sun it will definitely help.

Your Gemini Moon To Their Leo Sun

You adore their flamboyance and all the excitement that goes with it though you do not entirely understand their demanding need for constant attention. They may find your restless way of flitting around rather irksome. Your boredom threshold is much lower than theirs which could cause friction. You are much less snobbish and could be guilty at times of cutting them down to size which would not appeal to them.

Your Gemini Moon To Their Virgo Sun

Your moods would often be out of tune but you both share a basic fidgetiness which could draw you together. Neither of you likes boredom or standing still too long. You do not quite understand their conscientious need to double check all work sixteen times or to be quite as helpful. But they are not jealous and would not make you feel trapped. You would never be short of conversation together.

Your Gemini Moon To Their Libra Sun

You might envy their upwardly mobile ambitions in society but you do not share them and you certainly would worry about their delicately balanced sensibilities. You like slightly more robust types. But you do appreciate their initiative, drive, determination and ambition. They would not always take to your way of shocking others with your wonderfully direct opinions which sometimes rock the boat.

Your Gemini Moon To Their Scorpio Sun

You are wary of their constant attempts to possess and control you but you have a sneaking admiration for their way of driving hard for success, cutting corners if need be, and pulling the right strings to make their miracles work. You quite like a walk on the wild side and will happily supply them with ideas for their job, knowing full well that your enthusiasm span is too short for you to make them work. But you are different energies.

Your Gemini Moon To Their Sagittarian Sun

You share similar outlooks in life, wide ranging interests and you adore their constant up-beat enthusiasm for almost everything they are involved in. Your moods would not always be in tune since you are opposite signs in the zodiac. When you wanted to be together, they would want to work. When you wanted to have a stimulating chat they could be full of fiery passion. Neither of you is possessive. This could match well enough.

Your Gemini Moon To Their Capricorn Sun

You appreciate their drive, ambition, determination and resourcefulness though you think them a mite too serious, too conscientious. You would not object when they exhibited a ruthless to get to where they want since you have been known to cut corners yourself. They suit half of your needs but do not quite fulfil the bright, reckless, fun loving half of you. They might think you shallow and unreliable but you would certainly make them think more clearly.

Your Gemini Moon To Their Aquarius Sun

Just what you want - someone as flighty, chatty and devil-may-care as yourself. You would back them up to the hilt in their madcap schemes, ultra modern ideas and would never feel hemmed in because they are as spacey as you. You would wonder slightly at their staying power since they are more fixed than you but their range of interests is so wide that you would never become bored. They would appreciate your bright, inventive ideas.

Your Gemini Moon To Their Pisces Sun

You will be permanently perplexed at the way their minds work even although they are as adaptable as you. They never seem to think matters through. They intuit and float their way through life. Both of you are off the ground though in different ways. They would probably not satisfy your need for constant intellectual stimulation and you might feel a little cool and cutting to their sensitivities. But it is a better mix than some.

Your Cancer Moon To Their Aries Sun

You have a distant admiration for their flair, drive and ambition in the outside world but you are not remotely nourished by their ruthless way of trampling over the competition and your more tender feelings. They create noise and unrest which makes your head ache and your insecurities soar. You would make them feel trapped with your jealousy and swamped with the depths of your feelings unless they have a water moon as well.

Your Cancer Moon To Their Taurus Sun

You feel secured, contented and relaxed by their solid earthiness, their way of providing them and yourself with the worldly comforts, especially a settled home base. You will not always appreciate their obstinacy and slow, rather lazy pace of attacking work problems. You really want a mate with more drive and initiative. Neither of you minds the others' jealousy. It can be good this one.

Your Cancer Moon To Their Gemini Sun

Not a truly wonderful pairing since you like the wrap round factor and they want total freedom. You do admire mates who have ambition, resourcefulness and determination which they certainly have. They are restless, jack of all trades but they won't always make you feel really secure. Your possessiveness and emotional intensity would make them nervy. You need a mate with creative flair not just intellectual ingenuity. It would help if they had a water Moon as well.

Your Cancer Moon To Their Cancer Sun

Happy as two crabs together by the seashore you fit each other like hand and glove. You appreciate their creative flair, drive, ambition and initiative out in the world which is all directed towards setting up a settled home base. They will appreciate your tender love, care and support at the end of a hard day. You understand each other's moodiness and hyper sensitivities to criticism. You will soothe each other.

Your Cancer Moon To Their Leo Sun

You adore their flamboyant, extravagant lifestyle, their upmarket friends and their position in society, and their desire to settle with a family. So far so good. Though you do not understand why they have to be quite so grand or so pretentious. Their way of grabbing all the attention will not make you feel loved and wanted and at times they will not really understand your needs. But it can work with a little mellowing on both sides

Your Cancer Moon To Their Virgo Sun

You admire their quiet, refined, conscientious, practical way of going about their career. They never let anyone down or cut corners. You may not quite understand why they have to be so pernickety about details but at least you will never feel insecure. Their self sufficiency may at times make you feel cut out but they are warm, self sacrificing and keen to be of service. Eating with them will be a shared pleasure.

Your Cancer Moon To Their Libra Sun

Your moods may be out of sync and they will at times seem cool, detached and too unemotional but you are nourished by many things they also crave. Both of you like a good home life. You bring comfort and love. They bring, taste, elegance and harmony. You do admire their initiative, ambition and energy out in the world. They make things happen without creating too many waves. They certainly need a mate in life though not a possessive one.

Your Cancer Moon To Their Scorpio Sun

You are nourished to some extent by all their emotional intensity, courage, determination and deep, dark ambition. But you are wary of their stinging remarks which can wound you to the quick. Although this is a highly emotional connection you will never totally understand what goes on in their hidden depths and the sulks in your relationship could be long and brooding. But it can work for the long term with understanding on both sides.

Your Cancer Moon To Their Sagittarian Sun

You want a lover with initiative , ambition and a self starting mechanism. They are certainly fire flies but tend to race around agitatedly with their head in the clouds rather than focus on the central goal. They will also resent being forced to be practical or hand money over to set up home. You will make them feel fenced in and rather swamped by your feelings which they will not understand. Their blunt opinions will have you in the vapours. You'll need Fire in your chart to help this along.

Your Cancer Moon To Their Capricorn Sun

You certainly appreciate their ambition, determination and initiative and very much respect their conscientiousness. Both of you like upwardly mobile friends, are traditionalists at heart and like the grand lifestyle. But you need a mate who comes home occasionally, not one who works a 90 hour week. You always want sensitive handling because you are so emotional where they can be cool, not always sensitive when it comes to getting their own way.

Your Cancer Moon To Their Aquarius Sun

Ooh, this could throw up a few scratchy moments. You approach life in totally different ways. You admire traditional values while they are unreconstructed hippies, boffins or at least state-of-the-art merchants. They adore being eccentric, standing out as individuals at all costs, which will make you wince with embarrassment. You clutch and cling which will make then flee. Life to you is about relationship. An enjoyable life to them is avoiding too much intimacy. It would need a good deal of support from Suns and other planets to help this along.

Your Cancer Moon To Their Pisces

An adorable mix though you may slightly object to their rather vague way of proceeding in the world. But you admire their creativity, their intuition which is often inspired and their sensitive way of handling work relationships as well as you. You can help them find more ambition and drive without frightening them. With the happy home base you provide they will have more courage.

Your Leo Moon To Their Aries Sun

A rather roller coaster combination this. You certainly admire their fiery drive in the world, their competitive, adventurous spirit and if their need to win makes them successful, their ability to provide you with a sumptious lifestyle. But what nourishes you most is being centre of attention and being allowed to take the credit for all the successes going. They are not going to tread delicately round your fragile ego and your vanity. They are certainly not going to meekly hand over the winners 'rosette to you.

Your Leo Moon To Their Taurus Sun
On the upside you do appreciate their tenacity, their staying power and their practical skills which you almost totally lack. But you are both stubborn and dislike giving way. They can also be rather basic and earthy which does not suit your need for grandness. You would much prefer a mate who was a high flying person of some social standing. Taurus could not care less about appearances. They would point out your unrealistic streak and your arrogance. If you can overcome the hurdles and find flexibility and tolerance it has a good deal going for it.

Your Leo Moon To Their Gemini Sun
You certainly appreciate their versatile talents and way of making a success in life which are real plus points. Though you do not always adore their way of cutting corners. At times you fear they could cause you minor humiliation because they do not care about social respectability which you do deeply. They can dent your pride by being too blunt at times and maybe even by wandering off. Rejection makes you crumple. If they are soft Geminis it could work since oth of you like socialising and having a wide circle of friends.

Your Leo Moon To Their Cancer Sun
They have the drive, initiative, creative flair and resourcefulness in their career which you adore. They also mix in rather up market circles which suits you down to the ground. You will not understand their moodiness or rather emotional way of approaching work problems. They will not understand your need for constant exclusive attention. They quite like to be noticed as well.

Your Leo Moon To Their Leo Sun
At one level works brilliantly, since their flamboyance and love of a five star lifestyle will make you feel comforted and pampered. But it could prove very expensive and not the most practical of combinations unless you have other earthy planets to weight both of you down. There could also be a tiny clash of egos, since both of you adore the spotlight. But at best it will be a loyal, long term connection.

Your Leo Moon To Their Virgo Sun
They are not nearly grand enough, or flamboyant enough at work for you to really appreciate their meticulous talents. But on the other hand they will not be grabbing the spotlight from you and will sort out the tedious, practical details of your life. Their adaptability and willingness to be of service will turn them into a willing slave but at the end of the day you are highly different energies.

Your Leo Moon To Their Libra Sun
Wonderfully compatible mix. You love their resourceful, energetic, ambitious way in the world which still manages to be graceful and well bred. They are good at adapting to the needs of others and will put themselves out considerably for you. Both of you love a grand lifestyle, good taste, and snobbish friends. They will happily allow you to be centre of attention and their diplomatic, peace loving side will mean they never dent your vanity.

Your Leo Moon To Their Scorpio Sun
This could be tricky. You will certainly appreciate their staying power, stamina and hard driving ambition. But you cannot understand their overwhelming need for power, their secrecy or their need to manipulate. They could not care less whether they get attention or not (which you do) as long as they hold the whip hand. Their stinging tongue will reduce your fragile ego to a deflated balloon at times. Both of you are stubborn so both need to mellow and be more tolerant for this to work well.

Your Leo Moon To Their Sagittarius Sun
You applaud their courage, their way of following their fantasies and their idealistic aspirations. You even forgive them for their unrealistic ideas which are not always grounded in common sense. But you will wince at their sharp opinions which do not always take into account your tender ego. You hate criticism. They never stop to think of the effect of what they say. But they will adapt to your determined way of operating and give your life an added sparkle.

Your Leo Sun To Their Capricorn Sun

You find their ambitions to rise to the top of the pile admirable in the extreme. Both of you are traditionalist, rather snobbish, and always mix in the best circles. Your need for attention may cause you to complain when they spend long hours at the office so it can be a cooler combination than you might like. But you cannot have it all ways. They may complain about your extravagances since they have been known to be stingy.

Your Leo Moon To Their Aquarius Sun

You are polar opposites so you'll need to make an effort to bridge the gap. You cannot envisage how anyone could have such oddball ideas about work. You respect power, prestige, status and a glowing reputation. They thrive on humanitarian ideas, madcap schemes which would make you feel the laughing stock of the neighbourhood. Both of you are stubborn and would not give way. They would scorn your extravagances and deride your need to be so grand. Maybe you could learn from each other which might help.

Your Leo Moon To Their Pisces Moon

You will support them to the hilt if they are successful. They are superbly intuitive and can sometimes turn their dreams into reality. But if they are a vague, wispy, timid, non triers you are not the one to support their tentative efforts. They certainly will not be able to provide you with the lifestyle you need. Certainly they are elegant, sympathetic, kind creatures who will adapt to your needs except that you do need a regal mate of position in the world who can reflect well on you. If they have a Fire sparkle elsewhere in their chart it will definitely help.

Your Virgo Moon To Their Aries Sun

You respect hard workers, with practical common sense who are conscientious and helpful. So this could be tricky. You have picked a reckless adventurer who certainly can be successful but they never seem to take time to think let alone plan, have been known to push the competition ruthlessly aside and take great pleasure in winning. Their ego centredness makes you wince though you could do with more of it yourself. You would nag them endlessly. They would never be there when you needed them. Only if you can each take a little of the other's virtues will this work well.

Your Virgo Moon To Their Taurus Sun
All that earthy strength, solidity and common sense makes you purr. You envy their staying power which you lack though at times you may find them a touch ponderous and lazy. You adapt where they are obstinate. They have an honesty and straightforwardness which you find highly appealing and they never do anything which does not have a practical outcome. They smile amiably at your narking, are slow to rouse to irritation. You may find it difficult to get new projects rolling together but basically it is a great combination.

Your Virgo Moon To Their Gemini Sun
You light up at their quick wits, bright flow of ideas, snappy way with words and their non stop ability to keep three jobs on the go at once. What you are less chirpy about is their way of cutting corners sometimes at work, their impracticality and their short lived enthusiasms. You are fidgety but they can seem like a jack of all trades which is not your style. They do not understand your obsessive need for order. It could work well and you'll never be short of conversation that's for sure.

Your Virgo Moon To Their Cancer Sun
You appreciate their resourcefulness, initiative, creative flair and drive out in the world. They are not just home loving recluses. Their moodiness and emotional way of approaching problems is, however, not yours and can cause you to carp a little especially when they fall foul of workmates. You think they brew up storms that are unnecessary. Your narking does not go down well since they are deeply sensitive creatures. If you can stop worrying and they can less moody then it could work exceptionally well.

Your Virgo Moon To Their Leo Sun

You look with awe and wonder at their ability to grab all the spotlight for themselves which you would never do, their tendency to grab the credit even when they have not earned it. You basically do not respect what drives them on, their need for status and importance. What is important to you is a job well done which helps others. They will hate your nit picking and carping. Certainly you can be adaptable where they are stubborn, and self sacrificing so it can be made to work. But you need to worry less and demand more.

Your Virgo Moon To Their Virgo Sun
Ideal. You settle down, forget about nagging and worrying endlessly because you know they will do a job you can respect. They probably work too hard which means you see them less than you like but that is better than having a lazy, unemployed lump who hangs round your neck all day. Together you will pin every last tiny detail down and never have the paperwork out of place. The tension levels could sometimes rise a little and you might be indecisive together.

Your Virgo Moon To Their Libra Sun
You do like their elegant yet resourceful way of pushing their ambitions in the world. They may not always be as practical as you would like but they are hard working, fair minded and generally try to keep the peace. They will appreciate your helpful comments about detail though not being nagged because it ruffles their calm. They love your ability to keep order at home which makes them feel that life is in balance.

Your Virgo Moon To Their Scorpio Sun
You could have problems unless you are a Sun Scorpio since you not understand their driving need for power, their way of manipulating which never seems to you quite straight, or their in built secrecy. You respect hard working conscientious types who do a job well for its own sake and try to serve others fairly. They would scorn what they regarded as your obsessive principles. You certainly would adapt to their rather obstinate ways but maybe more out of fear than respect. It would take work to make life flow smoothly.

Your Virgo Moon To Their Sagittarian Sun

You certainly appreciate their wide ranging ideas and intellectually stimulating approach. You even slightly envy their eternal optimism but you have scant respect for their unrealistic, devil-may-care approach which often leaves jobs half done. Your constant need for order and endless worrying about detail would eventually weigh them down and dry up their inspiration. But if you can both find a balance then each of you will help the other with what they lack.

Your Virgo Moon To Their Capricorn Sun

An earth Moon to an earth Sun has distinct possibilities. You both share a respect for hard work, the practicalities of life, and when there is time, the indulgences of the body. You will not always have as much of them as you want because they are a workaholic even more than you. They can also be a touch sombre in their younger years which makes you anxious. You dislike their ruthlessness and attitude that the ends justify the means. They will never sympathise with your endless worrying. But it basically is a great match.

Your Virgo Moon To Their Aquarius Sun

This is a slightly cool combination with a few scratchy edges. You appreciate the solid, traditional virtues in life while they are wild, eccentric, ultra modern and not very grounded. Certainly you appreciate those who serve the world and they often are humanitarian. But you wince at their need to stand out as individuals and their uncompromising way of not bending to circumstance. They will fly away if you nag at them or try to tidy them up. But they will bring new friends into your life so it might be worth hanging on in there.

Your Virgo Moon To Their Pisces Sun

Successful they may be, but you will worry endlessly about how in their impractical muddle they manage to get results at all never mind repeat them. You will be constantly trying to bring order to their chaos which will help but it may not be entirely nourishing and relaxing for you. They are sympathetic and caring at heart which will soothe you. You may do more for them than they for you.

Your Libra Moon To Their Aries Sun

Your Moon opposes their Sun so you could find your moods permanently out of step. You basically respect people who are nice, fair in their dealings, diplomatic and do not make too much of a rumpus. So there are going to be a few rough edges at times. Aries crash through life being competitive, sweeping social niceties aside in their fight to be a winner. You would be on tenterhooks in your social life about what clanger they were going to drop next. They would dismiss your comments with scorn. But they'd certainly waken you up and life would never be boring.

Your Libra Moon To Their Taurus Sun

Their pace of operation will make your teeth ache but unless they are a thoroughly rough Taurus you will appreciate their pleasant, steadfast approach and their taste in the comforts of life. They can be lazier than you appreciate but they will bring a practical common sense to your rather up-in-the-head life. Sex may be a problem since they need constant physical reassurance while you do not.

Your Libra Moon To Their Gemini Sun

You like their bright, sparkling wit, their flow of ideas and their wonderful ways with words. An Air Moon to an Air Sun is a great combination. Though you will not always be sure whether you really respect their jack-of-all-trades versatility. You certainly do not appreciate the way certain Geminis cut corners or are less than straightforward in their dealings. They may pour scorn on your social ambitions and need for everything to be so nice all the time. They quite like walking on the wild side. But on the whole it will work well.

Your Libra Moon To Their Cancer Sun

Your moods will be out of sync and they may clutch more than you like but you do admire their ambition, drive, energy and creative flair out in the world. They are not just stay at home creatures. One problem may be that you do not understand their emotional moodiness or way of blowing up storms of misunderstandings with workmates. They are hyper sensitive where you would suppress your vulnerabilities just to keep the peace. They find you cool but adore you.

Your Libra Moon To Their Leo Sun
You'll be terribly grand together. You adore their extravagant lifestyle, classy friends and high social status. They may be stubborn, prickly, at times arrogant but your diplomacy can cope and they do have warm hearted moments. You could wish that they showed more initiative. They can be very fixed. They will like your way of adapting to their needs, your well bred manners and elegant tastes.

Your Libra Moon To Their Virgo Sun
You appreciate people who are hard working, refined and do not make waves. They may be a little dull for your rather more colourful, social tastes but it is not a bad match. When you throw parties they will do the work. They will not embarrass you by being too ruthless, dishonest and manipulative at work. They will appreciate your way of soothing them peacefully at the end of a long day. Neither of you is over emotional so it could work well.

Your Libra Moon To Their Libra Sun
Ideal. You adore similar things, have the same aims in life and fit together like a hand in a glove. You like people who have social aspirations, and energy, drive, initiative and creative flair. You need a mate you can converse with, who thinks deeply. They are wise and just, though a touch indecisive which you understand. It is a slight cool contact so you must watch when the stormy times come. Neither of you like handling difficult feelings.

Your Libra Moon To Their Scorpio Sun
You like 'nice', well bred, straightforward people who have justice as their aim. Scorpios certainly work hard which you appreciate but they can be dark, devious and manipulative about gaining their end - which is power. You will hate being dragged into their emotional depths. You

like a colourful, glittering life on the surface where all is calm and harmony. They will pour scorn on what they see as your superficiality. You'll need a Water Sun or Venus to keep this running smoothly.

Your Libra Moon To Their Sagittarian Sun
Conversations will sparkle until they start voicing over blunt opinions but there certainly is an intellectual rapport and a shared interest in the fate of society. You appreciate their mind. But you are not relaxed by their sometimes crazy lifestyle, short lived enthusiasms and rather reckless approach to career matters. You prefer a steadier, more respectable type. They will not understand your hyper sensitivity to other people's opinion and will tell you so in no uncertain manner. Your friends will be very different but they will liven you up and you'll smooth them down.

Your Libra Moon To Their Capricorn Sun
This is a cool but workable combination. You appreciate their hard work, initiative, determination and ambition since you loathe lazy loafers who sponge through life. Both of you are traditionalists at heart and slightly snobbish so you will share an elegant home, classy friends and a professionally useful social life. They work too hard and too long and you can be too laid back and unemotional. So it could eventually wither away from lack of attention and warmth. You need to keep the flame of passion alive.

Your Libra Moon To Their Aquarius Sun
An air moon to an air sign should work but you are very unlike Aquarius. You want niceness, social approval, an elegant home, classy friends and status in the community. They genuinely love being an oddball, have no social ambitions whatsoever, and will happily mix with anyone from tramps to kings. They would embarrass you with their eccentricities. You like to fit in harmoniously. They make a strenuous effort not to. You will converse well at the beginning but to make it last you both need to be tolerant and flexible.

Your Libra Moon To Their Pisces Sun
This can be just OK. They are not as resourceful or dynamic as you might like but they can have a way of floating intuitively towards success. You are nourished by their creative flair, their sympathy, caring and adaptability. You will like them if they do rise to the top but will not be so happy if they stay a wispy, timid recluse. You need standing in the eyes of the world. They will appreciate your way of creating peace at home.

Your Scorpio Moon To Their Aries Sun
This might have its sticky moments since you are so different. You are deep, dark, secretive and rather respect people who aim for power, are strategic, even devious. Aries are open, straightforward, crash ahead with little forethought and less planning never mind tactics. They can be successful since they like winning but they are not ultimately concerned with power. They also wander and hate being possessed so your jealous side would never be at peace. You'll need a water Sun or Venus to make this zing.

Your Scorpio Moon To Their Taurus Sun
You understand and admire their persistence though question their application at times. They can be lazy. Both of you are hugely stubborn and neither gives way easily. They do not quite have the edge of wit or cunning which you like and irritatingly will not be manipulated by you. Both of you can be deeply passionate though you are sexual in a feeling way where they are sexual in a highly physical way. They will certainly supply you with comforts aplenty.

Your Scorpio Moon To Their Gemini Sun
You may initially be attracted to their dark side, their agile wit, cunning and way of handling problems by bending every which way. But at the end of the day you will find them too changeable, lacking in staying power and real intuitive understanding of life. You need a more intense mate who can share your turbulent depths. Your jealousy would be set off by their wandering eye and their need not to be fenced in would eventually cause tensions. They need strong water planets for this to work well.

Your Scorpio Moon To Their Cancer Sun

You really appreciate their creative flair, ambition and resourcefulness out in the world as well as their interest in setting up a happy family base. Their interests are shorter lived than you might like. They are great starters not such great finishers but they do have more initiative than you which helps. Your emotional sensitivities are highly compatible so you can be of help to them and they will protect your vulnerabilities and not betray you.

Your Scorpio Moon To Their Leo Sun

At times you will feel at cross purposes. What you they like irritates you. You need a powerful mate of cunning, wit, strength and persuasiveness. Leo is open, attention seeking, an entertainer at heart and will seem naive or empty to you. You will never understand why they put appearances above everything else when you know it is what goes on behind the scenes that really counts. They will distrust the depths of your feelings, will assume you are always manipulating (rightly) and shy clear of your ruthlessness. You'll need Fire planets to keep this running amiably.

Your Scorpio Moon To Their Virgo Sun

You need a partner to grapple with and self sufficient Virgo may not be quite it. Certainly you respect their earthy persistence, their hard work and their way with details. But you can find them strait-laced at work and elsewhere. They want to be of service and will refuse to manipulate or power struggle to win. You need a mate who is willing to walk in the mud to find the gold nuggets. They seem too fastidious. They are fearful of your emotional depths and your stinging tongue. They will need a Scorpio Moon or Venus for this to be really compatible.

Your Scorpio Moon To Their Libra Sun

They are colourful, bright, straightforward, fair minded and live life on the surface. You live life in the depths and respect those who are willing to work in secret, who are good tacticians, willing to cut corners if necessary to gain power. Libra is too scared of losing social approval to do anything as risky and will loathe your stinging tongue. They need relationships but nothing too emotional or sexual. Unless they have a strong water Moon or Venus this could be problematic.

Your Scorpio Moon To Their Scorpio Sun
A match made, if not in heaven, then certainly in your favourite place. You adore their strength, their determination to work miracles against all the odds, their cunning and their ruthlessness. You also share a wildly sentimental outlook on family matters. Jealousy and obstinacy are the greatest drawbacks since neither of you budge or let go. But then neither of you minds a good tussle. They will give you all the passion you ever wanted.

Your Scorpio Moon To Their Sagittarius Sun
You'll struggle to bridge the differences here. They are either heady intellectuals or flyaway adventurers. You do not resonate to either greatly. People who think too much you tend to dismiss as lightweight. Those who do not have staying power come even lower down your love list. They dislike being fenced in, tied down or swamped with too many feelings. They want freedom not to be possessed. They live on the cloud tops not on the ocean floor. Both of you will need to learn to love their others domain before this can work well.

Your Scorpio Moon To Their Capricorn Sun
Certainly you admire their ambition, persistence, resourcefulness and way of getting to high positions of authority and power. But you do not appreciate a mate who works so hard they are never at home. They also incline to being cool emotionally. They do have a sensual, indulgent side but often it is repressed in favour of ambition. That is beyond your understanding. They would not quite trust the depths of your feelings and would always be suspicious because they think you manipulate. If they have a water Moon it will definitely help.

Your Scorpio Moon To Their Aquarius Sun
They represent most things you either do not understand or cannot respect. Power is not on their agenda, neither are

they cunning or ruthless. Certainly they have endurance which you like but they basically want to be one of a democratic group at work not the one pulling the reins of control. They dislike your need to possess and will run from jealousy at the drop of a hat. They'll bring round friends when you want intimacy. You'd need to soften your demands and they'd need to be more in touch with their feelings for this to work.

Your Scorpio Moon To Their Pisces Sun
This could work since you would help them be more robust but they would probably do less to feed your deeper needs. They can either be intuitive, creative successes in the world, though impractical, or they can be vague, wispy, rather indecisive. You would for ever be chivvying to make them stand up straighter and fight harder. They would care for you and bend round your wishes though shrink from your direct comments. If they are a strong Pisces the it could work.

Your Sagittarius Moon To Their Aries Sun
Your heart lifts at their fiery, adventurous escapades. Their wild schemes that can end in high flying successes and their crashing failures from which they dust themselves down and start again. They are not thoughtful but they will never, never fence you in. A fire Moon and a fire Sun guarantee the interest levels and noise levels will be high but boredom will be kept at bay. Neither of you is tactful or practical.

Your Sagittarius Moon To Their Taurus Sun
This could be tricky since you want an adventurer or a thinker. Someone who can soar in life. Taurus is rooted, placid, steady and very earthy. They have long term staying power which you cannot understand and write off as slowness. They would pour scorn on your brighter ideas as revenge for your blunt judgements on them. Their jealousy would make you feel fenced in and your wandering feet would give them a fit. You'd definitely need a cross over of other planets to keep this harmonious.

Your Sagittarius Moon To Their Gemini Sun

A wonderfully chatty pair, you would always be swapping titbits of information and discussing every subject under the sun. Their interests are slightly more superficial and shorter lived than yours but you genuinely respect their ability to hold down three jobs at once and their constant energy. You will be indecisive, impractical and rather harum scarum together but you certainly will not be bored.

Your Sagittarius Moon To Their Cancer Sun

A fire Moon and a water Sun are not great news together unless supported by other planets. You do appreciate their energy, drive and creative flair in the outside world but never understand their emotional moodiness. They fall out with workmates and create storms in a teacup you cannot fathom. They also dislike your rather blunt opinions. Their jealousy and need to set up a settled family base will make you run. You do not want to be fenced in. They'll teach you to be more emotional and understanding and you'll jolt them out of their glooms.

Your Sagittarian Moon To Their Leo Sun

A fire Moon with a fire Sun make for a spectacular firework display. You appreciate their flamboyance, their way of living an extravagant life. But you do not entirely understand their need to keep up appearances and their rather self centred approach to work and life. You are more adaptable, are fairly democratic, and cut straight through nonsense very sharply at times. Their fragile egos would deflate in a hurry. You'll need to soften down and be more tactful for this to be absolutely amiable.

Your Sagittarius Moon To Their Virgo Sun

Both of you are adaptable which helps and there are pros and cons. You genuinely admire their conscientious, practical way of working which is absolutely not yours. They can keep your life rolling along at an organisation level which is highly nourishing. But you do find them a little strait laced, dull even. They do not feed your need for excitement and adventure with their obsessive need for order and control. But they are self sufficient and will never fence you in though they will nag at your lack of realism.

Your Sagittarius Moon To Their Libra Sun
Can you keep your opinions toned down? Then this might just work though Libra can be a touch too calm, harmonious and well bred for your wilder tastes. You will certainly appreciate their initiative, resourcefulness and ambition in the outside world. They have sharp minds and a shared interest with you in the fate of society, so conversations should be deep and meaningful. But they can be a touch snobbish which you are not. Luckily they are fairly cool and will not fence you in which you'll appreciate.

Your Sagittarius Moon To Their Scorpio Sun
This is a rather chalk and cheese mix. You want a high flier, a straight forward, maybe reckless, certainly intellectual mate. You will envy but not understand Scorpio's staying power which you lack and certainly dislike their secrecy, cunning and manipulative way of getting power. You hate being crowded or possessed anywhere in your life and they will make you feel overwhelmed. You both in different ways have sharp opinions. The arguments would flare. You'll need to be more emotional and they'll need to mellow for this to be a success.

Your Sagittarius Moon To Their Sagittarius Sun
Ideal. You adore their fiery approach, bright mind, wide spread of ideas and share their love of travel. You approve of their idealistic way of tackling their career which may not always be realistic but is usually straightforward. Neither of you is practical which may cause problems but you are happy to muddle through. Conversation will never be lacking and neither of you will trap the other.

Your Sagittarius Moon To Their Capricorn Sun
A basic optimist with a basic pessimist is not usually an easy match. You certainly appreciate their energy, initiative, drive and resourcefulness at work though you seriously question whether anyone needs to put in those hours just for the sake of turning a buck. You are not as materialistic as them and they can be critical about your lack of practical

skills or realistic ambitions. You have much to offer the other if you can make the effort to stay the course.

Your Sagittarius Moon To Their Aquarius Sun
This is an appreciative mix since you like their eccentricity and complete disinterest in social approval. They are real one offs who do their thing for their own sake. They are more determined than you with more staying power but you are adaptable so that should not matter. Conversations will always sparkle since both of you have wide interests and a genuine feeling for humanity and the future of society.

Your Sagittarius Moon To Their Pisces Sun
An adaptable pair you can bend to each other but you will not understand their lack of courage or pushing power. You basically admire heroes who can go out into the world to make it happen. Pisces can be successful but they do it obliquely by avoiding confrontations. You will not understand their emotional intuition either though it often matches your fiery intuition. You would not find them straightforward enough while your bluntness would make them wince. If you become more sensitive to their needs and they find their vibrant side then it'll work.

Your Capricorn Moon To Their Aries Sun
You certainly need an ambitious, resourceful mate who will not fuss if you are never home, which Aries will not. But you really do not admire their rather slapdash, none too realistic way of proceeding. They leap into action without forethought or planning which offends your cautious nature. They can be lucky but you feel in the depths of your soul they have not earned it by solid toil. They would get cross with your eternally pessimistic outlook. But they would add sparkle to your life and you'd teach them a more practical approach.

Your Capricorn Moon To Their Taurus Sun
You adore their earthy practicality, their steadiness and rather envy their way of providing themselves with every comfort under the sun which you feel is too decadent for you. But they are less ambitious than you which may bring

on your stern disapproving face and they can be hugely stubborn. They could teach you to value yourself more by relaxing with your favourite indulgences but that is only if you would let them. They might help to boost your self esteem if you learn from their approach. They reckon they deserve it. There's a good deal that is positive here.

Your Capricorn Moon To Their Gemini Sun
This is a slight mix of opposites. You do appreciate their energy in tackling so many tasks at once. They certainly will not complain if you work non stop which you sometimes do since you don't always feel worthy of love if you do not achieve. But you really do not admire their grasshopper approach to career matters and your way of sometimes cutting corners. You also want social respectability which is not high on their list of priorities. Both of you need to move towards the other's values slightly for this to meld well.

Your Capricorn Moon To Their Cancer Sun
You certainly admire their drive, get up and go in the outside world. They are by no manner of means the stay-at-home cooks and knitters which they sometimes have the reputation for being. Their emotional moodiness leaves you puzzled but then your overly practical approach unsettles them. It is not ideal since they would resent being left when you skipped off to work. But it could be worse. Your moods would always be a little out of sync.

Your Capricorn Moon To Their Leo Sun
You warm to their grand ways and confident approach. Both of you are traditionalists, rather upmarket in ambition, so you would appreciate their way of introducing you to the right people. Your rather stingy streak would not remotely appreciate their extravagances which can be monumental. But never criticise sine their vanity will not take it. They would not teach you to love yourself more directly but by example. They radiate warmth and sunlight which certainly do you the world of good if you let it in.

Your Capricorn Moon To Their Virgo Sun
You purr with approval about their quiet, conscientious,

practical, workaholic approach to career matters. It is almost on a par with your own. Except that you crave position and possessions. They just like serving others. They are adaptable and would not stand in your way. Your vision (or slight lack of it) is a shared trait and both of you will always work with a purpose to a tangible end. They are refined and will not embarrass you. But it could be cool, too businesslike if you don't remember to indulge your indulgent sides every so often.

Your Capricorn Moon To Their Libra Sun

You are basically after the same aims in life which helps. You never feel quite loved or wanted and their tactful but rather detached way of handling relationships will help you gain self esteem. You certainly appreciate their resourcefulness, initiative and hard working streak. Especially after 29 they buckle to with a will. Though it could end up a cool pairing since neither of you is good at feelings. Make the effort and it will sing.

Your Capricorn Moon To Their Scorpio Sun

You certainly appreciate their determination to go at all costs for what they want career wise. Little is allowed to stand in their way and even if you would not use the same cunning you certainly think the end justifies the means. But you need to be more in your feelings and your body for this to work well. They are not just determined careerists, they are also highly intense sexual beings who live in the turbulent depths which you normally avoid.

Your Capricorn Moon To Their Sagittarius Sun

You tend to gloom, they enthuse. You like hard, dedicated workers. They fly through life at speed, not always with much common sense. They are certainly not practical. They can be highly intellectual or woolly idealists but you wonder if all these ideas have any real purpose. Your conscientious need to work long hours will suit them because they hate being hemmed in. But you are judgemental of their faults. You are not really in tune but they will brighten up your life and you'll keep their feet on the ground.

Your Capricorn Moon To Their Capricorn Sun

Same sign sun and moons should be an ideal pairing but in your case there are dangers - of two workaholics never meeting, of two pessimists stoking up each other's self doubt and gloom. Certainly you will have endless respect for their achievements, for their steady rise in the world, perhaps even to giving you the social position which you crave. But you need to watch you are not too narrow in your vision of the world together, maybe too materialistic. If you can find your earthy, indulgent side then it could be a long love in.

Your Capricorn Moon To Your Aquarius Sun

This has one thing going for it - you may never be home because you are a workaholic and they will never notice because the house will be full of friends. You are not basically on the same wave length since you are a traditionalist, a snob even, highly practical while they are democratic, egalitarians who have no sense of their social position. They are more tolerant than you of the world's lame ducks and humanitarian/ eco/green causes. They would also embarrass you with their oddball ways and friends. But they will teach you to be less straight edged and you'll make them more realistic.

Your Capricorn Moon To Their Pisces Sun

Their impracticality and vague approach to work will drive you to distraction but they are refined, kind, adaptable souls who can miraculously sometimes be successful which would suit you. Their lack of confidence exasperates you because you are fairly hard driving but they would in the gentle way teach you to value yourself more. You could help them greatly at work with your earthy sense of organisation.

Your Aquarius Moon To Their Aries Sun

You appreciate their courage, their sparkle, their sense of adventure but are rather concerned about their lack of staying power. They are great starters, terrible finishers while you really like mates who get on track and stay there. They are more ruthless than you appreciate. You are a humanitarian, democratic soul while they are out and out winners - me first. They love your independent stance and lack of jealousy but perhaps they might want for more excitement.

Your Aquarius Moon To Their Taurus Sun

This is a real mix of opposites. You certainly do appreciate their staying power and stamina but their aims seem so rooted, so materialistic,they do not give you any sense that there is inspiration, idealistic vision or humanitarian purpose behind them which are all important to you. Plus you like spacey relationships with few ties. They are possessive and jealous and hate insecurity. If both of you can be less extreme and more middle of the road it'll help.

Your Aquarius Moon To Their Gemini Sun

This is a zippy, chatty combination. You adore their bright, witty, agile minds and slick way with words. You may envy their way of doing three jobs at once. What you do not totally respect is their way of approaching certain matters which can be evasive, rather slippery and fairly opportunistic at times. You would prefer a steadier, more straightforward way. They will certainly not make you feel hemmed in and the conversation will never flag. It could end up being a touch too cool emotionally but you'll never be bored

Your Aquarius Moon To Their Cancer Sun

You admire anyone who can get results which with their energy, initiative and resourcefulness is very possible. But you do not understand their emotional moodiness which can brew up storms in a teacup with workmates. Their need for a happy home base can make you feel restricted and tied though they are not always keen on highly exclusive relationships as long as they have the family around. Your blunt, abrasive, not always sensitive way of expressing yourself can cause trouble since they hurt easily. You need to mellow and they need to become slightly more detached for this to work well.

Your Aquarius Moon To Their Leo Sun

Your Moon and their Sun are opposing each other across the zodiac which does not mean arguments just a feeling of being slightly out of step. You respect their steadiness, staying power and persistence. But their need to be flamboyant, grand, centre of attention and extravagant passes you by completely. They are ego centred where you are egalitarian. You like being part of a democratic group where they want to be the monarch. They want you to be at their feet all the time where you like space. Your outspoken opinions would offend them deeply. Your moods would always be out of sync so both of you will need tolerance.

Your Aquarius Moon To Their Virgo Sun
You really admire those who have courage to be a pioneer, to stand out as an oddball if necessary to fight for a just cause. Virgo will be self sacrificing and serve others but they can be rather timid, self effacing and slightly strait laced for your tastes. You do not understand their obsessive need to double check every detail and they certainly wince at some of your tactics. The conversations will be good because both of you are thinkers and communicators.

Your Aquarius Moon To Their Libra Sun
An air moon to an air sun should work well except that your rather unconventional needs and approach does not suit their terribly traditional, slightly class conscious way of living. You admire their thoughtful minds and their interest in justice. You appreciate their coolness and lack of jealousy. But you do not really take to their seemingly superficial social outlook. They want everyone to be harmonious, well bred and well washed. You adore oddballs, hippies, New Age Travellers and tramps. You'll loosen them up and they will make you more conventional.

Your Aquarius Moon To Their Scorpio Sun
Not only do you approach life from different directions, your needs run against each other's grain more than slightly. They have a deep, dark, secretive, power hungry way of attacking career aims and their love lives. You want space, the truth out in the open, no ties, and ambitions that do not include getting others under your thumb. Their jealousy would haunt you and you would raise their hackles instantly because you shy clear of exclusive relationships. You are

both stubborn and neither would ever give way. Only with great patience and tolerance will this work smoothly.

Your Aquarius Moon To Their Sagittarius Sun

An air Moon to a fire Sun promises plenty of sparkle, excitement, noise and good conversation especially here since they have wide ranging intellectual interests and a quite philosophical approach to life which suits you down to the ground. You do not entirely appreciate their rather restless approach to work. They never seem to stay long on track. But they will never make you feel hemmed in and even your abrasive opinions will wash over them.

Your Aquarius Moon To Their Capricorn Sun

This is not an instant hit since you do not appreciate their traditionalist lifestyle and upmarket aims. You also find them too materialistic and not caring enough about the philosophical issues which appeal to you. Certainly they are never going to crowd you since they work such long hours. So you can be free to wander. But you will never agree on friends. They like the leaders in the community. You adore oddballs, eccentrics and pioneers. If both of you can lean towards the other's values then it might just work.

Your Aquarius Moon To Their Aquarius Sun

This is ideal except that you may not meet very often. Both of you adore being one of a crowd or being out there doing your own thing. When your paths do cross the conversation will be lively, inventive and inspired. You like their steadiness, their way of disregarding convention to push ahead with ideas they consider important. Neither of you is jealous but both of you are hugely stubborn.

Your Aquarius Moon To Their Pisces Sun

In your heart of hearts you cannot understand their vague, meandering way of proceeding in the world. Certainly they can be successful but you never quite know how. You do share similar interests in helping to make the world a better place but you are very different types. They will not make you feel hemmed in because they disappear so frequently into their daydreams they may not notice your absence.

Though your sharp, sometimes tactless, opinions may upset them. It could work with supportive cross overs from Sun and Moon on the other side.

Your Pisces Moon To Their Aries Sun

You adore deeply sensitive, creative, kind, sympathetic souls. They hash, crash and bash their way through life in a fiery way, rather inconsiderate of the needs of others. You might envy their courage, their dash, their resilience in the face of setbacks because they just bounce back up. But they certainly do not nourish you where you need it most. You would withdraw into your shell and never come out. They would get exasperated. But they will teach you to have more courage and you'll soften them down.

Your Pisces Moon To Their Taurus Sun

You adore their earthy solidity, their protectiveness, even their jealousy makes you feel wanted. But you are not sure you want quite so much physical attention. You are highly different personalities so this is a complementary match. They help you by being practical. You are adaptable so will not stand in their way though you can feel a martyr. They are fairly self indulgent which could ultimately prove a problem since your needs where they differed would not be considered.

Your Pisces Moon To Their Gemini Sun

You love agile minds, versatile talents and restless souls so they suit you admirably though they can be a touch cool, detached and unemotional. You both have a fairly intuitive approach to career matters so neither of you is practical. Neither of you is great at making decisions either. But the drawback is that they will not stay around to give you the protection you need. Their wandering feet or minds will drive you back into your daydreams. But for all that it is not a bad match since you'll both adapt.

Your Pisces Moon To Their Cancer Sun

Lovely. You envy their initiative, drive, and creative flair out in the world. They make it all happen where you can be rather wandered and vague. Their nest building tendencies and emotional sensitivities will give you all the sympathetic protection you ask for. You are adaptable so will equally care for their needs. Neither of you is desperate to have a totally exclusive one-to-one relationship so that is fine as well.

Your Pisces Moon To Their Leo Sun
You adore the tinge of glamour, romance and adventure about their lives. They tend to try to live out their fantasies where you just dream yours. You positively envy their way of pushing themselves forward to demand attention though you do not understand it. You can adapt to their ego centred ways but you will end up getting precious little in return at times, since they assume you are there solely for their needs. But they will perhaps teach you to stand up for yourself better and you'll soothe them.

Your Pisces Moon To Their Virgo Moon
Opposite signs do not always complement but you probably do. Both of you are sensitive and refined. They have a practical streak which you lack and can help to give you a place in the world. They do nark on and worry almost as much as you which is not helpful. But they are ultimately kind hearted, wanting to serve. You can help them be more creative. They ground you. At times your moods will be out of sync but on the whole you can make this work.

Your Pisces Moon To Their Libra Moon
This is a lovely mix even though you are water to air. You want peace, bliss, harmony and taste in your life. So do they. You admire their drive, initiative, energy and ambition to get things done as gracefully as possible. They are not practical but they are good at starting new projects which you are not. They will work hard to provide the good life for both of you. Their diplomacy means you will never feel attacked. Your kindness will help bring them in touch with their feelings.

Your Pisces Moon To Their Scorpio Sun
A water Moon and water Sun should be fine together but you are terribly sensitive and they are fiercely robust. You

look with awe on their iron determination, miracle making talents, and ruthlessness about getting power which all makes you wilt. As long as you can persuade yourself that their strong, manipulative talents are all being used for you and not against you, then you could manage nicely. But you would always be slightly suspicious. They are sentimental at home so would surprise you with kindness.

Your Pisces Moon To Their Sagittarius Sun
You love variety in life but whether all this noise, excitement and strong opinion is really what nourishes you is questionable. Deeply sensitive water and rather inconsiderate fire do not generally make an easy mix. They mean well but they have a way of putting their foot in their mouths or rubbing you up the wrong way. Their reckless way of approaching some work problems also does not make you feel protected. Neither of you is practical which is a drawback. But they'll teach you to be more courageous and optimistic and you'll soften them down.

Your Pisces Moon To Their Capricorn Sun
There are distinct possibilities here but it is a cool match with you perhaps being locked away at home while they work manically long hours. They will not always appreciate your vagueness and you will not always take kindly to their rather judgemental, materialistic approach to life. What it has going for it is their practical, earthy ambitious side which could provide a solid home and solid lifestyle inside which you could feel protected.

Your Pisces Moon To Their Aquarius Sun
You feel for the suffering of the world while they actively work to help humanitarian causes. Neither of you in different ways wants a really committed, exclusive relationship so you will not mind if they wander off and they will not notice if you retreat in your dream world. But at the end of the day you are very different personalities and they may not give you quite enough emotional sustenance. They live in their heads, their ideas, their ideals and their inventive schemes.

Your Pisces Moon To Their Pisces Sun
This is ideal. Two deeply emotionally sensitive souls clinging to each other. You understand their fears, phobias and anxieties and will help them to put their dreams into action. They need someone other than you to give them practical help. But you will give them inner confidence and admiration. They in turn will never laugh at your worries and pain. You are just tuned into the same wavelength.